D0970326

Eudora Welty

Eudora Welty:
Two Pictures at Once in Her Frame

by

Barbara Harrell Carson

The Whitston Publishing Company
Troy, New York
1992

Library of Congress Catalog Card Number 91-75025

ISBN 0-87875-422-9

Printed in the United States of America

Chapter III herein was originally published in slightly different form, as "Eudora Welty's Tangled Bank" in *South Atlantic Review*, 48 (November 1983), 1-18; Chapter IV, in slightly different form, originally appeared as "Eudora Welty's Dance with Darkness: *The Robber Bridegroom*" in *The Southern Literary Journal*, 20 (Spring 1988), 51-68. Chapter VI was published in an earlier version as "In the Heart of Clay: Eudora Welty's *The Ponder Heart*," *American Literature* (December 1987), 609-625. The original version of Chapter VIII appeared as "Eudora Welty's Heart of Darkness, Heart of Light" in *South Central Review*, 4 (Spring 1987), 106-122.

For Robert Carson,
and for our daughters,
Ashley Anne and Bethany Jeanne

Acknowledgements

My debt to Charles R. Anderson, Caroline Donovan Professor of American Literature Emeritus of The Johns Hopkins University, goes back almost a quarter of a century. For that long he has encouraged, counselled, and prodded me through a variety of writing projects. I am grateful to him for his guidance and for his example. Past and present colleagues at Rollins College have given their support both by discussing the ideas that shaped these chapters and by reading early drafts. I am particularly indebted to Omar Castañeda, Hoyt Edge, Jack Lane, Judith Provost, and Roy Starling—and to my colleague in the Rollins Physics Department, Robert Carson.* A series of Jack B. Critchfield research grants helped at several stages in this study. And finally I am grateful to the following journals for permitting the publication of portions of this book which originally appeared in different forms in their pages: *American Literature, South Atlantic Review, South Central Review,* and *Southern Literary Review.*

Barbara Harrell Carson
Rollins College
Winter Park, Florida

* Several anonymous reviewers also made suggestions which are reflected in these pages. In addition, my thanks go to Elizabeth Kocan Pensiero for her editorial assistance.

Contents

Introduction

We have all seen these perceptual tests: what appear to be two profiles facing each other change in the blink of an eye into the outline of a vase—or a sketch of an old hag turns into an Aubrey Beardsley beauty. Both the profiles and the vase, the hag and the beauty are always "present" in the sketches—that is, the lines which compose them are there—but psychologists assure us that human perception is capable of receiving only one of the images at a time. The premise of this book is that, metaphorically speaking, Eudora Welty can see simultaneously the profiles and the vase, that the vision of the world projected in her work is holistic rather than dualistic.

In Welty's writings, life is not a matter of warring, irreconcilable opposites: subject-object, mind-matter, life-death, good-evil, past-present. Instead, hers is a vision of reality in which the traditional opposites exist in a polar unity. Reality is the whole, and the "parts" of any set are no more divisible, ultimately, than the positive pole of a magnet can be chopped away from the negative or a concave line can be drawn without simultaneously drawing a convex. In this view, one pole does not cancel out its "opposite," but rather is necessary for its existence and can even be seen as its very source, one giving rise to the other in the dynamic relationship that the East associates with the principles of yin and yang.

In *The Robber Bridegroom*, Welty's historical fairytale (the genre itself an example of her delight in linking the apparently irreconcilable), Welty makes one of her clearest assertions of life's polar unity. In this novella, the planter Clement Musgrove, who is repeatedly described as "innocent" in the ways of the world, displays another kind of wisdom when he speaks of the highwayman with whom his daughter has gone to live:

> If being a bandit were his breadth and scope, I should
> find him and kill him for sure. . . . But since in addition
> he loves my daughter, he must be not the one man, but
> two, and I should be afraid of killing the second. For
> all things are double, and this should keep us from tak-
> ing liberties with the outside world, and acting too
> quickly to finish things off.[1]

Even Jamie Lockhart, the robber bridegroom himself, comes to realize the heroism involved in his learning "to look both ways and to see a thing from all sides" (p. 185). Virgie Rainey, the main character in Welty's short story "The Wanderers," is another who possesses this heroic vision:

> Virgie never saw it differently, never doubted that all
> the opposites on earth were close together, love close to
> hate, living to dying; but of them all, hope and despair
> were the closest blood—unrecognizable one from the
> other sometimes, making moments double upon them-
> selves, and in the doubling double again, amending but
> never taking back.[2]

While the conclusions reached by Clement, Jamie, and Virgie may strike us as intuitively obvious, true to our *felt* relationship with the world, these ideas do not reflect the intellectual attitudes toward reality that are generally thought to have shaped Western civilization. Dualism, not holism, has been the prevailing viewpoint of the West at least since the Greek atomists decided that matter was essentially dead and passive, capable of motion only because of the existence of external forces that were probably spiritual, but certainly different in nature from matter.[3] For the next twenty-five hundred years, the principle of the fundamental opposition between mind and matter, soul and body—and their hierarchical relationship—stood as the basis of Western science and philosophy.

In the seventeenth century, Descartes' *Cogito ergo sum* codified the way most of us even today experience ourselves: as a mind locked inside an alien body. Descartes' division of all of nature into *res cogitans* (mind) and *res externa* (nature) drew the lines: matter was foreign to our real selves, dead, separate. It was, in fact, knowable to humans precisely *because* it was other. In the eighteenth century, this epistemological premise became the basis for the Newtonian mechanistic universe, the stage on which modern science unfolded. And scientific objectivity (observing, analyzing, taking apart in order to know and to control) became the intellectual desideratum of the twentieth century, in both of C. P. Snow's two cultures.

Through the centuries, the Aristotelian rule of noncontradiction has provided a neat philosophical underpinning for this view of reality: a thing cannot be both X and not-X at the same time. The settling for easy either-or distinctions dictated by this paradigm has expressed itself in Western culture in a willingness, unlike Clement Musgrove's, to "finish things off" by seeing people and things singly—as either the pagan or the true believer, the foreigner or the compatriot, the evil or the good, the false or the true, the ugly or the beautiful, the failure or the success, the stupid or the smart, the real or the imaginary.

The implications of a different view of reality, one where both X and not-X can coexist (easy to parrot, perhaps, on an *e pluribus unum* level) are intellectually elusive. Welty's recognition of the difficulty of achieving this perception may be behind her labelling it as heroic in Jamie Lockhart's self-evaluation in *The Robber Bridegroom*. The suspicion that such a holistic view would reduce all existence to an indistinguishable blob repels. Troubling, too, is the thought that attaining such a vision would result in paralysis: if apparent contraries are really united, if hierarchical relationships are denied (if neither X nor not-X can be regarded as "better" or "more important"), what would be the basis for making choices—the *sine qua non* of action?

However, the holism found in Welty's writing does not annihilate distinctions. Welty is well at home in the dualistic world we live in, and she knows that her characters—even the most perceptive—live within time, and in a society, and within their own skins (where it is proper—and necessary—that they perceive differences and make choices). Her precise and stunning use of the concrete specifics of her fictional times and places, so often applauded by critics, anchors her works in this everyday reality. What she offers her readers and what she endows her most enlightened characters with is the capacity to see vividly the world of everyday distinctions, dictated by the dualistic paradigm, while occasionally glimpsing that same world as a reality where ordinary distinctions do not apply.

Welty's holistic vision allows for the human experience of separateness, individuality, and conflict—and all the pain and triumph associated with these. It also, however, suggests that those who exercise another way of knowing, beyond analysis and discursive thinking, will see that there is no such thing as separateness: every part belongs inseparably to a larger whole.[4] From this perspective, boundaries blur—between self and other; between the human and the natural worlds; between past, present, and future. To perceive this wholeness results in a mind that can be at ease with ambiguity, that can confront apparent paradox without being driven to resolve its tensions.

Welty recognizes, however, that to have only this sense of union—with no awareness of distinctions—would mean the loss of all contact with the phenomenal world, of all capacity to function in it. The highest human vision, therefore, is one that perceives at once—or in close succession—union and distinction. This meeting place of contraries is, for Welty, the creative intersection: the nexus from which art and illumination arise.

Welty's comments on her sense of life's doubleness—in her fiction and non-fiction—have been so direct that critics have, of course, written before of the significance of this motif in her works. As early as 1944, Robert Penn Warren, in his famous essay "The Love and Separateness in Miss Welty," spoke of the contrasts repeated "from story to story" in Welty, contrasts he described as "basic," "not susceptible to a single standard resolution," "understood not in mechanical but in vital terms."[5] Twenty-five years later, he returned to this idea in a short tribute in *Shenandoah*. Musing on his "nagging curiosity" about why it is so easy to praise Welty and so hard to analyze "the elements in her work that make it so easy—and such a deep pleasure—to praise," Warren said:

> I came up with something like this. Eudora Welty's vision of—her feeling for—the world is multiple. She never even when she nods, sinks into what Blake called "the single vision and Newton's sleep." . . . [Hers] is a temperament so strongly and significantly itself that it can face the multiplicity of the world. Art is the appropriate expression of such a temperament—art not as an escape from the incoherence of the world, but as a celebration of its richness—secure in an instinctive trust of self and in the knowledge that only out of the strong shall come forth sweetness.[6]

Having introduced the proposition that Welty's vision of coexisting opposites is somehow fundamental to her art, Warren left it to others to develop. Through the years, critics have mentioned the idea repeatedly, but usually briefly, most often as the unexplored source of Welty's sense of life's rich variety and its mystery. Others have used the term "double vision," which occurs so often in discussions of Welty, to point either to Welty's penchant for linking comedy and tragedy or to her success in uniting fact with fantasy, external details with the inner reality of the artist's ideas.[7] When the theme has been discussed in greater depth, the analysis has almost always been limited to a single work.[8] Not surprisingly, the two most perceptive full-length studies of Welty—Ruth M. Vande Kieft's pioneering *Eudora Welty*[9] and Michael Kreyling's *Eudora Welty's Achievement of Order*[10]—offer the best introductions to this theme. Kreyling's is an astute and sensitive exploration of a variety of techniques leading to "the impression of unity" in Welty's works, focusing particularly on her bringing together what Kreyling calls the mythological and the historical visions.[11]

No one, however, has written more sensitively about Eudora Welty's fiction than Ruth Vande Kieft. The critical strategy that she posited in 1962 and reiterated in 1987 strikes me as still the most profitable approach to Welty (even though many would regard it as "dated," as Vande Kieft concedes): that is, "detailed explication with the free use of quotations," treating Welty's fiction with the "patient and loving scrutiny we apply to poems."[12] Using that technique, Vande Kieft explores the mystery at the heart of Eudora Welty's fiction. The source of that sense of mystery Vande Kieft locates both in the boundaries—the separatenesses—that Welty keeps pointing to, as well as in the "double truths, paradoxes, polarities, contradictions" characteristic of Welty's works.[13]

While my concern is also Welty's treatment of the apparently opposite and while we agree on many points, the emphasis of my approach to this motif in Welty—and my conclusions about its implications—are different from Vande Kieft's. The heart of our difference may be this: Vande Kieft sees the union of contraries as a fabrication of the human mind; I see Welty's works as suggesting a serious consideration of holism as a metaphysical reality, with specific psychological, ethical, and social consequences. Vande Kieft views the "terrible ambiguities and contraries," such as those in *The Optimist's Daughter*, as "finally impenetrable" and declares that "the curtain of green, as a symbol of nature . . . is never drawn back in Eudora Welty's fiction," resulting in her offering "no transcendental knowledge nor religious vision or hope . . . to comfort her characters."[14]

For Vande Kieft, Welty's fiction suggests that reality is only fragments; "the individual makes whatever meaning is to come out of chaotic reality."[15] The philosophical outlook implied by such a view Vande Kieft characterizes as "pessimistic and agnostic," leading to a vision of life as absurd.[16] In Vande Kieft's reading, the only relief from the pain occasioned by Welty's tragic stories comes from art itself: "the lyric beauty, mystery and fascination of Welty's prose, the perceptions of some kind of order in the work itself and of truth seen and faced, some equivalent of the catharsis of pity and fear. . . ."[17]

A recent compelling voice coming at Welty's work from a different critical vantage than Vande Kieft's, but arriving at a similar conclusion about the "wholly elusive" quality of reality in Welty, has been that of the French deconstructionist Danièle Pitavy-Souques. Like Vande Kieft, Pitavy-Souques sees Welty as dealing with "the illusions and displacements which the self creates to conceal the fracture, to uphold the fiction of a narcissistic whole."[18]

I will suggest, on the other hand, that Welty does point to a transcendental reality (though not a religious one), that her final word is not about chaos, but about order—the order of the unified whole—and that she intimates the essential wholeness, not just of art, but of life, even while recognizing that her characters usually see only fragments. It is the fragments which are the fictions, not the unity. The truly imperceptive characters in Welty accept the fragments as the reality. The more sensitive intuit "mystery," which becomes, in this reading, the human view of unified reality when it is still concealed by the curtain of dualistic perception, but when the viewer has some sense that the whole story has not been revealed. To experience the lifting of that curtain, even momentarily, is the privilege reserved for the passionate few—those who learn a way to knowledge that the rational mind cannot pursue. This approach to Welty's vision of reality argues against Derrida's idea of irreducibly plural meanings, by suggesting that even while Welty's works destroy the certainties of this world (as they do, by denying the possibility of reducing reality to binary categories), they also return us to the oldest and most embracing philosophical proposition—the notion of the essential unity of all reality.

Thus, my purpose in this study is to try to part a little further the curtain on this mystery at the center of Welty's art. In the following pages, I want to suggest that Welty does not offer us a glimpse just of life's mystery (though that and the human experience of the boundaries of knowledge so often accompanying a confrontation of mystery are important in themselves). Her writings also suggest specific features of the mystery. I believe Welty's repeated return to the theme of the union of contraries implies definite ontological and epistemological principles—insights into the nature of reality and the way we can know it that call for more than the respectful silence (or the generalizations) usually settled for. Her double vision affects Welty's psychology (that is, her understanding of how her characters work), her ethics (which involve, not the traditional attention to good and evil, but an evaluation of what contributes to or destroys wholeness), and her rhetorical strategies (especially her use of paradox and her choice of the symbols and imagery complexly revealing this vision). What I hope will emerge is a sense of much more specific interconnectedness among Welty's writings than has before been apparent—an interconnectedness of vision that in no way belies the independent and original insights of each work.

One thing this work will not attempt is to locate the source of Welty's interest in holism. Traceable in Western philosophy at least as far back as Plato's attempt to reconcile the opposition between the One and the Many (an attempt elaborated upon by the Neoplatonists), this is an idea that has been returned to regularly over the centuries, usually by people outside the mainstream of their society. Thus, the possible intellectual influences on Welty are endless. Possible causes—psychological and biographical—of her attraction to this motif are fascinating to consider, but finally impossible to determine. However, some sense of the range of these possibilities can be valuable in establishing a context for the ideas to be encountered in Welty's works.

One explanation of why the idea of holism is so central to Welty is suggested by studies of the nature of the creative mind, which associate creativity itself with the ability to bring contraries into union. In his presentation of this theory, Albert Rothenberg declares that one of the salient characteristics of creative genius is what he calls "janusian thinking." Named for the Roman god who had multiple faces turned in different directions (and thus, symbolically, the capacity to unite opposite visions of reality), janusian thinking is, according to Rothenberg, the ability to entertain contradictory visions simultaneously. Rothenberg explains: "In apparent defiance of logic or matters of physical impossibility, the creative person formulates two or more opposites or antitheses coexisting and simultaneously operating, a formulation that leads to integrated concepts, images and creations. . . . [I]t is a logical postulating of what, on the surface, seems illogical." Thus, Rothenberg says, a key step in Einstein's arrival at the general theory of relativity was his perceiving—Einstein called it "the happiest thought of my life"—that a person in free fall from a roof would be both in motion and (relative to objects falling with him) at rest. Applying Rothenberg's theory to Welty, we might postulate that the thematic emphasis on the union of opposites in her works is a philosophical extension of the creative impulse to bring opposites into artistic harmony.[19]

However, it might just as easily be argued that Welty's nondualistic approach to reality has its source in an essentially feminine perspective.[20] (Certainly, the men most often credited with this holistic vision—poets and mystics—have traditionally been considered effeminate in Western societies.) In her 1969 essay "The Human Continuum," Betty Roszak wrote of the

> male habit of setting up boundary lines between imagined polarities. . . . Masculine/feminine is just one of such polarities among many, including body/mind, organism/environment, plant/animal, good/evil, black/white, feeling/intellect, passive/active, sane/insane, living/dead. Such language hardens what is in reality a continuum and a unity into separate mental images always in opposition to one another.[21]

More recently, Carol Gilligan, Nona Lyons, Nancy Chodorow, and Jean Baker Miller have joined other voices in suggesting that women are more likely than men to define themselves in terms of relatedness to others and even to experience selfhood as a web of connections with others, so that for women the boundaries of self and other (generally considered antithetical) are not so rigid as for men.[22] In addition, feminist theories of epistemology point to women's ability to accommodate ways of knowing other than the rational and dualistic strategies privileged in Western culture.[23] We will see in Welty's works that insights into life's essential unity come only through such alternate cognitive approaches.

But if the impetus of the creative psyche or of a feminine perspective can be looked to as internal catalysts for Welty's holistic vision, external sources can also be identified in profusion. Welty's own association of Southernness with the ability to be at ease with the idiosyncratic suggests that the region of her birth contributed something to her holistic perspective.[24] She locates an even more intimate arena for her exposure to the pattern of united contraries in her parents—an idea that will be dis-

cussed below in the chapter on *One Writer's Beginnings*. But
beyond those immediate influences lay the intellectual milieu of
the century into which Welty was born—a time when some of
the liveliest minds in science, in the social sciences, and, occasionally, in philosophy were pursuing the question of the nature
of reality in ways that frequently brought them face to face with a
holistic view that introduced the possibility of a reduction of the
rigidity, at least, of the old dualistic paradigm.

The last half century has heard with increasing frequency
about the dismal human consequences of dualism. Many, for
example, have come to suspect that the detachment from nature
making possible our technological advances has led to our feeling ourselves strangers on the planet we work so hard to manage. Carl Jung—whose work Welty almost certainly knew[25]—
traced the modern sense of fragmentation to our dualistic, hierarchical relation with nature. Seeing ourselves as the summit of
life, a position won by beating out all challengers, we now feel
isolated in the cosmos, Jung said, because, since we no longer experience ourselves as "involved in nature," we have "lost emotional 'unconscious identity' with natural phenomena."[26]

Others have seen as a consequence of our dualistic thinking our temporal fragmentation, our isolation inside of time.
While members of "primitive" societies picture themselves as
part of revolving temporal cycles, we see ourselves as caught
within the slowly diminishing straight line of time. Our interest
in the past is largely a matter of pinpointing a person or an event
on that line; our sense of the future is dominated by an awareness of time's finitude. Western thought in general has given
little attention to our experiences in non-historical, non-linear
time, such as those met with in our responses to art, in our
imagination, in our deepest emotions, in our dreams.[27]

Still others in this century have emphasized the flaw in
the epistemology that drives dualism. Since being "objective" is
considered the most commendable intellectual attitude, whatever is under analysis—the self, others, nature—must be regarded as separate from the perceiver. This fragmentation of the
world into subject or object, the knower or the known makes it
inevitable, according to the physicist Sir Arthur Eddington, "that
knowledge of one-half of the world will ensure ignorance of the
other half."[28] Acting as if this were the only kind of knowledge,
we have neglected another way of knowing that demands a
melting of the borders between subject and object. Eddington described the two approaches this way:

> We have two kinds of knowledge which I call symbolic
> knowledge and intimate knowledge. . . . [The] more cus-
> tomary forms of reasoning have been developed for
> symbolic knowledge only [i.e., knowledge by a subject of
> an object]. The intimate knowledge will not submit to
> codification and analysis; or, rather, when we attempt
> to analyze it the intimacy is lost and it is replaced by
> symbolism.[29]

The philosopher Michael Polanyi designated this second
type of knowing as "personal knowledge," requiring not intellectual detachment, but "the passionate participation of the knower
in the act of knowing."[30]   Changing slightly Martin Buber's dictum that "all real living is meeting," this approach to knowledge
sees all real knowing as union.   While in our culture we have
been taught that we can know X only by ceasing to be X, the other
kind of knowledge has widely been available to "uncivilized"
people, "who," Owen Barfield said,

> participated mentally and physically in [nature's]
> inner and outer processes. The evolution of man has
> signified not alone the steady expansion of con-
> sciousness (man getting to know more and more about
> more and more); there has been a parallel process of
> contraction—which was also a process of awakening—a
> gradual focusing or pinpointing down from an earlier
> kind of knowledge, which could also be called
> participation. . . . [W]e have come to know more and
> more about less and less.[31]

None of this is to suggest that Welty was familiar with all
or even most of these thinkers.   The point is, rather, that ideas
like these were very much in the intellectual air.   In fact, their
centrality to the period is indicated by the historian Thomas
Kuhn's identification of the twentieth century as the time of the
"paradigm shift."   Responding to the growing sense of the in-
completeness of the dominant dualistic vision of reality, there
began to develop, according to Kuhn, a new framework for perceiving the world and humanity's relation to it, introduced by
this century's new science.   Some scientists spoke explicitly of
the philosophical implications of this scientific revolution, but
even without such explanations the laity found in it metaphors
for a new way of approaching reality.   This new paradigm is like
Eudora Welty's vision in that it acknowledges the dualistic
world of appearance and deals with reality as we usually experi-

ence it, while also recognizing that there is another way of seeing the world that is distinctly non-dualistic.

The first dramatic step in this direction—the one most obvious to the public, at any rate—was taken by Einstein. His theory of relativity not only showed that mass and energy are but different forms of the same reality (what were once considered opposites, now are seen as one—at least from one perspective); it also taught us that a body could be both in motion and at rest at the same time (depending on who is observing it), that space is equivalent to time, and that time itself is relative.[32] After Einstein, the door to non-dualism in science opened even wider when Niels Bohr pronounced that electrons and light are both waves *and* particles, categories once considered mutually exclusive (since a particle is confined in space and a wave is spread out). Then Heisenberg's uncertainty principle blurred the line dividing subject and object, with its assertion that the characteristics of an object cannot be separated from the act of measurement and thus from the measurers themselves. Sounding distinctly non-Newtonian, the physicist Erwin Schroedinger declared: "Subject and object are only one. The barrier between them cannot be said to have been broken down as a result of recent experience in the physical sciences, for this barrier does not exist."[33] (In the visual arts a similar challenge to dualism had been expressed, in the closing decades of the nineteenth century, in Impressionism and Post-Impressionism, and, in the first decade of this century, in Cubism—all of which undercut the notion of a clear distinction between subject and object.[34])

The new physics was creating a picture of the cosmos as a whole, composed of atomic particles and space. The atoms making up each person or tree or rock were more or less dense, but the atoms in every person, tree, or rock were "filled" with more space than matter. What, exactly, determined where the "edge" of the person or tree or rock was, when the atoms of all could be pictured as flowing together within the whole? And the atom itself, once thought to be the smallest building block of matter, was found to be composed of yet smaller particles, and those particles were discovered to be constituted, not of things, but of "probabilities of interconnections," as Fritjof Capra explains:

> Quantum theory thus reveals a basic oneness of the universe. It shows that we cannot decompose the world into independently existing smallest units. As we penetrate into matter, nature does not show us any isolated "basic building blocks," but rather appears as a compli-

cated web of relations between the various parts of the whole.[35]

The difficulty in using a dualistic language to express ideas about holism—a problem that Welty would have to deal with in her fiction by subverting the language through paradox, symbolism, and metaphor—is exemplified in Capra's statement by his use of the terms "part" and "whole." As Arthur Koestler mused:

> . . . what exactly do we mean by the familiar words "part" or "whole"? "Part" conveys the meaning of something fragmentary and incomplete. . . . [A] "whole" is considered as something complete in itself. . . . "[P]arts" and "wholes" in an absolute sense do not exist anywhere. . . .[36]

Alfred North Whitehead, mathematician, philosopher, and student of the new science, added his own voice to those speaking out against the reduction of reality to separate, mutually exclusive categories. In his philosophy of "organism" and "vibratory existence," Whitehead declared (using Ken Wilber's summary) that

> all the things and events we usually consider are irreconcilable, such as cause and effect, past and future, subject and object, are actually just like the crest and trough of a single wave, a single vibration. For a wave, although itself a single event, only expresses itself through the opposites of crest and trough, high point and low point. For that very reason, the reality is not found in the crest nor the trough alone, but in their unity. . . .[37]

In the last decade, the study of holography has provided another model for the essential identity of the part and the whole that the new physics keeps implying. David Bohm—the man Einstein predicted would arrive at the unified field theory he himself had been unable to reach—has considered the fact that if you tear off just a piece of holographic negative and shine a laser beam through it, what you get is not the image of a part, but a picture of the whole. Using this not as evidence but as analogy, Bohm postulates the existence of

> an encoding pattern of matter and energy spreading ceaselessly throughout the universe—each region of space, no matter how small (all the way down to the

single photon, which is also a wave or "wave packet"),
containing—as does each region of the holographic
plate—the pattern of the whole, including all the past
and with implications for all the future. . . . Everything mirrors everything else: the universe is a looking-
glass.[38]

(Western science and Eastern mysticism meet in their own polar
unity in the similarity between the hypothesis Bohm is contem-
plating and The Flower Garland Sutra of Zen Buddhism: "In the
heaven of Indra there is said to be a network of pearls, so ar-
ranged that if you look at one you see all the others reflected in
it. In the same way each object in the world is not merely itself
but involves every other object, and in fact *is* every thing
else."[39])

   We can imagine that Carl Jung might have found in the
hologram a model for his suprapersonal unconscious. Jung saw
each individual as like Bohm's atom, encoded with the whole,
carrying a memory of identity with all humanity. This memory
code is "distributed throughout the brain-structure . . . like an
all-pervading, omnipresent, omniscient spirit. It knows man as
he always was, and not as he is at this moment; it knows him as
myth. . . . [It] means an extension of man beyond himself. . . ."[40]
Jung's collective unconscious shatters barriers between individuals and societies, as well as between the human past, present,
and future. So basic was holism to his vision that Jung defined neurosis as "self division" and saw the purpose of therapy
as "healing the split." He counselled those working toward
regaining their wholeness to be wary of "left hemisphere
imperialism"—domination by the rational, linear, reductionist,
dualistic side of the mind.[41]

   Another non-physicist whose work reflected the new
holistic paradigm was the psychological anthropologist Gregory
Bateson. Known for his description of the double-bind theory of
schizophrenia (there is no schizophrenic individual, only
schizophrenogenic relationships), Bateson saw the only real self
of any human being as composed of all of the personal relationships of that individual plus society plus the individual's natural environment. What is more, Bateson believed that we experience ourselves as this network of relationships.[42]

   In biology we can hear Lewis Thomas sounding the theme
of holism in his book *The Lives of the Cell*:

A good case can be made for our nonexistence as entities.
We are not made up, as we had always supposed, of suc-
cessively enriched packets of our own parts. We are
shared, rented, occupied. At the interior of our cells,
driving them, providing the oxidative energy that
sends us out for the improvement of each shining day,
are the mitochondria, and in a strict sense they are not
ours. They turn out to be little separate creatures, the
colonial posterity of probably primitive bacteria that
swam into ancestral precursors of our eukaryotic cells
and stayed . . . with their own DNA and RNA quite
different from ours. . . . My cells are no longer the pure
line entities I was raised with: they are ecosystems
more complex than Jamaica Bay.[43]

Erich Jantsch arrived at a similar denial of our separate
existence, working from the general systems, or context, theory.
According to Jantsch, while John Doe's mitochondria and
various organs and physiological systems are transformed from
"energy flow" into the being designated "John Doe," John is, in
terms of other flowing systems—family, religion, profession,
culture, country, ecosystem, solar system—simply a part of the
dynamic, flowing energy creating that whole.[44]

In short, startling ideas coming in this century from a variety of disciplines have been intimating a view of the world astonishingly different from that described by the Greek atomists
or by Newton. The breadth and vigor of the new movement
toward a non-dualistic paradigm suggests two things of significance to this study. It reminds us, first of all, that Welty could
have heard voices all around her echoing (and supporting) her
own holistic ideas. Secondly, it suggests that the holistic view
Welty evokes in her fiction should not be dismissed as naïvete
or philosophical evasion or aesthetic preciosity, unconnected to
the real challenges of life.

However, even without the confirming words of the scientists and philosophers mentioned, Welty could have found
another source confirming the validity of her holistic vision.
That lies in the intimation most of us have from time to time—
especially perhaps in our encounters with art and in our most
intense personal relationships—that there *is* a level of truth
where paradox reigns, where opposites exist together in a creative and not an antagonistic tension, where the rule of non-
contradiction does not apply. (In these moments we acknowledge, as Morris Berman has said, that "we love and hate the
same thing simultaneously, we fear what we most need, we recognize ambivalence as a norm rather than an aberration."[45])

We recall also that in mystical traditions, Eastern and Western, the liberated or enlightened person has always been one who recognizes the unity behind the illusions of opposites. According to Joseph Campbell, the mystical and the mythmaking consciousnesses share "one great story"—the "singularity" behind the apparent duality of reality. In different forms, they furnish the world with reminders that

> we have come forth from the one ground of being as manifestations in the field of time. The field of time is a kind of shadow play over a timeless ground. And you play the game in the shadow field, you enact your side of the polarity with all your might. But you know that your enemy, for example, is simply the other side of what you would see as yourself if you could see from the position of the middle.[46]

Indeed, the greatest of our literature may always have offered intimations of the same holistic vision, at least since Homer taught us to admire both Hector and Achilles—both the serenity and the commitment to civilization and order on the part of the Trojan and the "demonic egoism" (as Norman Rabkin calls it) on the part of the Greek.[47] In the *Divine Comedy*, Rabkin reminds us, Dante's central point is "that no event can be looked at from a single point of view. The journey in time must be seen in the light of the journey beyond time; every moment achieves full sense both in time and out of time, both as historical fact and as figure."[48] We suspect that paradoxes in Shakespeare such as the witches' "Fair is foul and foul is fair" delight us because we know the truth implied extends beyond the political and moral confusion of Macbeth's Scotland—and this in spite of the dualistic philosophy that dominates the surface level of Shakespeare's plays.

The notion of an organic cosmic unity was more obviously at the center of the poetry and poetic theory of the English Romantics, echoing in Blake's "And twofold Always May God us keep / From Single Vision and Newton's Sleep" (the quotation Robert Penn Warren referred to in his discussion of Welty's doubleness) and in Coleridge's confident declaration that it would take a lifetime to investigate "all the instances and exemplifications of the proverb 'extremes meet.'"[49] For the Romantic poets, the ability to entertain opposites simultaneously was the mark of the creator—supernal or human. Expressing itself cosmically, according to Shelley, in the ultimate unity of all things beyond the dome of many-colored glass, the reconciliation of opposites appeared in the poets' own creations in the Romantic emphasis on the union of subject and object, and in such techniques of imagistic blending as synaesthesia.

In America, Emerson spoke most explicitly of the philosophy of polar holism, which informed all he wrote and laid the foundation for his belief in the law of compensation, as well as in the Over-Soul, within which all apparent opposites—including human and divine—were resolved. Whitman's *Song of Myself* is a paeon to this holistic vision, an assertion of his union with the grass, the prostitute, the child, the president. Declaring himself both "the acme of things accomplished and the encloser of things to be," Whitman anticipates David Bohm's dictum that "the cause for any one thing is everything else."[50] And speaking of Welty's fellow Mississippian, James Snead has reminded us that "the futility of applying strictly binary categories to human affairs is the main lesson of Faulkner's novels. . . ."[51] Faulkner's repeated theme of the victim who is also the victimizer is one expression of the inseparability of apparent opposites; another is his treatment of the union of all time, even the apparent opposites, past and future: "Yesterday today and tomorrow are is: indivisible: one," Faulkner insists.

In short, the idea of the harmony of contraries may be the *leit motif* of much of Western literature. So if we are looking for sources of Welty's holistic vision, we might need to look no further than to a sensitive reading of the best writing our culture has produced. Indeed, the identification of this underlying motif in such a wide range of literature might suggest that there is nothing extraordinary about Welty's focus on holism. This is not the case, however. While for many writers this idea plays beneath the surface or on the periphery of their works, in Welty it is at the very heart. Her writings are marked by the unusual frequency with which this motif occurs; by its centrality to her plots, her characterizations, her themes; and by the astonishing variety and complexity of techniques she uses to express the idea, making each work unique, so that the linking vision never comes across as a repetitious sermon, but instead offers continually fresh insights into what life is.

One reason for its freshness, of course, is that she does not write to propound a philosophy, but simply to describe life as she sees it—and she sees it whole. The consequences of this vision for her art are multiple. It contributes an attitude toward life and toward people characterized by acceptance rather than judgment. For Welty an "insight" is not a fixed truth, but is rather "an act or angle of perception."[52] It makes possible a tone of comedy or genial affirmation or gentle wonder even in the face of the rape, murder, suicide, and the general cruelty of human to human that punctuate her stories. Here is the stuff of black comedy, but she knows that darkness is merely one side of a whole that includes light—and her goal is to help us to sense the wholeness. Because she is capable of such leaps beyond the apparent—seeing nobility in the grotesque legs of Clytie scissoring out of the water barrel where she killed herself; finding love in Howard who murdered his wife; unearthing the richest of all treasures in the bare life of the hill people the travelling salesman meets in his final journey—Welty's works are all tinged by the sense of mystery she speaks of so often in her essays. She knows that reality is not something merely to be analyzed, that there is more to people than what we see between their hats and shoes, and that the solemnest—and most joyous—challenge faced by writer and by reader is to penetrate the shadow that divides Us from Them or It.

The following chapters take a look at various ways Welty strikes at all sorts of dividing lines, beginning with her most direct statements of the theme in her autobiographical *One Writer's Beginnings* and then (in Chapter Two) in her essays and reviews collected in *The Eye of the Story*. Many of the changes Welty rings on this theme in her short stories are developed more fully in her longer works. I have chosen to emphasize seven of her stories involving initiation into holistic awareness—or the failure to complete that initiation. The discussion of *The Robber Bridegroom* analyzes Welty's mixture of fairy tale and history to expose the human desire to see life as *simplex*, while reality dances around us in all its multiplicity. The next chapter, on *Delta Wedding*, explores the epistemology of holism: the kind of knowing that puts us in touch with a unified reality and contributes most to a sense of personal wholeness. In the chapter on *The Ponder Heart*, the focus is on Welty's comic exploration of one woman's integrated self, a union of apparent opposites superior to the extremes between which she is torn. In *Losing Battles*, Welty engages in her own most extended battle to subvert our dualistic language to the expression of holism. That chapter will analyze the series of remarkably complex image patterns Welty creates to symbolize the unity that words cannot express directly. And in the final chapter, I will explore the insights *The Optimist's Daughter* offers into what may be the most difficult to achieve of all holistic per-

ceptions: the recognition of the necessary and creative connection between life and death.

Notes

[1] *The Robber Bridegroom* (Garden City, NY: Doubleday, Doran, 1942),
p. 126.
[2] *The Collected Stories of Eudora Welty* (New York: Harcourt, Brace
and World, 1980), pp. 452-53.
[3] For the following summary of the history of Western dualism and
modern scientific movements to holism, I am indebted to these books: Morris
Berman, *The Reenchantment of the World* (Ithaca: Cornell University Press,
1981); John P. Briggs and F. David Peat, *Looking Glass Universe: The Emerging
Science of Wholeness* (New York: Simon and Schuster, 1984); Fritjof Capra, *The
Tao of Physics* (New York: Bantam Books, 1984); Paul Davies, *God and the
New Physics* (New York: Simon and Schuster, 1983); Gary Zukav, *The Dancing
Wu Li Masters: An Overview of the New Physics* (New York: William Morrow,
1979).
[4] For the discussion of the implications of holism, I am indebted to J. C.
Cooper, *Yin and Yang: The Taoist Harmony of Opposites* (Wellingborough,
Northamptonshire: The Aquarian Press, 1981), pp. 9-21.
[5] *Kenyon Review*, 6 (Spring 1944), 256.
[6] "Out of the Strong," *Shenandoah*, 20 (Spring 1969), 38-39.
[7] For example, Margarette Sather, "Man in the Universe: The Cosmic
View of Eudora Welty," unpublished doctoral dissertation (University of
Louisville, 1976). Other general studies which consider Welty's double vision
or her frequent linking of opposites include J. A. Bryant, Jr., *Eudora Welty*
(Minneapolis: University of Minnesota Press, 1968); Chester E. Eisinger,
"Eudora Welty and the Triumph of the Imagination" in *Fiction of the Forties*
(Chicago: University of Chicago Press, 1963), pp. 258-83; Jennifer Lynn Randisi,
A Tissue of Lies: Eudora Welty and the Southern Romance (Lanham, MD: University Press of America, 1982). See also Richard C. Moreland, "Community
and Vision in Eudora Welty," *The Southern Review*, 18 (Winter 1982), 84-99. In
his *Eudora Welty's Chronicle: A Story of Mississippi Life*, Albert Devlin focuses on the union of quite specific opposites: historical fact and the artistic
imagination (Jackson: University Press of Mississippi, 1983).
[8] See, for example, on *The Golden Apples*, Merrill Maquire Skaggs,
"Morgana's Apples and Pears"; on *The Robber Bridegroom*, Warren French, "All
Things Are Double: Eudora Welty as a Civilized Writer"; on *Losing Battles*,
Seymour Gross, "A Long Day's Living: The Angelic Ingenuities of *Losing Battles*"—all collected in *Eudora Welty: Critical Essays*, ed. Peggy Whitman
Prenshaw (Jackson: University Press of Mississippi, 1979). In the same volume,
see Jane L. Hinton, "The Role of Family in *Delta Wedding, Losing Battles,* and
The Optimist's Daughter." Dealing with the idea of the ambiguity created by
the conflict of opposites in three works, Hinton sees the purpose of this collision
as an initiation into the mutability and uncertainties of the world. Other critical studies touching on Welty's union of apparent opposites in a single work include John Allen, "The Three Moments" in *A Still Moment: Essays on the Art of*

Eudora Welty, ed. John F. Desmond (Metuchen, NJ: The Scarecrow Press, 1978); J. A. Bryant, Jr., "Seeing Double in *The Golden Apples,*" *Sewanee Review,* 82 (Spring 1974), 300-15; and Elaine Upton Pugh, "The Duality of Morgana: The Making of Virgie's Vision, the Vision of *The Golden Apples,*" *Modern Fiction Studies,* 28 (Autumn 1982), 435-51.

[9] New York: Twayne, 1962; revised 1987.

[10] Baton Rouge: Louisiana State University Press, 1980.

[11] p. xiv.

[12] "Preface," 1962, n.p.; "Preface to the Revised Edition," n.p.

[13] 1987, p. 194.

[14] 1987, pp. 177, 196.

[15] 1987, p. 21.

[16] 1987, pp. 19, 69.

[17] "Further Reflections on Meaning in Eudora Welty's Fiction" in *Critical Essays on Eudora Welty,* ed. W. Craig Turner and Lee Emling Harding (Boston: G. K. Hall & Co., 1989), p. 303.

[18] "A Blazing Butterfly: The Modernity of Eudora Welty" in *Welty: A Life in Literature,* ed. Albert J. Devlin (Jackson: University Press of Mississippi, 1987), pp. 128, 124.

[19] "Einstein's Creative Thinking and the General Theory of Relativity: A Documented Report," *American Journal of Psychiatry,* 136 (January 1979), 38-43. See also Albert Rothenberg, "Janusian Thinking and Creativity" in *The Psychoanalytic Study of Society,* eds. W. Muensterberger et al. (New Haven: Yale University Press, 1976) and *The Emerging Goddess: The Creative Process in Art, Science and Other Fields* (Chicago: University of Chicago Press, 1979). Coleridge had a similar explanation for creativity in his view of imagination as the threshold between mind and matter, self and other, consciousness and the unconscious. Perhaps the most famous statement of the association between creativity and the capacity for unitary vision is Scott Fitzgerald's declaration that "the test of a first-rate intelligence is the ability to hold two opposed ideas in the mind at the same time, and still retain the ability to function" (*The Crack-Up,* ed. Edmund Wilson [New York: New Directions, 1945], p. 69).

[20] In her ground-breaking essay, "Woman's World, Man's Place: The Fiction of Eudora Welty," Peggy Prenshaw makes clear that Welty's fiction deals primarily with a woman's world, that its concerns are the matriarchal concerns of biological life, and that her heroes are more often women than men (*Eudora Welty: A Form of Thanks,* eds. Louis Dollarhide and Ann J. Abadie [Jackson: University Press of Mississippi, 1979], pp. 46-77).

[21] *Masculine/Feminine,* eds. Betty Roszak and Theodore Roszak (New York: Harper and Row, 1969), p. 304. Cf. Mary Daly's declaration that "*Gyn/Ecology* requires a constant effort to see the innerconnectedness of things" (*Gyn/Ecology: The Metaphysics of Radical Feminism* [Boston: Beacon Press, 1978], p. 19). See also Lynda Glennon, "Synthesism" in *Women and Dualism: A Sociology of Knowledge Analysis* (New York: Longman, 1979), pp. 97-118, and Rosemary Radford Reuther, *New Woman, New Earth: Sexist Ideologies and Human Liberation* (New York: The Seabury Press, 1975).

[22] Carol Gilligan, *In a Different Voice: Psychological Theory and Women's Development* (Cambridge: Harvard University Press, 1982); Nona Lyons, "Two Perspectives on Self, Relationships and Morality," *Harvard Education Review,* 53, 125-45; Nancy Chodorow, *The Reproduction of*

Mothering (Berkeley: University of California Press, 1978); Jean Baker Miller, *Toward a New Psychology of Women* (Boston: Beacon Press, 1976).

[23] Mary Field Belenky et al., *Women's Ways of Knowing: The Development of Self, Voice, and Mind* (New York: Basic Books, 1986). See also Ann Garry and Marilyn Pearsall, eds., *Women, Knowledge, and Reality: Explorations in Feminist Philosophy* (Boston: Unwin Hyman, 1989) and Sandra Harding and Merrill B. Hintikka, *Discovering Reality: Feminist Perspectives on Epistemology, Metaphysics, Methodology, and Philosophy of Science* (Dordrecht, Holland: D. Reidel Publishing Co., 1983).

[24] Linda Kuehl, "The Art of Fiction XLVII: Eudora Welty" in *Conversations with Eudora Welty*, ed. Peggy Whitman Prenshaw (Jackson: University Press of Mississippi, 1984), pp. 74-75.

[25] See Charles T. Bunting, "'The Interior World': An Interview with Eudora Welty" in *Conversations*, p. 58.

[26] "Approaching the Unconscious" in Carl G. Jung, ed., *Man and His Symbols* (London: Pan Books, 1978; first edition, 1964), p. 85.

[27] For ideas in this paragraph, I am grateful to Anthony Stevens, *Archetype: A Natural History of the Self* (London: Routledge and Kegan Paul, 1982), pp. 283-84, and Berman, pp. 56-57, 306. Berman quotes Alfred von Martin as saying that by the thirteenth century people had begun to feel that time was "'slipping away continuously. . . . After the thirteenth century the clocks in the Italian cities struck all the twenty-four hours of the day. It was realized that time was always short and hence valuable, that one had to husband it and use it economically if one wanted to become the "master of all things." Such an attitude had been unknown to the Middle Ages; to them time was plentiful and there was no need to look upon it as something precious'" (p. 56).

[28] Cited in Ken Wilber, *The Spectrum of Consciousness* (Wheaton, IL: The Theosophical Publishing House, 1977), p. 29.

[29] Cited in Wilber, *The Spectrum of Consciousness*, p. 40.

[30] Michael Polanyi, *Personal Knowledge* (Chicago: University of Chicago Press, 1958); cited in Belenky, p. 141.

[31] *The Rediscovery of Meaning, and Other Essays* (Middletown, CT: Wesleyan University Press, 1977), p. 17.

[32] Paul Davies explains that in relativity "there is no universal present, and the entire past and future of the universe are regarded as existing as an indivisible whole. The world is four-dimensional (three of space, one of time) and all events are simply *there*; the future does not 'happen' or 'unfold'" (p. 137).

[33] Cited in Wilber, p. 38.

[34] Betty Jean Craige, *Reconnection: Dualism to Holism in Literary Study* (Athens: University of Georgia Press, 1988).

[35] Capra, p. 57.

[36] *Janus: a Summing Up* (London: Hutchinson and Co., 1978), p. 27.

[37] Wilber, p. 23.

[38] Briggs and Peat, p. 111.

[39] C. Eliot, *Japanese Buddhism* (New York: Barnes and Noble, 1969), pp. 109-10.

[40] *Civilization in Transition* in *The Collected Works of C. G. Jung*, vol. 10, trans. R. F. C. Hull (London: Routledge & Kegan Paul, 1964), p. 10.

[41] Stevens, p. 258.

[42] Wilber, p. 25.

[43] Thomas Lewis, *The Lives of a Cell* (New York: Viking, 1974), pp. 3-4.

[44] Briggs and Peat, p. 18.

[45] Berman, p. 36.

[46] Joseph Campbell and Bill Moyers, *The Power of Myth*, ed. Betty Sue Flowers (New York: Doubleday, 1988), pp. 49, 54-55. Campbell distinguishes the mythology of the rest of the world from that of the religions of the Near East (which begin with an emphasis on unity in the Garden of Eden, but move to a dualism in which "you identify with the good and fight against the evil"), pp. 54-56.

[47] *Shakespeare and the Common Understanding* (New York: Free Press, 1967), p. 14. See also Robert Grudin, *Mighty Opposites: Shakespeare and Renaissance Contrariety* (Berkeley: University of California Press, 1979).

[48] Rabkin, p. 15.

[49] Samuel Taylor Coleridge, *The Friend*, ed. B. E. Rooke, vol. 2 (Princeton: Princeton University Press, 1969), p. 74.

[50] Briggs and Peat, p. 96; David Bohm, *Causality and Chance in Modern Physics* (London: Routledge & Kegan Paul, 1957). See also Bohm, *Wholeness and the Implicate Order* (London: Routledge & Kegan Paul, 1980).

[51] James A. Snead, *Figures of Division: William Faulkner's Major Novels* (New York: Routledge, Chapman & Hall, 1987), p. ix.

[52] Briggs and Peat make this point about David Bohm (p. 99).

I

Confluence: *One Writer's Beginnings*

The final sentences of Eudora Welty's latest work, the autobiographical *One Writer's Beginnings* (1984), offer a striking paradox: "As you have seen, I am a writer who came of a sheltered life. A sheltered life can be daring as well. For all serious daring starts from within."[1] This sheltered daring is part of a pattern of yoked opposites threading their way through the autobiography, beginning with Welty's earliest recollections. It is tempting, therefore, to look to *One Writer's Beginnings* for evidence of the biographical sources of Welty's fascination with harmonious contraries. And certainly the work appears to heap up such evidence. However, the inescapable fact is that this account of her life has passed through the filter of Welty's adult mind, a mind whose shaping paradigm, as her fiction suggests, is the idea of life as a dynamic pulsation of united opposites.

In the end, whether *One Writer's Beginnings* actually locates the source of Welty's holism is not important. What is important is that, in the process of looking back and consciously thinking about those "certain patterns in my work [which] repeat themselves without my realizing" (p. 98), Welty clearly sees her own life again and again in terms of the unifying vision that colors her fiction. Indeed, she comes close to acknowledging the significance to her of this particular pattern, when, toward the end of the work, she speaks of "the wonderful word *confluence*" (p. 102). But even without an explicit reference, the frequency of her return to that idea is evidence of its continuing centrality to her life as well as to her art.

In her parents, Welty says, she first experienced the harmony of contraries. Here is perhaps the simplest and most obvious exemplification of that difficult philosophical idea: two very different people united in loving tension, their differences undiluted, whirling at antipodes and drawing energy from their opposition. The creative potential of such a relationship is evidenced not only in its effects on the husband and wife, but also on their daughter. This was an idea she introduced in 1970 in an interview with Walter Clemons when, with comic exaggeration, she declared that while her mother was Southern, her father was a Northerner—"A Republican," Clemons says she added "in a mock hushed tone" before continuing: "It was a good family to grow up in. I learned there wasn't just one side that was right."[2] *One Writer's Beginnings* develops the contrast more seriously and in more detail.

Her father was the practical one, interested in technology and in instruments that instruct. He read for information, distrusting fiction "because fiction is not true" (p. 82). An optimist, he believed "in progress, in the future" (p. 5). Yet even his nature was a composite of apparent contraries, since, although an optimist, he always took chain, rope, and ax into hotel bedrooms, worked for an insurance company, and worried that his children might be lost or hit by lightning. In him united "the energetic practice of optimism" and "an abiding awareness of mortality itself" (p. 91), a double vision into which he was initiated, perhaps, when his mother wrote in his memory book her admonition that he be a good boy and meet her in heaven— and then died.

His wife—"with her different gifts," as Welty emphasizes (p. 5)—stood at the opposite pole. The first words Welty gives her mother in this work are "Well, I'm *not*"—in response to the declaration that Welty's father was "a pretty good weather prophet" (p. 4). Mrs. Welty was a lover of fiction who took hedonistic pleasure in novels; she was a teller of family tales (while her husband told not one). But she was like her husband in uniting contraries within herself. Although she was a pessimist, she faced life with exuberant courage, exemplified by her lack of fear of lightning: back home in West Virginia she had, in sheer exhilaration, "spread [her] arms wide and *run* in a good big storm" (p. 4). And like her husband, she bore the double memory of a beloved parent—in her case, the memory of her father, "half of it adoring dream, half brutal memory of his death" (p. 53).

While the book begins by establishing the opposition between Welty's parents, what the work as a whole emphasizes is the union created, not in spite of, but because of those differences. Nothing could be clearer from the epigraph Welty chooses for *One Writer's Beginnings,* an expression of the *concordia discors* in which she grew up:

> When I was young enough to still spend a long time buttoning my shoes in the morning, I'd listen toward the hall: Daddy upstairs was shaving in the bathroom and Mother downstairs was frying the bacon. They would begin whistling back and forth to each other up and down the stairwell. My father would whistle his phrase, my mother would try to whistle, then hum hers back. It was their duet. I drew my buttonhook in and out and listened to it—I knew it was "The Merry Widow." The difference was, their song almost floated with laughter: how different from the record, which growled from the beginning, as if the Victrola were only slowly being wound up. They kept it running between them, up and down the stairs where I was now just about ready to run clattering down and show them my shoes.

Even the title of their song—or the one Welty recalls—reflects the harmony of opposites.

As Welty remembers it, her education in this way of perceiving reality continued outside her home as well. The same united doubleness pops up again and again in her memories of growing up in Jackson, Mississippi: for example, the cheerful tunes of the Methodist hymns about damnation (p. 31); Saturday at the movie theatre watching *The Cabinet of Dr. Caligari* where the children "screamed with laughter, laughing at what terrified us" (p. 37); the parade that detoured by the house of a boy who soon died, creating forever in Welty the association of processions with ominous gaiety (p. 37). In their linking of joy and sorrow, fear and pleasure, these experiences underscore the young Eudora's continuing exposure to a reality that she was not yet ready to deal with intellectually. (As Morris Berman has suggested, experiencing the fact that the principle of Aristotelian non-contradiction does not apply to human emotions may be the most universal personal encounter with *concordia discors.*[3])

Intimations of a union of opposites far more challenging for the ordinary mind to take in—the polar balance of life and death—also came early, when the young Eudora asked her mother where babies come from and learned not the secrets of birth, but the secret of a baby's dying. What she glimpsed, uneasily, in that experience was that "the two secrets, told and still not told, [were] connected in her [mother's] deepest feelings" (p. 17). Welty's attempt, as a writer, to come to terms with the nature of the union of life and death plays throughout her works until it reaches its fullest exploration—and, for her, a resolution—in *The Optimist's Daughter*.

The tension between mother and daughter described in the account of Eudora's effort to learn where babies come from (seen initially in her mother's comic evasion and ending in Eudora's vague sense of guilt and her mother's heartbreaking confession) prefigures their later relationship. That relationship provided Welty with what was apparently the richest and the most painful youthful experience of polarities: her first recognition that the need to be freed of love is but the other pole of loving. Giving up her ticket to *Blossom Time* so Eudora could see the play, waiting in Jackson while her daughter went to New York, "telling me she missed me but only wanted what was best for me" (p. 94), Mrs. Welty taught her daughter "that bliss for me would have to imply my mother's deprivation or sacrifice." "I don't think it would have occurred to her what a double emotion I felt . . . ," Welty writes; " . . . I could hardly bear my pleasure for my guilt." "There is no wonder," she continues, "that a passion for independence sprang up in me at the earliest age. It took me a long time to manage the independence, for I loved those who protected me—and I wanted inevitably to protect them back. I have never managed to handle the guilt" (pp. 19-20).

Rejecting neither her need for independence nor her mother's love, Welty continued those trips to New York in spite of the guilt and pain they caused her and her mother. Looking back in *One Writer's Beginnings* on this complex relationship, Welty focuses on the creative wholeness that emerged from the tension of the "double emotion" evoked by her mother. Precisely here, Welty declares unequivocally, was the catalyst for the direction her creativity took: "In the act and the course of writing stories, these are two of the springs, one bright, one dark, that feed the streams" (p. 20).

As we shall see, it is in Welty's fiction, in *The Optimist's Daughter*, that she confronts more explicitly the anger that is only glancingly acknowledged in *One Writer's Beginnings*, in its descriptions of her feelings of guilt.[4] In the novel, Welty expresses, through the lesson Laurel Hand learns, her own recognition of anger's role in psychic wholeness.[5] But the Welty of *One Writer's Beginnings* is on the other side of that anger (as

Welty believes artists must be when they are creating[6]), possessed of an understanding of the rightness of both the anger and the love.

The closest Welty comes in *One Writer's Beginnings* to revealing, symbolically, her youthful rejection of her mother's complicated love is in her description of her revulsion at her grandmother's pigeons. This is just like Laurel's response, in *The Optimist's Daughter*, to *her* grandmother's pigeons, which she remembers as "sticking their beaks down each other's throats, gagging each other, eating out of each other's craws, swallowing down all over again what had been swallowed before. . . ."[7] In *One Writer's Beginnings*, Welty associates this image with her mother's love—a love that sacrifices self and then silently requires sacrifice of the loved one, a love that nurtures and then demands sustenance in return. Welty tells us, too, however, that she has learned that her own "agitation and apprehension" about the pigeons (which the child Eudora had interpreted as hatred of them) was really love (p. 56). In her maturity she can articulate what the child intuited: the psychological truth of the intersection of love and hate, of generosity and neediness. Indeed, the pigeons provided Welty with a homey symbol of the uroboric image of life itself, like the mythic snake that gets its nourishment by feeding on itself (or, in this case, on that extension of self, one's offspring).

It is little wonder that the family, the apparent source of her intimate knowledge of life's doubleness, is at the center of almost all that Welty has written. She explains in *One Writer's Beginnings* that she now recognizes that even an early story, "Acrobats in a Park," which had at the time seemed "exotic, free of any experience as I knew it," was really about family, and "I've been writing about the structure of the family in stories and novels ever since." Though "artificial and oddly formal," the image of the family developed here conveys Welty's sense of *concordia discors*: the family of acrobats erect "a structure of their bodies that holds together, interlocked, and stands like a wall," a union created by the tension of pushing against each other (p. 86). The family is the ideal studio for learning another lesson in polarity: how self can retain its individuality and yet unite with other; indeed, that only in such a union can it be fully self.

Years later when she took photographs for the WPA of the Mississippi poor and still later when she began writing, Welty discovered that art, too, requires the shattering of the barrier between self and other. In photography, first "getting

[her] distance," she drew nearer and nearer her subject, until she was able to learn their secrets by plunging into her own heart (pp. 21-22). This may be the clearest explanation possible of what is meant for the artist by "the self becoming other." Repeatedly in *One Writer's Beginnings*, Welty returns to the paradox of a character's becoming most other—"in his own right another human being on the page"—when the author writes "most entirely" out of self (p. 100). Welty is using the idea of "self" here in a very Jungian sense. For Jung the "individuation" process—becoming a self—involves bringing to consciousness greater and greater depths of the unconscious, which, for Jung, contains the collective unconscious. Here, in this "trans-personal" self lies the source, in Jungian thought, "of all our understanding of the deepest mysteries."[8] Plunging into that self is for Welty, as for Jung, the path to the visions of the creative person. It is what makes possible the "vaunting," as Welty calls it, of "imagin[ing] yourself inside another person," which, she says, "is what a story writer does in every piece of work; it is his first step, and his last too, I suppose" (p. 39).

In a variation on this idea, Welty gives us a vivid account of an early encounter with the artist's perception of the union of the created and the instrument of creation, in her description of Eudora in kindergarten drawing three daffodils. (The impli-cation of the passage is clear if we consider the pencil she is literally describing as a metaphor for the artist as the instru-ment.) She writes: " . . . while I was drawing, my sharpened yellow pencil and the cup of the yellow daffodil gave off whiffs just alike," the sharp edges separating the two fading (p. 9). Welty continues: "That the pencil doing the drawing should give off the same smell as the flower it drew seemed part of the art lesson—as shouldn't it be? Children, like animals, use all their senses to discover the world. Then artists come along and discover it the same way, all over again. Here and there, it's the same world. Or now and then we'll hear from an artist who's never lost it" (pp. 9-10).

The artist's need for connection with the world of other becomes one of the themes of the last section of *One Writer's Beginnings*, which Welty called "Finding a Voice." She speaks there of "the need I carried inside myself to know—the appre-hension first, and then the passion, to connect myself to [the world out there]" (p. 76). She associates this passion with her growing awareness of the relativity of self and other, and of the possibility of their union. Initially, the relativity of that relationship struck her most forcefully on those occasions when she experienced herself as other to yet other selves.

As a child travelling with her father, she had always seen the "world passing my window. It was when I came to see it was *I* who was passing that my self-centered childhood was over" (p. 76). What may have been her first adult experience of this exchange occurred on one of her trips to New York City during World War II. The train had stopped inexplicably in "a long, high valley, a green peaceful stretch of Tennessee." Then, a soldier sitting near her had, without a word, simply got off the train, not even taking his cap, and walked away. Welty remembers: "The train in time proceeded, and as we left him back there in the landscape, I felt *us* going out of sight for *him*, diminishing and soon to be forgotten" (p. 96). These accounts have the feeling of literary versions of Einstein's descriptions of his discovery of the special theory of relativity in his "vision" of himself as both in motion and at rest, depending on his point of view.

In her early story "A Memory," Welty was to approach the interchange of self and other in another way: a young dreamer is painfully dragged from her position of observer, from which she had viewed the world through the small frame of her fingers as she had learned in painting class. The shocking realism that she observes from this new perspective permanently changes her. In *One Writer's Beginnings*, Welty writes of this story: "It has something of my own dreaming at the train window. But now the dreamer has stopped to look. After that, dreaming or awake, she will be drawn in" (p. 89). For the artistic mind, subject and object cannot remain separate.

The passion for connection which dominates the last third of *One Writer's Beginnings* is not limited to Welty's desire to unite with her artistic subjects. She speaks also of detecting in retrospect connections of theme, motifs, and characters among her works (one of those retrospective discoveries of connection resulting in the collection of seven of her stories in *The Golden Apples*): "In writing, as in life, the connections of all sorts of relationships and kinds lie in wait for discovery, and give out their signals to the Geiger counter of the charged imagination, once it is drawn into the right field" (p. 99). In life, the Geiger counter of Welty's imagination led her to detect the connections in the lives of her parents:

> Connections slowly emerge. Like distant landmarks you
> are approaching, cause and effect begin to align

themselves, closer together. Experiences too indefinite
of outline in themselves to be recognized for themselves
connect and are identified as a larger shape. And
suddenly a light is thrown back, as when your train
makes a curve, showing that there has been a mountain
of meaning rising behind you on the way you've come, is
rising there still, proven now through retrospect.

It seems to me, writing of my parents now in my
seventies, that I see continuities in their lives that
weren't visible to me when they were living. . . .
Writing fiction has developed in me an abiding respect
for the unknown in a human lifetime and a sense of
where to look for the threads, how to follow, how to
connect. . . . (p. 90)

One wonders, indeed, whether it is writing that has led
Welty to her holistic vision or an aptitude for perceiving life
holistically that inclined her to writing. Yet, as she says, cause
and effect finally come together, making such distinctions
unnecessary. Whatever its source, the implications of this
vision open in the last chapter of *One Writer's Beginnings*, like
the century plant in *Losing Battles* showing its rare and startling
beauty. The connections between her artistic self and her
fictional characters, the continuities in the lives of her parents,
the links between her own life and her family—these all become
part of a larger pattern of wholeness. The homemade Andrews
family tree Welty had examined as a child serves her as a symbol
not only of the union of individual part and whole, but of the
whole's organic, dynamic, ever-changing, ever-constant nature:

The leaves weren't stiffly drawn or conventional
ellipses, all alike, but each one daintily fashioned
with a pointed tip and turned on its stem this way or
that, as if this family tree were tossed by a slight
breeze. The massed whole had the look, at the time to
me, of a children's puzzle, in which you were supposed
to find your mother. I found mine—only a tiny leaf on a
twig of a branch near the top, hardly big enough to
hold her tiny name. (p. 50)

Welty's sense of being a part of a larger non-familial, even nonhuman whole is suggested in her description of the time she
stood in her father's Lamar Life office, looking down over all of
Jackson, "spread to its seeable limits, its green rim, where the
still river-like Pearl River and the still-unpaved-over Town
Creek meandered and joined together in their unmolested

swamp, with 'the country' beyond. We were located where we stood there—part of our own map" (p. 83).

If she can see the line blur between subject and object, between person and person, between part and whole, between natural world and human, it is only a step to the overthrow of the final dualistic barriers—those between past, present, and future, and finally between life and death themselves. Photography had taught her, she says, that transience could be captured, in a paradoxical yoking of movement and stasis (p. 84). Life and writing combined to teach her the subjectivity of time, that events taking a linear order from one perspective can be perceived from another perspective in a completely different order: "The events of our lives happen in a sequence in time, but in their significance to ourselves they find their own order, a timetable not necessarily—perhaps not possibly—chronological. The time as we know it subjectively is often the chronology that stories and novels follow: it is the continuous thread of revelation" (pp. 68-69).

Such a passage makes clear the centrality of epistemology to Welty's philosophical holism: *this* is the reality that the intensely feeling, illuminated mind perceives and experiences. In such a mind, in moments of insight, memory removes apparent temporal distinctions, and, as a consequence, past and present—contraries necessarily kept separate in our conduct of everyday business—are seen as existing together. In other works (particularly in descriptions of the natural world conveyed from the point of view of an omniscient narrator), Welty will suggest that the vision so perceived parallels a united external reality that exists independent of the perceiving mind.

One Writer's Beginnings opens with a description of the many clocks in Welty's childhood house on North Congress Street. It ends with an assertion of freedom from "that clock time which spaces us apart so inhibitingly, divides young and old, keeps our living through the same experiences at separate distances" (p. 102). Her description of this alternative perception of life is as unifying, as creative, as dynamic as a straight-line perception of time is static, divisive, and entropically destructive. Her image is a spiral; the movement is kaleidoscopic; the goal is connection:

> It is our inward journey that leads us through time—
> forward or back, seldom in a straight line, most often
> spiraling. Each of us is moving, changing, with respect
> to others. As we discover, we remember; remembering,

we discover; and most intensely do we experience this
when our separate journeys converge. Our living experience at those meeting points is one of the charged
dramatic fields of fiction. (p. 102)

Finally, having done away with these divisions, Welty
speaks in *One Writer's Beginnings* of "the wonderful word" that
exists "as a reality and a symbol in one. . . . the only kind of
symbol that for me as a writer has any weight, testifying to the
pattern, one of the chief patterns, of human experience" (p. 102).
That magical word for Welty—we might be tempted to call it the
"key" to her fiction and to her view of her own life if such a
term were not so reductive—is *confluence*, containing in its
etymology the implication of both unity and of dynamic
motion.[9] Welty locates her clearest fictional treatment of this
theme in the closing pages of *The Optimist's Daughter*, which
she discusses at length in *One Writer's Beginnings*. By the end
of that novel, Laurel Hand has made it through her father's
funeral and the reawakened memories of the deaths of her
mother and her husband. She has burned her father's letters to
her mother and is preparing to give up her family home to her
father's unfeeling young widow.

Then she has a dream that she is a passenger on a train
with her husband, riding over a bridge. When she awakens,
dream and reality merge as she recalls that she had made just
such a trip when she and Phil had come by train from Chicago to
Mount Salus for their wedding. From their train window, they
had seen what Welty presents as the perfect symbols of life's
multiple-layered, but united reality. Laurel and Phil had looked
out first on "the water . . . reflecting the low, early sun," then on
"the confluence of the water, the Ohio and the Mississippi."
Because "they were looking down from a great elevation"—the
perspective required for a sense of the whole—

> . . . all they saw was at the point of coming together,
> the bare trees marching in from the horizon, the rivers
> moving into one, and as he touched her arm she looked
> up with him and saw the long, ragged, pencil-faint line
> of birds within the crystal of the zenith, flying in a V
> of their own, following the same course down. All they
> could see was sky, water, birds, light, and confluence. It
> was the whole morning world.
> And they themselves were a part of the confluence.
> (p. 103)

Earthly reflects heavenly; eastern and western waters join to flow south; birds mirror the patterns of the rivers below; human beings unite with each other and with nature. The message Laurel receives from this moment of enlightenment seems at first to have been inaccurate: "They were riding as one with it, right up front. It's our turn! she'd thought exultantly. And we're going to live forever" (p. 103). Yet the war had left Phil "bodiless and graveless of a death made of water and fire"—an apparent contradiction of the promise of her vision of confluence. What Welty knows and Laurel learns is that Laurel's early interpretation was true. The barrier between life and death fades as she realizes that Phil could live for her, even in death: "For her life, any life, she had to believe was nothing but the continuity of its love" (p. 103). (Laurel knows, too, that without the continuity of love, people who are alive can be as good as dead.)

What is striking about Welty's symbolic use of the rivers is its contrast to other familiar and more conventional symbolic renderings of flowing water, which emphasize change, loss, irrecoverable transience. St. Augustine's is typical: "Time is like a river made up of events which happen, and its current is strong; no sooner does anything appear than it is swept away."[10] In Welty's imagery, the rivers are certainly associated with dynamic movement, too. Yet because the birds, Phil, and Laurel are travelling with the water, relative to themselves there is no movement, no loss of each other, no change. And as long as Laurel keeps them all together in her mind (that is, by internalizing what was external), time is conquered by memory. Phil will always be with Laurel, as will be this moment of convergence and all other moments and people vivified by her mind.

One Writer's Beginnings—the book that begins with the ticking of the clock and the outlining of contrasts—leaves us at the end with a declaration of reality's constant change and ultimate unity:

> Of course the greatest confluence of all is that which makes up the human memory—the individual human memory. . . . Here time, also, is subject to confluence. The memory is a living thing—it too is in transit. But during its moment, all that is remembered joins, and lives—the old and the young, the past and the present, the living and the dead. (p. 104)

Looking back on her life, Welty discovered variations on the theme of polarity that are developed (in even greater complexity and with greater subtlety) in her fiction—not merely the coexistence of opposites, but the harmony potential in the opposition, the dynamic tension of the poles, the creativity implicit in that tension, and the recognition of wholeness that can shatter the barriers between such opposites as self and other, past and present, life and death.

Notes

[1] *One Writer's Beginnings* (Cambridge, MA: Harvard University Press, 1984), p. 104. References to this work will hereafter be given in the text of this chapter.

[2] "Meeting Miss Welty," *The New York Times Book Review*, 12 April 1970, 2, 46; rpt. in Prenshaw, ed., *Conversations*, p. 33.

[3] Berman, p. 36.

[4] Carolyn Heilbrun criticizes *One Writer's Beginnings* for falling into "the old genre of female autobiography, which tends to find beauty even in pain and to transform rage into spiritual acceptance" (*Writing a Woman's Life* [New York: W. W. Norton, 1988], p. 12). For a discussion of this and other criticisms of Welty's failure to challenge social injustices in her work, see below, pp. 25-26.

[5] For a perceptive discussion of the role of anger in Laurel's accession to wholeness in *The Optimist's Daughter*, see Helen Hurt Tiegreen, "Mothers, Daughters, and One Writer's Revisions" in Devlin, ed., *Welty: A Life in Literature*, pp. 188-211.

[6] *The Eye of the Story: Selected Essays and Reviews* (New York: Random House, 1978), pp. 149-51.

[7] *The Optimist's Daughter* (New York: Random House, 1972), p. 140.

[8] The phrase is Benjamin G. Lockerd, Jr.'s, in *The Sacred Marriage: Psychic Integration in 'The Faerie Queen'* (Lewisburg: Bucknell University Press, 1987), pp. 23, 33, 25.

[9] "I'm crazy about that word," Welty exclaimed in a 1978 interview with Martha van Noppen ("A Conversation with Eudora Welty," in Prenshaw, ed., *Conversations*, p. 242).

[10] Cited in Paul Davies, *Other Worlds: Space, Superspace and the Quantum Universe* (London: Sphere Books, 1982), p. 46.

II

Inside the Labyrinth: *The Eye of the Story*

While *One Writer's Beginnings* offers evidence of how
Welty views her own life in terms of polarity, *The Eye of the
Story* (1978) shows us that the same vision operates when Welty
looks outward. Welty repeatedly finds in the fiction of authors
she admires the holistic themes that resound in her own works.
And when she turns to explanations of her theories of writing,
she reveals that the idea of the coexistence of opposites in art
underpins her aesthetics. At least half of the essays in *The Eye of
the Story*, collected from a period of forty-two years, contain
some reference to this motif.

Together, these essays offer Welty's clearest and most explicit statements about this vision of reality, its relevance to her
theory of art, its significance in the development of the self, and
its potential role in human relationships. Of course, it is not
Welty's purpose, in any of these essays, to present a philosophy
of non-dualism. Sometimes, indeed, the idea appears in just an
image, or in a sentence or two, or in a couple of paragraphs. But
almost always it appears, just below the surface of the essays, a
leitmotif supporting the essays' major themes.

The earliest essay in the collection, "Ida M'Toy" (first published in 1942), suggests that from the beginning of her career the
theme of the harmony of opposites informed Welty's view of
life and of art. "Ida M'Toy" is the description of "an old Negro
woman, for a long time a midwife in my Mississippi town and
for another long time a dealer in secondhand clothes in the
same place."[1] Although this is the only essay in the whole collection focused on a person who is not a writer, Ida M'Toy herself becomes one of Welty's earliest symbols of the artist. The
metaphors Welty attaches to the midwife-merchant leave little

question about this: she is a skyrocket or meteor ("radiant of [her] own substance and shower[ing] it about regardlessly"); one who has "a hand in the mysteries"; a "cross between a transcendentalist and a witch"; a visionary (pp. 336, 338, 345, 347).

Like the writer she represents, Ida keeps a ledger where, she declares, "you could find anything in the world . . . if you turn enough pages and go in the right direction" (p. 341). At the end of her life, she lives "directly in symbols" (p. 348). And, like powerful bards always, Ida "sometimes, owing to her superior wisdom . . . is a little malign, but much oftener she will become excruciatingly tender, holding, as if in some responsibility toward all the little ones of the world, the entire population to her great black cameoed breast" (p. 346). One wonders if the Welty of today would not be able to see characteristics of her own art in this description of Ida's domain: "Her house turns year by year into a better labyrinth, more inescapable, and she delights in its complication of aisles and curtains and its mystery of closed doors with little signs on ruled paper, 'Nobody can come in here'" (p. 340).[2]

What is important for this study is that the dominant characteristic of this symbolic artist, a characteristic identified so early in Welty's career, is her capacity for uniting opposites, for triumphing over apparent duality. Welty writes: "Ida's life has been divided into two (it is, in many ways, eloquent of duality); but there is a thread that runs from one part into the other, and to trace this connection between delivering the child and clothing the man is an interesting speculation" (p. 337). Although she does not use the term "polarity," Welty's careful differentiation between the apparent duality and the unitary reality of Ida's life makes clear her awareness of the philosophical distinction between "duality" (mere doubleness or multiplicity) and polarity, the transcendence of doubleness in union.

The thread stitching into a whole the parts of Ida's life is Ida's vision of the *united* doubleness of all of life. Welty says of her:

> . . . you cannot help believing that she sees them all, her children and her customers, in the double way, naked and clothed, young and then old, with love and with contempt, with open arms or with a push to bar the door. She . . . sees her customers as a procession of sweet suppliant spirits that she has birthed, who have returned to her side, and again sometimes as a bunch of scarecrows or even changelings, that she wishes were well gone out of sight. (p. 345)

In Welty's fiction, too—as, indeed, Welty believes, in all true art—people are perpetually and simultaneously sweet suppliants and scarecrows.

Ida's relationship with her mother (of whom she speaks in pity and amazement) is also shot through with doubleness. It shows the same combined light and darkness that later in *The Optimist's Daughter* mark Laurel's relationship with her mother and that we see tingeing Welty's relationship with her mother in *One Writer's Beginnings*. (This may, of course, be the razor's edge of all human connectedness.) Ida tells how she had given her mother a grand party before her death with "four turkeys, four hens, four geese, four hams, red cake, white cake, chocolate cake, caramel cake, every color cake known" only to hear her mother demand, "Where my coffee? Bring on turnip and cornbread. Didn't you make a blackberry pie?" Ida had finished her story "laughing and crying," an appropriately polar response to life (p. 347), very like the responses elicited by Welty's fiction. Ida's agonizing relationship with her mother becomes for Welty a reminder that creativity itself may have its source in what is usually thought of as an opposite, destructive power: " . . . perhaps," she says, "all vision has lived in the house with cruelty" (p. 347). Certainly this recalls Welty's identification, in *One Writer's Beginnings*, of the source for the double streams of her own creativity in the love and guilt her mother evoked.

In other essays in *The Eye of the Story*, Welty speaks even more directly of art as the point at which opposites can unite. A good writer, Welty declares in "Place in Fiction," "is always seeing double, two pictures at once in his frame. . . ." On the simplest level she refers to the meeting in art of imagination and external reality. The two pictures Welty speaks of are "[the writer's] and the world's. . . . [The writer] works best in a state of constant and subtle and unfooled reference between the two. It is his clear intention—his passion, I should say—to make the reader see only one of the pictures—the author's—under the pleasing illusion that it is the world's; this enormity is the accomplishment of a good story" (p. 125).

But the double vision of the artist expresses itself in other ways as well, ways that more subtly and complexly depend on the idea of a holistic philosophy. Welty discusses, for example, how the novel becomes universal by being first of all vividly local (on the face of it, quite contradictory ideas), because roots that reach deep touch finally "the deep and running vein, eternal and consistent and everywhere purely itself, that feeds and is fed by the human understanding" (p. 133). Furthermore, in "Some Notes on River Country" she ventures that in intense involvement in place, time ceases to be linear, so that it is possible to believe that even now the Natchez Trace is home to "Indians, Mike Fink the flatboatman, Burr, and Blennerhassett, John James Audubon, the bandits of the Trace, planters, and preachers . . ." (p. 299).

Comedy itself, Welty's chosen genre, she characterizes by its capacity to unite opposites,[3] but all the arts communicate by their power to link self and what seems not-self, addressing "our common feeling" (p. 354) or (she uses almost Jungian terms) our "common memory" (p. 26). They join all times, overcoming the dual opposition of now and not-now, because (as she writes of Jane Austen's novels), the arts "pertain not to the outside world but to the interior, to what goes on perpetually in the mind and heart" (p. 11). " . . . by the shock of what first seems new," she writes in her essay on Henry Green, " . . . we are led . . . truly to recognize the familiar" (p. 19).

Just as art rises out of a triumph over dualism, so, Welty believes, one of its most important functions is to correct the either-or view of reality which distorts the vision most of us have. Living dualistically, we divide our reality into opposites and spend our lives pursuing one side of the pair. Our humanity thus reduced (because we experience only part of our selves and of our relationship to other), we become acclimated to isolation, expressed in human alienation, or in violence, or in failure to find meaning in life. According to Welty, much of modern fiction participates in this deception: "For many of our writers . . . for the purpose of writing novels, most human behavior is looked at through the frame, or the knothole, of alienation" (p. 10).

Welty sees the role of the best fiction as reuniting the separated poles of reality. Such art can help us overcome our sense of isolation from others by reminding us of our union in common humanity. It can help us overcome our isolation from ourselves by pointing out our total being—a person who combines good and bad, heroism and cowardice, wisdom and folly. It can help us overcome our isolation from reality by giving us glimpses of life's mysterious doubleness, making us dissatisfied with one pole only of reality.

Welty expresses this aim in "Place in Fiction," calling up the image of the china night-light that she had earlier used in *Delta Wedding* and that later she would speak of in *One*

Writer's Beginnings. In the 1956 essay she explains its symbolism this way:

> Some of us grew up with the china night-light, the little lamp whose lighting showed its secret and with that spread enchantment. The outside is painted with a scene, which is one thing; then, when the lamp is lighted, through the procelain sides a new picture comes out through the old, and they are seen as one. A lamp I knew of was a view of London till it was lit; but then it was the Great Fire of London, and you could go beautifully to sleep by it. The lamp alight is the combination of internal and external, glowing at the imagination as one; and so is the good novel. Seeing that these inner and outer surfaces do lie so close together and so implicit in each other, the wonder is that human life so often separates them, or appears to, and it takes a good novel to put them back together. (pp. 119-20)

Inner and outer lives, London calm and London afire, are "implicit" in each other, as the negative magnetic pole is implicit in the positive. So in Welty's characters, tender feeling is implicit in the most hard-hearted (Little Harp in *The Robber Bridegroom*); cruelty is implicit in love (Howard in "Flowers for Marjorie"); nobility is implicit in the reviled and degraded (the deaf mutes in "The Key" or Phoenix Jackson in "A Worn Path" or Clytie in the story of that name); and a beginning is embedded implicitly in every conclusion (*Delta Wedding, Losing Battles, The Optimist's Daughter*). It is the illumination of the imaginative mind that allows the two to glow as the one they truly are.

The theme of the artist's apprehension of holism underlies every essay in the section "On Writers" in *The Eye of the Story*, offering further evidence that this is one of the basic constructs of Welty's aesthetics. What Welty seems most interested in is the variety of ways other artists have of expressing, in spite of the dualism of language itself, the essential unity of apparently contradictory parts of reality. She detects this in other writers' narrative structures, in their characterizations, and in their moral vision. Stephen Crane's "The Bride Comes to Yellow Sky" has, Welty writes, "a construction simple as a seesaw, and [is] not without a seesaw's kind of pleasure in reading" (p. 87), an image that makes visible the irrevocable unity—and dynamic interdependence—of the fates of the marshal and Scratchy Wilson in Crane's tale. According to Welty, the plot of Katherine Mansfield's "Miss Brill" has "two sides, or two halves, or two opposites, or two states of mind or feeling side by side" (p. 88), but both unite in the title character. In D. H. Lawrence's "The Fox," the two women represent

> the conventional separation at work in the two halves of the personality—the conscious and the unconscious, or the will and the passive susceptibility, what is "ready" and what is submerged. March and Banford may well be the two halves of one woman, of woman herself in the presence of the male will. (p. 98)

In Jane Austen, more than in any other, Welty identifies the spirit of wholeness: "Her habit of mind of seeing both sides of her own subject—of seeing it indeed in the round—is a little unusual, too, to writers and readers of our day" (p. 7). This capacity—so often absent in our fragmented, isolated, alienated modern society—Welty attributes to Austen's sense of oneness with her society, her *"belonging to her world"* (p. 10).

Chekhov's ability to see in the round Welty also traces to a tolerant, non-dualistic vision. Because of that vision, Chekhov was able to change the short story into what Welty describes as "something open to human meaning and answerable to that meaning in all its variety" (p. 62). His was the basic holistic truth: for him, Welty writes, reality is not one thing,

> invariable, or static, or ironclad, or consistent, or even trustworthy. . . . What is real in life—and what a Chekhov story was made to reflect with the utmost honesty—may be at the same time what is transient, ephemeral, contradictory, even on the point of vanishing before our eyes. So it isn't just *there*. (p. 63)

Welty's explanation of what Chekhov's reality *is* sounds very much like the ancient Taoist comparison of the non-dual whole to a garland of flowers or a cluster of mutually reflecting jewels. Welty writes:

> And so reality is no single, pure ray, no beacon against the dark. It might be thought of as a cluster of lesser lights, visible here on earth like the windows of a village at night, close together but not *one*—some are bright, some dim, some waywardly flickering. All imply people; there are people for every light.
> . . . all bear some relationship to one another—it is, again, a matter of human connection, a state of kinship or at least of neighborliness. (p. 63)

And reality itself is not any one light, but all the lights together, each distinct within the unity—another expression of the idea behind the china lamp with London at peace and ablaze.

Such a vision makes both ends of a paradox real, allowing Chekhov to say, "Life is terrible and marvelous" (p. 62), allowing him to show that fantasy is real—"because the existence of [a person's] feelings is real; and they are all he has" (p. 64); allowing him to demonstrate that "success and defeat are aspects of the same thing" (p. 80). The tolerance for evil consequent to such a view is beyond the capacity of most people: Welty recalls that Chekhov refuses to judge and condemn even a woman's scalding to death another woman's baby, accepting "even this unbearable act . . . as only one with the rest of human acts . . ." (p. 77). This unsettling example is the most vivid evidence in Welty's essays that what she is asking of the artist is the taking of a cosmic perspective, a god's-eye view of human existence. From this vantage point, questions of human justice and legal judgments do not enter into consideration. Without denying the appropriateness (and even necessity) of such judgments on the human level, the artist regards unblinkingly all reality, including all human actions, as part of the whole. We think in Welty's own works of her acceptance of Salome and Little Harp in *The Robber Bridegroom,* of both Solomon and Cash in "Livvie," of Faye in *The Optimist's Daughter,* of Homer Champion and Curly Stovall in *Losing Battles.*[4]

Among twentieth-century writers, Welty locates this attitude in Henry Green, whom she describes as "a man of reason . . . fascinated by the irrational," an artist who conveys the "extraordinary" quality of ordinary lives (p. 18). Writing from "inside the labyrinth of everyday life" (again, that image, introduced in "Ida M'Toy," of the heart of the maze, a kind of *axis mundi* where opposites unite), Green is privy to this non-dualistic secret: " . . . frivolity . . . is part of the everyday world along with the murder in the next street and the rose in the garden— with us, within us" (pp. 20-21). Carl Jung made a similar point when he wrote in *Civilization in Transition:*

> None of us stands outside humanity's black collective shadow. Whether the crime occurred many generations back or happens today, it remains the symptom of a disposition that is always and everywhere present— and one would therefore do well to possess some "imagination for evil"; for only the fool can permanently disregard the conditions of his own nature. In fact, this negligence is the best means of making him an

> instrument of evil. Harmlessness and naivete . . . lead
> to projection of the unrecognized evil into the "other."
> . . . [T]he projection carries the *fear* which we in-
> voluntarily and secretly feel for our own evil over to
> the other side. . . . [O]ur lack of insight deprives us of
> the capacity to deal with evil.

Jung points out that this has been a problem for Christians who seek to avoid a tabooed evil by projecting it onto a scapegoat, an act which ignores the fact that evil is essentially internal, not external, and cannot be avoided.[5] To perceive that what is with us—murder or rape or petty meanness or failure to understand—is also within us is at the heart of Welty's compassion, too.

Other of Welty's essays offer yet further examples of her fascination with the theme of the coincidence of contraries. Katherine Anne Porter's despair is both dark and light: "robust and sane, open to negotiation by the light of day" (p. 35). Balancing "passion and self-possession," Porter unites caring and cruelty, for "real compassion is perhaps always in the end unsparing . . ." (pp. 36, 34). In her discussion of Willa Cather's works, Welty underscores Cather's expression of the union of past and present in such well-known scenes as the fusion of Coronado's sword with the plow against the sun in *My Ántonia* and Thea's touching, on the rock ceilings, soot from the cook stoves of the ancient settlers of the West in *The Song of the Lark* (p. 43). In Ford Madox Ford's fiction, Welty sees the synthesis of his response to his "double" heritage and the "double pressure . . . pulling him in opposite directions" (p. 241). (We recall Welty's evocation of her own double heritage in *One Writer's Beginnings.*)

In *The Eye of the Story* Welty speaks with delight about the character in Ross Macdonald's *The Underground Man* who has been "'strung out on an Einstein trip,'" which is "'when you go all the way out, past the last star, and space loops back on you'" (p. 253). The reality Welty discovers in her favorite authors and the vision she offers in her fiction can seem as threatening to our usual logic as Einstein's universe, where matter and energy, space and time are one. However, Welty believes that one of the secret ills of contemporary life is that it has confused unreality with reality, a problem that, she says, Macdonald identifies in *The Underground Man* (p. 256).

The cure for our ills, then, must be confrontation with the truly real; that is, with what is whole or complementary. Welty saw an awareness of such a reality in E. B. White's *Charlotte's Web*. In her review of White's book, she observes: "The characters are varied—good and bad, human and animal, talented and untalented, warm and cold, ignorant and intelligent, vegetarian and blood-drinking—varied, but not opposites; they are the real thing" (pp. 203-04). The real thing. In White's embracing of opposites, Welty is pointing out a way of viewing reality unlike the one we operate from everyday, where choices between X and Y are not only useful, but necessary. (It is handy in *this* world to be able to sort out the blood-drinkers!) For Welty, that other reality makes no demands that X and non-X be sorted out; it is capable of holding in unity all the extremes of life.

And how, according to *The Eye of the Story*, do we know this reality? Not, it is clear, by logic or analysis, which suggests a single answer arrived at by classification (that is, attempting to discover X by throwing out all the non-X, a futile effort, since ultimately speaking there is no non-X). In life as in fiction, Welty says, there are no clear (that is, single) answers to any questions worth asking, and certainly there is no single way to pursue knowledge (p. 149). As Welty knows: " . . . opposite things are very often done in getting at the truth" (p. 98). The goal, in fact, Welty declares in "Words into Fiction," is not "to solve this mystery," but to "rediscover the mystery" (p. 137). "Solve" suggests discovery of a rational, dualistic "answer." Because ordinary knowledge does not apply in encounters with mystery, Welty points to another way of knowing that can part the curtain: "rediscovery," unlike a "solution," implies a felt, not an intellectual, experience of the reality. What we must do—and what Welty's heroes must do to be exemplars of this way of life—is to give up simplistic demands for neatly divided X's and Y's. " . . . you can't," Welty insists, "explain 'difficult' things 'ordinarily.' And what is not difficult?" (p. 20).

In several essays, Welty speaks in almost Coleridgean terms of different types of knowledge: transient and deceptive knowledge comes from the conventional, subject-object relationship; real knowledge is immediate, intimate, non-discursive. "The contemporary mood," she writes, " . . . can affect the way we see life but not the way we *know* it" (p. 11). The first way of knowing is the one we bring to bear on our everyday, dualistic existence. The second leads to union with the thing to be known, an impossibility for those reductionist Western philosophers for whom knower and known had to remain split, by whom, indeed, we have been taught that we can know *only* if we observe objectively. Welty explains her epistemology this way in "One Time, One Place":

> We come to terms as well as we can with our life-long exposure to the world, and we use whatever devices we may need to survive. But eventually, of course, our knowledge depends upon the living relationship between what we see going on and ourselves. If exposure is essential, still more so is the reflection. Insight doesn't happen often on the click of the moment, like a lucky snapshot, but comes in its own time and more slowly and from nowhere but within. The sharpest recognition is surely that which is charged with sympathy as well as with shock—it is a form of human vision. And that is of course a gift. (p. 354)

The shift in imagery here implies a movement from regarding the world as other—as object to which one is *exposed*, which one *uses*—to experiencing the world as part of the self. One *reflects* on the world, an image suggesting not only thinking about the world but also embuing it with light from the self. Thus external reality is brought into a "living relationship" with the perceiver rather than existing as a dead objectification. Unitive sympathy following disjunctive shock creates the knowing which is vision.

This is not counting-house knowledge or taxonomical wisdom. We can think of how many of Welty's characters fail at truly knowing because they substitute for a living relationship an analytical approach to life: Miss Julia Mortimer in *Losing Battles* telling Gloria that she can reduce Jack to the averages in a gradebook; Miss Sabina in "Asphodel" attempting to subdue the emotions of an entire town with the strangle hold of her reason; Grandpa Ponder in *The Ponder Heart* responding to Uncle Daniel's wild tales with the reporter's "Who? What? When?"

Other characters attain at least momentary enlightenment because they step beyond reason—but precisely what they learn as a consequence of that experience none of them can express. Joel Mayes, the deaf boy in "First Love," epitomizes the experience shared in some way by characters as varied as Mrs. Lawson in "A Curtain of Green," Eugene in "Music from Spain," the couple in "No Place for You, My Love," Ellen Fairchild in *Delta Wedding*, Edna Earle in *The Ponder Heart*, and Granny Vaughn in *Losing Battles*. Their experiences seem in accord with Jung's saying: "The needful thing is not to *know* the truth but to *experience* it."[6] It is left, finally, to the artist, through metaphor and symbol and through dislocation of our dualistic language, to offer intimations of what is experienced in such moments of enlightenment.

For Welty, the critic who approaches a piece of literature as if shaking a button out of a baby (confident that somewhere down there is *the* interpretation of the story)[7] is working from the simplistic, safe, conventional epistemology. Whether this is our approach to art or to life, what we are doing is removing the mystery, the wonder, the experiential whole. As Welty reminds us in her essay on Henry Green: " . . . everybody who can read knows that by fishing a sentence out of a novel, to spread like a captured sea serpent on the bank with the color going out of it, the creature's scales can be counted; but in the element where it lived it was, to begin with, not a monster" (p. 29). Analytical knowledge has its place, of course, depending on what one wants to know. The trick is not to confuse counting the monster's scales with knowing the creature itself. The best the critic can hope (including, and perhaps especially, the critic who analyzes Welty's holism) is that the reader will not stop with the lower type of knowing that is the critic's metier, but, reminded there of the mystery of the original, will—as Welty advised at the end of her review of Faulkner's *Letters*—go to the fiction itself: "If you want to know all you can about that heart and soul, ... [r]ead that" (pp. 219-20). In taking such a step the reader will have moved from the dualistic world of the critic, back to the holism of art.

Because knowledge in the world of polar, holistic reality comes not discursively nor analytically, but experientially, Welty's fiction emphasizes the need not for mere exposure to, but for living involvement in, all of life's muddle and majesty. The pattern Welty sees in the stories of Patrick White's *The Cockatoos* is the same that informs so many of her own:

> Accidentally set free by some catastrophe, general or personal—war, starvation, or nothing more than a husband's toothache—Patrick White's characters come to a point of discovery. It might be, for instance, that in overcoming repugnancies they are actually yielding to some far deeper attraction; the possibilities of life have been those very things once felt as its dangers. Or they may learn, in confronting moral weakness in others, some flaw in themselves they've never suspected, still more terrifying.
>
> The common barriers of sex, age, class, nationality *can*, in uncommon hands, operate as gates, which open

(for his characters) to experience beyond anything yet
travelled, hope of which may have beckoned from earliest years and gone ignored, only haunting dreams and
spoiling the day at hand. (p. 264)

So Eugene in "Music from Spain" is suspended over the Pacific
by the silent foreign musician; Jenny Lockhart in "At The Landing" leaves her protected home to be violated by the Dionysian
Billy Floyd; William Wallace in "The Wide Net" dives to the
bottom of the Pearl River searching for his wife Hazel; Judge
Moody joins Jack Renfro, just escaped from the penitentiary, on
top of Lover's Leap; and on and on. All come to insight, not by
grasping for it, but by letting go.

The gravest threat to holistic knowledge is what Welty
calls in the essay "Writing and Analyzing a Story" the "courting
of imperviousness" (p. 113). Because those who value invul-
nerability choose a single vantage point from which to view life,
they effectively avoid life, whose reality is always multiple. The
self can develop only as it becomes entwined in what appears to
be non-self. (As Martin Buber said: "Through the *Thou* a man
becomes *I*.[8]) "Vulnerability," Welty writes, "is a personal and
valuable and selfish possession—perhaps more; perhaps in effect
it is the self" (p. 16). If we attempt to reduce this paradox to a
formula, what we arrive at is something like this: Self=invasion
by the non-self (i.e., vulnerability). The magic of this paradox is
echoed in Welty's declaration in "Place in Fiction" that "the
open mind and the receptive heart . . . are at last and with fortune's smile the informed mind and the experienced heart"
(p. 130): the open mind, once filled, contains both self and other.

On the other hand, what may seem to be safety, a desire
for self-protection, will end in destruction of that very self. In
"Place in Fiction," Welty discusses the writer's need to take
chances, but her comments have far broader applications:
"Although it is in the words of a witch—or all the more because
of that—a comment of Hecate's in *Macbeth* is worth our heed:
'Security / Is mortal's chiefest enemy.' In fact, when we think in
terms of the spirit . . . is there a conception more stupefying than
that of security?" (p. 130) This rushing to "sanctuaries of extremes"—this search for protection by viewing life through a
single lens—Welty associates with "daydreams," that is, unreality. Such a retreat to the extreme, Welty writes, "can end only in
violence" (p. 230), because it is based on a conception of life as
competition, conflict, a matter of Them or Us.

The courting of imperviousness finds comic expression in Welty in such works as "Lily Daw and the Three Ladies" and "Why I Live at the P.O." (where Sister is indeed "one-sided," but in a way that Stella-Rondo did not mean when she passed the word to Mr. Whitaker). In *The Eye of the Story* Welty discusses the centrality of this theme to the plot of "No Place for You, My Love" (p. 113). The ability to accommodate extremes, to see the two ends as part of a united whole, is the fairy-tale message of *The Robber Bridegroom* and the serious idea behind the joke in *The Ponder Heart*. It is at the core of the paradoxically titled *Losing Battles*, where the Renfro family experiences the truth of past, present, and future as one time; welcomes at their table the man who sent the family favorite to jail; and learns that no important battle is ever really lost—or ever finally won. It is also the secret Laurel Hand learns in *The Optimist's Daughter* with her discovery of Welty's magic word, *confluence*.

What this view of reality makes impossible is passing final judgment—because judgment implies an either-or decision or a setting up of barriers between the judge and the accused. This philosophy has led Welty into what some readers have seen as at best a tricky moral position and at worst, an indefensible one. They find her too accepting, too non-judgmental. Reviewing Welty's first novel, Diana Trilling, for example, accused Welty of ignoring the classism and racism of the southern society she writes about,[9] and, more recently, Carolyn Heilbrun has criticized *One Writer's Beginnings* for its absence of anger at the patriarchal society that "has for so many years imprisoned women without [Welty's] genius or her rewards." Heilbrun sees in Welty a "docile acceptance of what is given," resulting, in *One Writer's Beginnings*, in a rewriting of what Heilbrun describes in her discussion of May Sarton's *Plant Dreaming Deep* as the "old genre of female autobiography, which tends to find beauty even in pain and to transform rage into spiritual acceptance."[10]

Of course, some writers, looking at the social injustices that Trilling and Heilbrun pointed to, *have* taken up the gauntlet of the social crusader, as Alice Walker, for example, did in her early novels. Others, like Faulkner, have viewed the same scene with the eye of tragedian. Welty has always made clear that what she is about is different. And what she is about comes close to the approach of the myth-maker, whose attitude toward life Joseph Campbell contrasted to that of the moralist and the writer of tragedy in this way:

> Where the moralist would be filled with indignation
> and the tragic poet with pity and terror, mythology
> breaks the whole of life into a vast, horrendous Divine
> Comedy. Its Olympian laugh is not escapist in the
> least, but hard, with the hardness of life itself—
> which, we may take it, is the hardness of God, the
> Creator. Mythology, in this respect, makes the tragic
> attitude seem somewhat hysterical, and the merely
> moral judgment shortsighted. Yet the hardness is bal-
> anced by an assurance that all that we see is but the re-
> flex of a power that endures, untouched by the pain.
> Thus the tales are both pitiless and terrorless—suf-
> fused with the joy of a transcendent anonymity regard-
> ing itself in all of the self-centered, battling egos that
> are born and die in time.[11]

In Welty, belief in a transcendent power is substituted for by a
sense of an encompassing unity that transcends every part, but
that provides a basis, like the one Campbell speaks of, for the
hardness and the joy that characterize her works, too.

When Welty herself tried to explain her resistance to the
demand, heard often in the Sixties and Seventies, that the novelist be a crusader for social change, she turned to her belief that
reality always embraces what strike most people as contraries.
Argument and logic belong to a dualistic world where right and
wrong battle it out, the winner being designated possessor of The
Answer. The one thing a novel is not, Welty insists in "Must
the Novelist Crusade?", is an argument. Its territory is not logic,
but life, where mystery is part of the meaning (pp. 150-51).
"There is absolutely everything in great fiction but a clear answer," Welty declares, because there *are* no clear—that is, un-
paradoxical, non-polar—answers (p. 149). The problem with a
"blueprint for sanity and of solution for trouble" is that it
"leaves out the dark" (p. 151). That light exists only by virtue of
the presence of darkness Welty suggests when, commenting on
the omission of "the dark" from social blueprints, she muses
parenthetically: "(This is odd, because surely it was the dark that
first troubled us)" (p. 151). From the artist's god's-eye view, the
dark is as necessary to the whole picture as the light.

Welty also refuses to pass judgment on others because she
knows how intimately other and self are linked. Her belief that
art is an act of human identity, not judgment, is seen in her
comments on "Where Is the Voice Coming From?" This is one
of just two stories (the other is "The Demonstrators" [1966]) written by Welty in response to a social problem and the only one,
she confesses, that came to her out of anger and not love. Even

this story, however, had its inception in her attempt to over-come her separation from the murderer of Medgar Evers, to enter "into the mind and inside the skin of a character who could hardly have been more alien or repugnant to me."[12]

But if Welty's vision makes simplistic judgment impossible, what it makes possible is wonder, a response to what from the human vantage point is life's mystery, its intersecting, inter-penetrating, ever-turning prism-beams, its multiple and inex-pressible *Suchness*, as the Taoists say. This, finally, is what Welty sees as the purpose of her fiction, a purpose that she learned first as a photographer for the WPA in northern Missis-sippi and wrote of in the essay "One Time, One Place":

> In my own case, a fuller awareness of what I needed to find out about people and their lives had to be sought for through another way, through writing stories. But away off one day up in Tishomingo County, I knew this, anyway: that my wish, indeed my continuing passion, would be not to point the finger in judgment but to part a curtain, that invisible shadow that falls between people, the veil of indifference to each other's presence, each other's wonder, each other's human plight. (pp. 354-55)

Notes

[1] *The Eye of the Story: Selected Essays and Reviews* (New York: Random House, 1978), p. 336. Hereafter, references to this edition will be given in the text of this chapter.

[2] Ruth Vande Kieft suggests the aptness of the labyrinth image to Welty's own work when, independent of any discussion of the Ida M'Toy essay, she writes: "One cannot undertake to write about the stories of Eudora Welty without feelings of trepidation and hope because she has provided her readers and critics both with ominous warnings and with delightful allurements. It is as if the welcome mat were clearly out before her door while the sign on the gate post read 'Keep out,' or as if she had given us a map to reach her but had not promised it wouldn't turn out to be the sketch of a labyrinth in which we would get hopelessly lost" (Vande Kieft, 1962, p. 25).

[3] In "The Radiance of Jane Austen," Welty speaks of comedy as being "sociable" (p. 6); in "Reality in Chekhov's Stories," she asks, "What but the comic vision could accommodate so much, bring it all in?" (p. 80).

[4] For a discussion of parallels in Chekhov's and Welty's subject matter and techniques, see Jan Nordby Gretlund, "The Terrible and Marvellous: Eudora Welty's Chekhov," in Dawn Trouard, ed., *Eudora Welty: Eye of the Storyteller* (Kent, OH: The Kent State University Press, 1989), pp. 107-18.

[5] *Civilization in Transition*, p. 297.

[6] *The Collected Works*, vol. 18, p. 558.

[7] "How I Write," *Virginia Quarterly Review*, 31 (1955), 244. This image does not appear in the revision of this essay published in *The Eye of the Story*.

[8] *The Writings of Martin Buber*, ed. Will Herberg (New York: World, 1973), p. 51.

[9] "Fiction in Review," *The Nation*, CLXII (May 11, 1946), 578. Trilling wrote: "[Welty] leaves her honest cultural observations in rosy poetic solution exactly because she does not wish to precipitate them as moral judgment."

[10] *Writing a Woman's Life*, pp. 12-15.

[11] *The Hero with a Thousand Faces*, Bollingen Series XVII (Princeton, NJ: Princeton University Press, 1973; 1st edition, 1949), pp. 45-46. Reynolds Price makes a point similar to Campbell's in his discussion of *The Optimist's Daughter*: " . . . comprehension . . . is always comic. All patterns are comic . . . because the universe is patterned, therefore ordered and ruled, therefore incapable of ultimate tragedy (interim tragedy is comprised in the order but cannot be the end . . .) . . ." ("The Onlooker, Smiling: An Early Reading of *The Optimist's Daughter*," *Shenandoah*, 20 [Spring 1969], 58-73).

[12] *One Writer's Beginnings*, p. 39.

III

The Tangled Bank: Stories of Initiation

In a number of her short stories, Eudora Welty treats the parting of the curtain hiding holistic truths in terms of an initiation into another way of experiencing reality. That this reality exists, independent of human perception, that holism is not just a narcissistic fiction is implied in a variety of descriptions of the natural world conveyed by omniscient narrators, all ascribing to nature the capacity for uniting apparent opposites. Seven of these stories—"A Curtain of Green," "Moon Lake," "At The Landing," "No Place for You, My Love," "Death of a Traveling Salesman," "Music from Spain," and "The Wide Net"—display an amazing similarity in their treatment of the initiation motif, sharing with significant frequency major features of the archetypal ritual.

In each of these stories a character is prepared to receive a new view of reality by increased vulnerability, usually a reduction of self-confidence caused by some loss. The character withdraws from ordinary life into the silence of a dream-like state, entering a wild, natural area that Welty's narrator pointedly describes as being "walled" off from the regular world. This untamed place in Welty's stories suggests what J. E. Cirlot says the natural tangle so often symbolizes: the unconscious, the repressed, the forgotten, the past. As Cirlot explains: "The Garden is the place where Nature is subdued, ordered, selected and enclosed. Hence, it is a symbol of consciousness as opposed to the forest, which is the unconscious. . . ."[1] Welty's symbolism is clear: if holistic reality is to be encountered, it will be by the non-rational part of the self.[2]

At the center of this arena stands a tree (Welty's version of the Tree of Life and Death), and always water flows nearby,

suggesting the potential of renewal, in this case a return to a forgotten view of reality. For the initiate, the natural world inside
the wall is confusing and even threatening. But the complex
landscape into which the character retreats provides both the
stimulus for initiation and symbols of the truth into which the
character is initiated: that the simplistic order humans impose
on life hides its true multiplicity and that the apparent duality of
life masks an unseen unity.

This is a relationship with nature and a vision of reality
that many of Welty's characters fight tooth and nail. Cassie
Morrison of "The Wanderers" is one of these. At the end of that
story, Cassie encounters Virgie Rainey who, freed by her
mother's death, is finally on her way out of town. Made vulnerable and open to change because of that death, Virgie has experienced a kind of baptism into holism in the Big Black River,
where "all was one warmth, air, water, and her own body . . . a
translucent one, the river, herself, the sky all vessels which the
sun filled."[3] Now, armed with the knowledge that "all the
opposites on earth were close together" (p. 452), she is setting out
on a quest for what she can find of fullness in her personal life.

In a not very subtle rebuke for Virgie's being able to put
aside her mother's death with such apparent ease, Cassie invites
Virgie to return to Morgana the coming year so that she can see
Cassie's mother's "Name in the Spring." Cassie has meticu-
lously planted a garden of narcissus, bordered with hyacinths
and violets, to spell out the first name of Catherine Morrison,
the apparently happy young matron who one day had walked
out of the room and killed herself. Cassie's is an act of order
memorializing a life whose end shouts complexity. And
Cassie's narrow, constrained life has, through the years, expressed a similarly dogged stand against that multiplicity that
Virgie seems always to have intuited.

Other characters in Welty's short stories (Miss Sabina in
"Asphodel," for example, and Solomon in "Livvie") try in a
similar fashion to deny the tangled reality of life by attempting to
simplify and control the landscape around them.[4] Still others
seem to have intimations of a fullness of being beyond their ordinary lives, but pursue that wholeness in ways that cannot lead
to illumination. Chief of these is the wanderer King MacLain,
who, instead of setting out on a spiritual or psychological quest,
turns to sex and travel, which have perennially offered human
beings the illusion of wholeness. It is appropriate that King's
children—legitimate and illegitimate—number prominantly

among those who figure in the initiation stories. Among these offspring are King's son Eugene; certainly the black boy Exum McLane; most likely the orphan Easter; and quite possibly Loch Morrison.[5]

In the seven parallel initiation stories, characters who allow themselves to enter Welty's tangled banks—whether literally an unchecked garden or a forest or a river's edge—step beyond the imposed orderliness and distinctions of daily life to encounter the multiplicity of cosmic reality. They enter a forgotten corridor of the world we know, experiencing what Joseph Campbell has called "multi-dimensional meaning" in a two-dimensional world.[6] This is Welty's *axis mundi*, the world navel, the point through which "the energies of eternity break into time."[7] No wonder the suggestively named Twosie warns in "Moon Lake": "Yawl sho ain't got yo' eyes opem good, yawl. Yawl don't know what's out here in woods wid you" (p. 348).

The purpose of Welty's initiations is, indeed, the goal of all initiations: to remind us, in Mircea Eliade's words, "that the ultimate reality, the sacred, the divine, defy all possibilities of rational comprehension; that the *Grund* [Ground of Being] can only be grasped as a mystery or a paradox. . . ."[8] Welty's characters experience what Alan Watts calls "the implicit unity of all poles."[9] Nicolas of Cusa, writing five hundred years ago of this *coincidentia oppositorum*, cautioned that awareness of such unity comes only to one who seeks truth by "entering into darkness . . . beyond all the grasp of reason," since the door of "the wall of Paradise" is "guarded by the most proud spirit of Reason, and, unless he be vanquished, the way will not lie open."[10] When Welty's characters leave reason and dualistic classifications behind and step beyond the dividing wall, they discover that life and death, love and hate, compassion and violence, beauty and horror, pain and joy, self and other are one.

The initiation inside the tangled bank occurs most obviously in "A Curtain of Green," where the garden is the exact opposite of Cassie Morrison's controlled plot. Mrs. Larkin has isolated herself in this garden after her husband is killed by a falling chinaberry tree. The mystery of a natural world that could so senselessly take her husband's life has driven her to look for meaning where none seems to exist. That she is ready for a revelation is suggested by her meekness before nature: she "kneel[s]" among the flowers all day long, then leaves the garden at the end of the day "with a drooping, submissive walk" (pp. 107, 108). She is "lost" in the garden (p. 108)—a good condition for finding herself and her relation with what passes as other.

The sense of the garden's enclosure is heightened by its having a border of hedge "high like a wall" (p. 107). Within this wall, garden—with its usual implication of human control—has become virtually jungle. Welty describes it as "this slanting, tangled garden, more and more over-abundant and confusing" (p. 107). Yet Mrs. Larkin does not attempt to control the landscape. Instead of "cop[ing] with the rich blackness of this soil" by "cutting, separating, thinning and tying back" and thus keeping the plants from "overreaching their boundaries and multiplying out of all reason," she allows "an over-flowing, as if she consciously ventured forever a little farther, a little deeper, into her life in the garden" (p. 108). She stops thinking about order, stops worrying about what her neighbors' garden club might consider appropriately harmonious as she begins to move from the world controlled by reason.

Yet Mrs. Larkin still asks: "Was it not possible to compensate? to punish? to protest? (p. 111) Such dualistic questions imply a conception of life as divided into nature and humanity, victim and victimizer, life and death. The tangled bank itself, however, is witness to the other truth: that all apparent opposites are really one. And Mrs. Larkin becomes another symbol of this, dressed as she is in "stained overalls, now almost of a color with the leaves," "her hair streaming and tangled" like the landscape (pp. 108, 107). She is becoming one with the reality she tries to penetrate. (Or, more precisely, she is beginning to experience a unity that has always been there.)

At the very center of the garden is further evidence of the harmony of opposites. There, the pear tree, heavy in April with its brilliant green foliage, forms the retreat Mrs. Larkin seeks when it rains. The sheltering pear tree in bloom is paralleled in memory by the tree that had crushed her husband. Thus, the garden contains both the Tree of Life and the Tree of Death. But at this mythopoeic axis of the world, we realize that they are two expressions of the same life force.[11] Even the tree that had brought her husband's death had been the "fragrant chinaberry"—perhaps made top-heavy by its own abundant blossoming, its very vitality in such a case causing death.

The rain at the end of the story brings a final expression of the identity of contraries in the garden. Its first effect is to emphasize individuality: " . . . everything appeared to gleam unreflecting from within itself in its quiet arcade of identity. . . . One by one, as the rain reached them, all the individual little plants shone out, and then the branching vines" (p. 111). Even Jamey, the yardman, whom Mrs. Larkin had been on the verge of killing when she had viewed him as a "mirage," emerges as an individual, turning "his full face toward her . . ." (pp. 110, 111). But while the rain brings individuation, it brings also merger.[12] Drenched with rain, Mrs. Larkin faints, falling down among the flowers. In Welty's cosmic picture, individuality is real, and so is union. So, too, life and death have one source, and Nature is both protector and destroyer.

In "Moon Lake" the tangled bank is not a wild garden, but the dense swamp on the side of the lake opposite the girls' camp. Here Loch Morrison, impressed into duty as a lifeguard, moves in resentful silence, swinging through the trees, crashing in the foliage. Here Easter, the orphan who, according to Jinny Love Stark, acts like a deaf-and-dumb, retreats within herself, pretending she is alone even when other campers are around. And here, too, wanders the most isolated of all—the black boy Exum McLane:

> Exum was apart too, boy and colored to boot; he constantly moved along an even further fringe of the landscape than Loch, wearing the man's stiff straw hat brilliant as a snowflake. They would see Exum in the hat bobbing along the rim of the swamp like a fisherman's cork, elevated just a bit by the miasma and illusion of the landscape he moved in. It was Exum persistent as a little bug, inching along the foot of the swamp wall, carrying around a fishing cane and minnow can, fishing around the bend from their side of the lake, catching all kinds of things. (p. 362)

And with them—or ahead of them—moves the significantly androgynous Cat who "edged the woods onward, and at moments vanished into a tunnel in the briars. Emerging from other tunnels, he—or she—glanced up at them with a face more masklike than ever. . . . Cat always caught something; something was in his—or her—mouth . . ." (pp. 353, 359).

Nina Carmichael, wanting to "catch" something too, penetrates the walls (or the "curtains," in the imagery of the omniscient narrator) of the swamp, following Easter. Trudging down the slope, she and the non-initiate Jinny Love,

> moved single file between two walls. . . . They were eye to eye with the finger-shaped leaves of the castor bean

plants, put out like those gypsy hands that part the
curtains at the back of rolling wagons, and wrinkled
and coated over like the fortune-teller's face. . . .
    Sweet bay and cypress and sweetgum and live oak
and swamp maple closing tight made the wall dense,
and yet there was somewhere still for the other wall of
vine. . . . Closer to the ear than lips could begin words
came the swamp sounds—closer to the ear and nearer to
the dreaming mind. (pp. 351-52)

While Nina has to fight her way through the natural tangle, Easter responds to the dreamlike world of the swamp as she
does to the literal world of dreams at night, concurring with its
message without struggle, opening her hand to its darkness.
Easter—"untouchable and intact" (p. 368), self-named, free of
rules and of the need for external validation, free from disap-
pointment and from expectation—is hierophant in this story.
She reflects the unity of Welty's vision in her oneness with the
natural world, "her dress stained green behind" (p. 352), "her lips
stained with blackberries" (p. 353). Leading Nina (and the tag-
along Jinny Love) deeper into the tangled bank, Easter is the perfect guide to a revelation of the harmony of opposites: she looks
"both ways" as she nears the apocalyptic ground and moves
"inward" by both "rising" and "sinking" (pp. 354, 353).

At the center is Moon Lake—the same lake into which the
campers have daily taken their sedate and regimented Dip, Dip,
Dips, but it now offers the girls "a different aspect altogether"
(p. 354). The paradox of Heraclitus works for this lake as it does
for streams, particularly since Welty associates with it imagery of
movement and flux (" . . . Moon Lake streamed out in the night.
By moonlight sometimes it seemed to run like a river" [p. 361]).
Other descriptions of the lake underscore the union of contraries: it is quiet, but "where the sun shone right on it the lake
seemed to be in violent agitation, almost boiling"; although it
is in the bright sunshine, "the world looked struck by moonlight" (p. 354); earth and sky join in a "crucible of sun-filled
water" (p. 357). Mircea Eliade points out that in some myths
access to the Other World is to be found only "'where Sky and
Earth embrace' and the 'Ends of the year' are united," since only
at a point of union of opposites is there entry to Reality where
opposites are one.[13]) Lying in a boat, Easter both floats and is
moored, placidly accepting drift and stasis, while Nina—not yet
privy to the mystery—struggles to set the boat free.

However, as soon as she is truly immersed in the swamp,
the mud kissing her toes, the roots lacing her feet, Nina has a vi-

sion of one facet of life's harmony. She perceives, on the one hand, the beauty of life and, on the other, life's precariousness (and, hence, its painfulness and even horror). The unifying epiphany is expressed—once more—in the symbol of a pear tree, or at least its fruit:

> Again she thought of a pear—not the everyday gritty kind that hung on the tree in the backyard, but the fine kind sold on trains and at high prices, each pear with a paper cone wrapping it alone—beautiful, symmetrical, clean pears with thin skins, with snow-white flesh so juicy and tender that to eat one baptized the whole face, and so delicate that while you urgently ate the first half, the second half was already beginning to turn brown. To all fruits, and especially to those fine pears, something happened—the process was so swift, you were never in time for them. It's not the flowers that are fleeting, Nina thought, it's the fruits—it's the time when things are ready that they don't stay. (pp. 355-56)

Nina has come close to the central vision of Welty's world: the interface of beginnings and endings; the beauty and the frailty of life; the joy and the sorrow that exist together, neither contradicting the other, and, indeed, each giving rise to the other.

This ability to see unity behind apparent diversity remains with Nina when she returns to camp. Thinking that night of a boat floating on the water, she sees it as uniting motion and fixity. And, thinking of herself thinking of the boat, she experiences an exchange of self and other as she muses: " . . . in the boat, it was not so much that they drifted, as that in the presence of a boat the world drifted, forgot. The dreamed-about changed places with the dreamer" (p. 360).[14]

Attempting to translate these visions of unity into action, Nina tries to break the barrier of the self—to become other:

> The orphan! she thought exultantly. The other way to live. There were secret ways. She thought, Time's really short, I've been only thinking like the others. It's only interesting, only worthy, to try for the fiercest secrets. To slip into them all—to change. To change for a moment into Gertrude, into Mrs. Gruenwald, into Twosie—into a boy. To *have been* an orphan. (p. 361)

Nina stretches her hand out toward the sleeping Easter, begging the personified, secret-laden giant Night to come to her instead of to the orphan. But the union is not achieved, perhaps because Nina is willfully pursuing what must come unconsciously.[15] (Later, she is granted her wish for empathetic identity, arrived at without conscious effort, when she faints and is lifted to the table to lie beside the nearly drowned Easter.) But if Nina is now denied precisely the union she desires, she is given another demonstration of the oneness of life: "In the cup of her hand, in her filling skin, in the fingers' bursting weight and stillness, Nina felt it: compassion and a kind of competing that were all one, a single ecstasy, a single longing" (p. 362). The coincidence of love and strife has been revealed to her. When she wakes, the hand she had held out to Night and to revelation is asleep. Hitting and biting it to bring it back to life, she enacts the union of violence and life-giving that Loch will later dramatize over Easter's body.

Underscoring the fact that holistic reality is always present, even when unperceived, the narrator describes the scene outside the camp as Nina sleeps. Nature acts out, in Moon Lake, the unity that Nina has had intimations of:

> Beyond the cry of the frogs there were the sounds of a boat moored somewhere, of its vague, clumsy reaching at the shore, those sounds that are recognized as being made by something sightless. When did boats have eyes—once? Nothing watched that their little part of the lake stayed roped off and protected; was it there now, the rope stretched frail-like between posts that swayed in mud? That rope was to mark how far the girls could swim. Beyond lay the deep part, some bottomless parts, said Moody. Here and there was the quicksand that stirred your footprint and kissed your heel. All snakes, harmless and harmful, were freely playing now; they put a trailing, moony division between weed and weed—bright, turning, bright and turning. (p. 361)

The frailty of the human impulse to simplify reality is represented perfectly in the hopeful rope that can neither keep out the snakes nor prevent a person like Easter from plummeting to the depths of the lake.

While she had served as hierophant for Nina, Easter herself becomes an initiate into yet deeper mysteries when she plunges into the lake as a result of the prodding fingers of Exum, the most isolated wanderer and "catcher" in the swamp. In her near-drowning, Easter comes to the meeting point of life and death. Loch, in resuscitating her, shows another paradox: the coalescence of violence and compassion, which causes onlookers to decide that death would almost be preferable to such brutal life-saving (this is particularly the opinion of the prim Miss Lizzie Stark, to whom the resuscitation looks like the sex act).

And in the strangest of all metamorphoses, Easter, in the moments before her revival, is herself changed into a tangled bank. The girls standing by wonder if "Easter, turned in on herself, might call out to them after all, from the other, worse, side of it? Her secret voice, if soundless then possibly visible, might work out of her terrible mouth like a vine, preening and sprung with flowers. Or a snake would come out" (pp. 369-70). Such a transformation suggests that the wild, natural spot from which comes evidence of cosmic oneness is parallelled by a region of the self—a forgotten realm of the psyche. The onlookers' fear of word from the other side and their decision that other is necessarily worse suggest how loath we are to penetrate the wall that both separates (cutting us off from the security of ordinary values and distinctions) and unites.

The union of love and violence, life and death is also revealed to Jenny Lockhart in "At The Landing." Until the wild Billy Floyd leaps across the ravine to join Jenny in the cemetery—an area again curtained off from the world by woodbine and hanging moss and ropelike grapevines—, Jenny's life is as circumscribed as her grandfather desires. As the voice of rational control, her grandfather "deprecated raving simply as raving, as a force of Nature and so beneath notice or mention" (p. 242). When, years before, his daughter, Jenny's mother, had been driven mad by the rigid life he had prescribed, he had simply rung "a bell and told the cook to take her off and sit by her until she had done with it, but in the end she died of it" (p. 242).

Since then, Jenny has spent her days wandering through her grandfather's house, counting the plates in the china closet; gazing at the backs of books without titles; or sitting with her grandfather in a pavilion circled with "an ancient . . . thorny rose, like the initial letter in a poetry book" (p. 242). This cultivated flower, as imprisoning as the roses that keep young maidens inviolate in fairy-tale castles,[16] contrasts with the liberating landscape, uncontrolled by human cultivation, where Jenny meets Billy Floyd. Before that meeting, the only hint Jenny has that there is more to life is suggested by the infinite regression of vases decorated with landscapes "endlessly rising in front of her" as they reflect in two mirrors (p. 242) and by the prisms that hang everywhere in her house, put there, we suspect, by her mother.

Jenny pointedly refuses to touch the prisms. But when the air stirs them, they give off faint musical notes and break into their rainbow colors—a symbol of the union of the One and the Many and of the multiple possibilities of beauty beneath the staid surface of life.

Freed from her grandfather's control by his death and then driven from her home by the flooding river, Jenny is made vulnerable for her initiation. As in the case of the other initiates, her epiphany is preceded by a dream-like state. When she announces that she is sleepy, Billy Floyd takes her in his boat to the enclosed cemetery, where—without speaking—he violates her. Her communion with this other side of reality is symbolized in her eating the wild meat he offers. Near the graves of her forebears, her new life has begun. The first part of her revelation comes to her: "She knew from him nevertheless that what people ate in the world was earth, river, wildness and litheness, fire and ashes. People took the fresh death and the hot fire into their mouths and got their own life" (pp. 251-52). Alone in her home after the flood, Jenny continues to muse on the implications of her new vision. The result is her acceptance of unity and multiplicity in love:

> But it was when love was of the one for the one, that it seemed to hold all that was multitudinous and nothing was single any more. She had one love and that was all, but she dreamed that she lined up on both sides of the road to see her love come by in a procession. She herself was more people than there were people in The Landing, and her love was enough to pass through the whole night, never lifting the same face. (pp. 255-56)

Another vision of the union of opposites in love is brought to her, significantly, by a tree—this time, "an old mimosa closing in the ravine" leading to the cemetery (p. 256). This "ancient fern, as old as life" combines within itself the messages of the Trees of Life and Death, bearing witness to the single source of the utmost sorrow and the deepest joy. For the mimosa is the sensitive plant, "grotesque in its tenderness," shrinking from every touch: "All nearness and darkness affected it, even clouds going by, but for Jenny . . . no tree ever gave such allurement of fragrance anywhere" (p. 256). The sweetness that comes from the pain of feeling too much—that is its paradoxical disclosure.

Leaving her home to search for Billy Floyd, Jenny reenters the tangled bank where trumpet and muscadine and passion

flower vines close about her. At the river, she steps out of the
enclosure to be surrounded now, not by a curtain of vines, but by
"veil behind veil of long drying nets hung on all sides," reflecting in spiraling circles the light of the sky. As if caught in a
vortex where earth and heavens meet, Jenny experiences again
the revelation of unity: "All things, river, sky, fire, and air,
seemed the same color, the color that is seen behind the closed
eyelids, the color of day when vision and despair are the same
thing" (p. 257). Then, in a stunning shift from the lyricism of
this moment, Welty describes Jenny's rape by the rivermen in a
grounded houseboat. If there can be any protection for Jenny
from such a horror, it must come from her realization of the
union of vision and despair, the hint that insight can come from
suffering.

Nevertheless, this is one of the most troubling scenes in
Welty's fiction, especially because of the statement that Jenny's
cries "could easily have been heard as rejoicing" (p. 258). The
implication that somehow Jenny's rape is a positive thing causes
only outrage in any reference to real life. Making the ending
even more chilling is the narrator's statement that the crude
laughter of Jenny's rapists merges with her cries in sounding
like rejoicing. Never again in Welty is the reader so challenged
by the demands of philosophical holism as here, when we are
asked to see the unity of this fragile victim and her callous attackers. (It is Welty's equivalent of Chekhov's acceptance even
of the mother who killed another's child.)

For most readers, this ending makes sense only when the
fairy-tale quality of the entire story is recalled and the tale is responded to as myth rather than mimesis, a symbolic statement
of philosophy—almost an allegory—with fewer ties than most
of Welty's stories to the literal world in which we live. Given
that approach, Welty's symbolism becomes clear, especially
when considered in terms of her belief that "Security / Is mortal's chiefest enemy." For Jenny, who has had the courage to
leave behind the sanctuary of imperviousness created by her
grandfather, this violation is at least life—while the rose-pro-
tected bower of her former existence had been as life-less as a
fairy-tale existence. Now the hanging willow branches by the
river form another enclosure appropriate for initiation, suggesting why the cries sound like rejoicing.

But the unsettling truth is that the symbolism of the story
also requires us to take seriously the implication of the unity of
Jenny and her attackers. The visionary who is capable of a truly

holistic perspective would, no doubt, be able to see all these players—Jenny and the rivermen—as united, not only because the act of the men makes possible Jenny's further initiation, but also because they are, finally, alike. Equal and identical in their need for a fuller life, they all set off from The Landing, from their own individual emptinesses, pursuing in their different ways their quests for life's wholeness. That Welty, as a metaphysical observer, is capable of such a judgment (so different from our judgment in the field of time[17]) is indicated in another of her short stories, "Music from Spain," in the version originally published in *The Golden Apples*. There she has Eugene MacLain briefly seized with the desire to go about telling people that "Convicts are Christ."[18]

The bank of the Mississippi River is the location of yet another encounter with non-dual reality in "No Place for You, My Love." Once again, the initiates are cut off from ordinary human communication and are made susceptible to new insights by their less than satisfactory lives. Both outsiders in the South and strangers to each other, the unnamed woman and man have each apparently suffered a recent weakening of their ties with those they love. Her bruised temple suggests a troubled love affair; his wife's suggestion that he stay out from underfoot while she entertains old college friends speaks of a less than harmonious marriage. Together the strangers retreat from Galatoire's to Baba's Place in the Delta, a trip to a locale that seems "out of this world," "a sort of dead man's land, where nobody came" (pp. 467, 468). In the process, each enters that familiar dream-like state characterizing Welty's initiates. Signalling the diminishment of civilized order and restraint, he loosens his collar and tie; she momentarily loses her hat. Clearly this is, as he declares, a "Time Out" from their usual lives (p. 472).

The levee holding back the Mississippi becomes one wall effecting their enclosure (which, as is the case in all of the initiations, is accompanied by a sense of exposure to naked reality). The feeling of insularity is increased by the "uprooted trees . . . drawn across their path, sawing at the air and tumbling one over the other" (p. 471). The tangled bank they enter is straight from scenes of primordial chaos. As Mircea Eliade points out, all initiations involve a re-enactment of creation and "every ritual repetition of the cosmogony is preceded by a symbolic retrogression to Chaos."[19] This return to the original condition before division into parts has been, of course, part of the *raison d'être* of all of Welty's retreats to the tangled bank. In "No Place for You,

My Love," just as before the first order of creation, earth and water blend together. The river itself feels "like the sea" and looks
"like the earth" (p. 470). The land is "strange . . . amphibious—
and whether water-covered or grown with jungle or robbed entirely of water and trees . . . , it had the same loneliness" (p. 479).
At the end of the road "there was water under everything. Even
where a screen of jungle had been left to stand, splashes could be
heard from under the trees. In the vast open, sometimes boats
moved inch by inch through what appeared endless meadows of
rubbery flowers" (p. 472).[20]
    Even the animals littering their way belong to both
worlds: scuttling and dragging crayfish and other shell creatures
("little jokes of creation"), turtles and terrapins—and "back there
in the margins . . . crawling hides you could not penetrate with
bullets or quite believe, grins that had come down from the
primeval mud" (p. 468). Other images continue the pattern of
merged identities. Road and heat and river blend together, and
snakes are described as like colored stones and birds.
    At the end of the road, the man and woman enter Baba's
Place, at first glance a surrealistic inferno with its cloud of pep-
pery steam escaping from a cauldron,[21] its noise and confusion,
its sapient animal (the goose read to by a man), its grotesque
people (Baba with his knife, the child with the lizard hanging
from his shirt, the massive black of indefinite sex). Yet even
here the real message is of the coexistence of contraries. For
Baba's cafe—with all its chaos and implied violence—is also a
place of good will (Baba's friendliness, the apology offered for an
unheard insult) and joy (the promised Shrimp Dance, the pleasure of the cardplayers). As if in celebration of this reality, of a
world where violence and friendship coexist, where a goose can
be wise, and where strangers can act like lovers, the man and the
woman end their visit to Baba's by dancing—the perfect image
of the dynamic tension between union and separateness. Welty
writes: "They had found it, and had almost missed it: they had
had to dance. They were what their separate hearts desired that
day, for themselves and each other" (p. 478).
    They do not, after all, fall in love. But the trip to the end
of the road—because of its spoonlike cul-de-sac also the beginning—has been efficacious. Having seen doubleness on the
other side of the wall, they begin to come to terms with doubleness in their own lives. To return with such an insight makes it
appropriate that the man declares: "We're all right now" (p. 480).
As the story ends, she goes to meet the man who possibly gave

her the bruise, apparently accepting the synchronism of love and violence—like Jenny Lockhart's rape, hard to take on the literal level, but resonant with symbolic implications. And he recalls a time when in his youth he had been able to see promise behind horror: " . . . he remembered for the first time in years when he was young and brash, a student in New York, and the shriek and horror and unholy smother of the subway had its original meaning for him as the lilt and expectation of love" (p. 481).

But while these two may have brought back from their encounter with unitary reality both the insight and the will to change (or embrace) their lives in the "two-dimensional" world, this is not always the case. In "Death of a Traveling Salesman," the salesman is so stricken by the difference between the unity in the central arena and the isolation of his own life that he flees to his death. "Music from Spain" is usually read as if it also is about failed initiation—and certainly it results in no long-sustained insight. Close attention to that story's focus on the harmony of opposites may suggest, though, that Eugene Mac-Lain brings back with him from the tangled bank more than has been recognized.

The pattern of initiation in these two stories is essentially like that of the others. In "Music from Spain," Eugene MacLain's psychological defenses have been weakened by the recent death of his daughter and by his growing frustration with the tedium of a life whose perfect, linear orderliness is suggested in his occupation: he is a repairer of time pieces. The routine breaks and he takes his first step toward a new vision of reality on the morning when he slaps his wife, skips work, and decides that "no familiar person could do him any good" as he moves "in this new direction" (p. 400). Feeling both panic and exultation (an initial encounter with unified opposites), he decides to seek a stranger.

R. J. Bowman in "Death of a Traveling Salesman" has, like Eugene, lived until recently a rational, orderly, linear life. For fourteen years, he has driven the roads of Mississippi selling shoes, distrusting roads without signposts, avoiding asking the way of strangers. But now, not thinking "clearly" because of a recent sickness, he has begun to question the value of his long record (p. 119). Time, which had directed his life, seems frozen as he makes his way along an unfamiliar road under an apparently unmoving sun. As was the case in "No Place for You, My Love," his trip has taken him to "the road's end" (p. 120), where, in a variation of the motif fitting for a traveling salesman, his car falls into the tangled bank before he does. (Welty underlines the imagistic identity of car and driver by describing the car in the tangled grapevines as like a "grotesque child" and then declaring that Bowman moved toward the house on the hill "with almost childlike willingness" [p. 121].) Only after this first encounter with enclosing nature can he admit to himself that he is lost—and thus a candidate for being "found."

Both Eugene MacLain and R. J. Bowman are accompanied to the center by silent strangers: Eugene by the Spanish guitarist; Bowman by the hill people, Sonny and his wife. For Eugene, the variation on the isolated, tangled natural area is a walled walkway, "wild and narrow," overlooking the exploding surf of the Pacific shore (pp. 418-19). The path leads finally to the ritual vortex, a spot "entirely out of use," where "paths ran everywhere now, a network of threads over waste and rock" (pp. 419, 420). Bowman's initiation begins in the dark hill-country house, where the woman has before her a half-cleaned lamp. The familiar stream flows nearby. (Writing about "Death of a Traveling Salesman" forty-three years after its publication, Welty said of this water: "Clearly I was trying to suggest that he'd come near, now, to the stream of life. . . ."[22])

The lamp the woman is cleaning brings Bowman his first hint of the union of opposites: "It showed its dark and light. The whole room turned golden-yellow like some sort of flower, and the walls smelled of it and seemed to tremble with the quiet rushing of the fire and the waving of the burning lampwick in its funnel of light" (p. 127). This enlightenment continues when Bowman enters another version of the tangled bank, a thicket where he is ordered onto his knees to crawl through a tunnel made of bushes. The whiskey retrieved from this enclosure has been made by Sonny, himself the image of the union of contraries: his pants are covered with mud, signalling the harmony of human and natural; he wears an old military coat from the Civil War, an image of the jointure of past and present. The revelation that comes to Bowman after drinking the communion whiskey is that the enviable secret possessed by Sonny and his wife is simply human unity: "A marriage, a fruitful marriage. That simple thing. . . . The only secret was the ancient communication between two people" (p. 129).

In "Music from Spain" the wild, isolated arena also brings its vision of harmonious opposition, signalled first by the sky and the sea. The sky, divided by "a kind of spinal cloud," is both clear and cloudy; the sea burns silver and white under the clouds, but is dark beneath the clear sky; and the waves rushing to shore appear frozen in stillness as they come in (p. 419). At this cosmic center, even rocks seem endowed with vitality. Here, too, Eugene senses that the wind can be both adversary and aid, a force to stop his breath or a fortification he can lean on for support.

And here, where so many evaluations and identities double and change, Eugene exchanges identities with the Spaniard, accusing him of assaulting his own wife.[23] At that moment Eugene comes close to some understanding of himself, but, as is always true in visionary moments, words fail him. Instead of articulating his insight, Eugene grasps the Spaniard and holds him over the cliff; then the Spaniard holds him in the same precarious balance. Suspended above the Pacific, Eugene is granted one more encounter with unity, described in a passage in which almost every physical detail has its balancing opposite:

> As he gasped, the sweet and the salt, the alyssum
> and the sea affected him as a single scent. It lulled him
> slightly, blurring the moment. The now calming ocean,
> the pounding of a thousand gentlenesses, went on into
> darkness and obscurity. . . . Now the second hat blew
> away from him too. He was without a burden in the
> world. (pp. 422-23)

In this moment of great vulnerability, he experiences the "vision" that potentially could change his life: he sees his wife—the vulgar, shallow, ordinary Emma—as youthful, tender, mysterious, and loving. In a posture reminiscent of Easter's open-handedness, he is relaxed and "open-armed," annointed with sea spray, thinking only of the possibility of renewed love with Emma (p. 423).

What has happened to Eugene is precisely what he had earlier dreaded when he mused:

> . . . it would be terrifying if walls, even the walls of
> Emma's and his room, the walls of whatever room it
> was that closed a person in in the evening, would go soft
> as curtains and begin to tremble. If like the curtains of
> the aurora borealis the walls of rooms would give even
> the illusion of lifting—if they would threaten to go up.
> That would be repeating the Fire—of course. That
> could happen any time in San Francisco. It was a spe-
> cial threat out here. But the thing he thought of
> wasn't really physical. . . . (pp. 407-8)

Here on the walled overlook, other walls—separating people and things into neat compartments—have begun to dissolve. And those disappearing walls, though terrifying, bring hope of union on the other side.

It is easy to see, however, why readers have concluded that the vision on the cliff is lost when Eugene returns home. Emma nags about his lost hat and petulantly displays the hand she splattered with grease that day. When Eugene mentions that he has seen the Spanish guitarist, she suggests that the Spaniard suffers from indigestion. Yet if we decide—as most critics have—that because of her vulgarity, her apparent superficiality, her lack of empathy, Eugene's vision on the cliff is dashed, we lapse ourselves into the dualistic thinking that the epiphany denied. Reality, Welty keeps insisting, is not an either-or proposition. Indeed, she hints that Eugene retains—at least for a time—something of this insight. The story ends as, with a certain cockiness, he tilts back his chair and watches "Emma pop the grapes in" (p. 426). The image of the grape with its enclosed seed—used by Welty in other stories to emphasize a character's hidden, even Dionysian potential[24]—suggests that Eugene can now see into Emma's emotional interior, where the tender and passionate self he had envisioned on the cliff remains a possibility.

It is not, admittedly, a vision he manages to sustain. The final story in *The Golden Apples* reveals that Eugene returns to Morgana, alone, and dies of tuberculosis. Eugene's tragedy has not been his failure to see into the reality revealed by the Pacific nor his incapacity to allow (at least momentarily) that reality to illuminate his relationship with Emma. His tragedy instead— implied in the change in Eugene between the events of "Music from Spain" and what we hear of him in "The Wanderers"— arises from his inability (humanly very understandable, given Emma's apparent insensitivity and vulgarity) to keep that vision alive.

For R. J. Bowman, however, there is not even a short-lived hope of transferring the vision into his own life. After dreaming briefly that the child expected by the hill couple is his, he leaves under the half-cleaned lamp all his money—the only expression of human connection he knows—and runs from the home in shame. Overwhelmed by his own isolation and by his inability to achieve such a "simple" thing as the union he has seen, he dies, covering his exploding heart with his hands in a final gesture of isolation.

Since "The Wide Net," the final story of this initiation

group, is a comedy, it is fitting that it treat with comic reversal the vision at the center of the other stories. Here William Wallace goes to his initiation confident of his ability to unite with the mystery of the other. He is absolutely sure he understands his wife Hazel. What he learns instead is the other, but equally true, side of reality: that beneath apparent human unity there is always the mystery of individual separateness.

The other main components of the ritual remain the same. William Wallace is readied for a new view of life by the shock of his wife's supposed suicide. Preparing to drag the Pearl River for her body, he and his friends enter "in silence" the deep, dim, still woods, stepping "among the great walls of vines and among the passion-flowers" (pp. 175, 176). By the river stands the now familiar tree, this time a magnolia, under which William Wallace and his companions take shelter. The magnolia responds to the pounding of the rain by releasing its fragrance without yielding its strength.

As in the other stories, symbolic revelations of unity cascade before the initiate. Doc (the hierophant here) suggests that they are at that interface between time and eternity, at the meeting point of life and death, ripeness and decay, when he describes the world as all of one color, frozen gold for just one moment before the changes of autumn occur. (The image works in much the same way as Nina's description of the perfect pear in "Moon Lake.") At the Pearl River, silence turns out really to be its opposite: "The thing that seemed like silence must have been the endless cry of all the crickets and locusts in the world, rising and falling" (p. 177). Doc (who is never really concerned that Hazel has killed herself, but who knows that William Wallace has to discover reality for himself) voices the ultimate paradox when he says: "The excursion is the same when you go looking for your sorrow as when you go looking for your joy" (p. 181). And in a transformation symbolic of the union of the human and natural worlds, each member of the search party is plastered with wet leaves, causing the young boy Sammy to wail, "Now us got scales. . . . Us is the fishes" (p. 183). Later, William Wallace manifests a similar unifying vision when, walking home, he sees all the women he has known as "all one young girl standing up to sing under the trees the oldest and longest ballads there were" (p. 187).

This is one truth from the center: the Many are really One. However, the insight William Wallace really needs is that each individual one is really that, separate and impenetrable. (Welty is following seriously Doc's sarcastic advice: "Now that's the way to argue, see it from all sides . . ." [p. 175].) William Wallace has too smugly assumed that he understands Hazel, taking her message literally and thinking that he will find her by diving into the Pearl River, oblivious to the implication of Doc's query: "Who says Hazel was to be caught?" (p. 186)

William Wallace's first hint that even the familiar must remain unknown comes when, suddenly struck by the wonder of the Pearl, he asks the name of the river he has lived near all his life. Just as the mystery of the river defies naming, so the sure identification of Hazel's trouble may have escaped him:

> Had he suspected down there, like some secret, the real, the true trouble that Hazel had fallen into, about which words in a letter could not speak . . . how (who knew?) she had been filled to the brim with that elation that they all remembered, like their own secret, the elation that comes of great hopes and changes, sometimes simply of the harvest time, that comes with a little course of its own like a tune to run in the head, and there was nothing she could do about it—they knew—and so it had turned into this? It could be nothing but the old trouble that William Wallace was finding out, reaching and turning in the gloom of such depths. (p. 180)

Who knows, indeed? For William Wallace, too, is a mystery—even, Welty suggests, to his author.

After diving into "the deepest place" in "the dark clear world of deepness," he boasts, "I'm the only man alive knows Hazel"—a comic undercutting of our expectations after an initiation into awareness of human separateness (pp. 180, 186). However, back home, greeted by Hazel's "mysterious" look, William Wallace experiences once more the reality of the unknowable other. The story closes with William Wallace frowning—just as he had when he wondered about the name of the river—and trying "to look where [Hazel] looked. And after a few minutes she took him by the hand and led him into the house, smiling as if she were smiling down on him" (p. 188).

The cure for comic cockiness—for overweening confidence that because people are united on the surface (in marriage, say) they are also united in empathetic understanding of each other's mysterious selfhood—is, Welty suggests in "The Wide Net," initiation into the truth that the other is always other, to be respected as an integrity inviolable. In the other initiation stories, as a solace for the tragic vision that self is isolated, cut off from others, from nature, from cosmic meaning, Welty offers the opposite reality, equally true: that ultimately humanity and nature, self and other, the forces of life and death are one. The strength of Welty's paradoxical vision in these stories is her ability to sustain simultaneously a belief in both truths, seeing life as like that tree at the center of the tangled bank, the tree which unites earth and heaven, shelters and kills, and which, being assaulted itself by natural forces, gives out the fragrance of its blossoms.

Notes

[1] *A Dictionary of Symbols*, trans. Jack Sage (New York: Philosophical Library, 1962), pp. 93, 110.

[2] On the initiation motif in the short stories, cf. F. Garvin Davenport, Jr., "Renewal and Historical Consciousness in *The Wide Net*" in Prenshaw, ed., *Critical Essays*, pp. 189-200. Davenport associates the consequent "awakening or renewal" of characters with the playing out of the old antagonism between individuality and community.

[3] *The Collected Stories of Eudora Welty* (New York: Harcourt, Brace, Jovanovich, 1980), p. 440. All subsequent references to Welty's stories will be to this edition and will be given in the text of this chapter.

[4] Before Miss Sabina's house "not one blade of grass grew in the hard green ground." Solomon has seen to it that "every vestige of grass [has been] patiently uprooted and the ground scarred in deep whorls from the strike of Livvie's broom" (pp. 201, 229). In "A Memory," garden imagery also clearly symbolizes a way of approaching—and attempting to contain and control— reality. The narrator says: "My father and mother . . . believed that I saw nothing in the world which was not strictly coaxed into place like a vine on our garden trellis to be presented to my eyes . . ." (p. 75).

[5] There is, of course, no question about the paternity of Eugene, King's son by his marriage to Snowdie. King is almost certainly also the father of Easter of "Moon Lake," who is probably one of those Katie Rainey describes in "Shower of Gold" as "children of [King's] growing up in the County Orphans" (p. 264). The paternity of the young black boy Exum McLane, who also plays a role in the initiation in "Moon Lake," is indicated in his last name (p. 261). Evidence that Loch Morrison (of "June Recital" and "Moon Lake") is another of King's byblows is less concrete. Loch's sister Cassie recalls in "June Recital" that their mother always slipped off by herself when the town gathered for "speakings"—making her a wanderer, too, as well as suggesting the possibility of her slipping off for romantic assignations. Mrs. Morrison's calling Loch "*my* child" is probably also significant, as Ruth Vande Kieft has suggested (1962, p. 121). Further evidence of her romantic involvement with King lies in that missed beat in Mrs. Morrison's response in "June Recital" when Cassie tells her mother that "Mr. King MacLain was here, and now he's gone" (p. 326). There is

widespread critical agreement about Virgie Rainey's spiritual kinship with King (see, for example, Vande Kieft, 1987, p. 114, and Louise Westling, *Sacred Groves and Ravaged Gardens* [Athens: The University of Georgia Press, 1985, p. 99]). I believe, however, that Virgie is quite likely King's natural child as well. We recall that King once offered Katie Rainey—Katie Blazes, as King tellingly remembers her in his old age—any gift she wanted, giving her the swivel chair that perhaps only partially justified King's declaring, "I set her on a throne!" (p. 444). In addition, Katie Rainey admits in "Shower of Gold" that she "could have streaked like an arrow to the very oak tree" where King kept his trysts with his wife Snowdie (p. 264), and near the end of her story Katie tells us that Snowdie does not like Katie's baby Virgie any more (a feeling that seems insufficiently justified by the reason Katie offers: that Katie was at Snowdie's the Halloween King appeared and left without seeing his wife). Katie concludes her tale by declaring: " . . . I bet my little Jersey calf King tarried long enough to get him a child somewhere. What makes me say a thing like that? I wouldn't say it to my husband, you mind you forget it" (p. 274). Hints of Katie's sexual exploits outside of marriage appear in her own memory that as a bride she had "more than they guessed" (p. 431) and in the town gossips' snide declaration that Virgie's mother even in old age "ain't lost her appetite" for wild birds (p. 429). Both Loch and Virgie leave Morgana, becoming wanderers as King was for part of his life.

6 Joseph Campbell, *The Hero with a Thousand Faces*, Bollingen Series, XVII (1949; rpt. Princeton, NJ: Princeton University Press, 1973), pp. 217-18.

7 Campbell, *The Hero with a Thousand Faces*, p. 41.

8 Mircea Eliade, *The Two and the One*, trans. J. M. Cohen (Chicago: University of Chicago Press, 1965), p. 82. Joseph Campbell also points out that part of the revelation of all initiations is the secret of the essential unity of all, hence, the emphasis in initiation rituals on bisexual forms, on the identity of time and eternity, and of the divine and human (Campbell, p. 171).

9 Alan Watts, *The Two Hands of God: The Myths of Polarity* (New York: Collier Books, 1963), p. 186.

10 Nicolas of Cusa, *The Vision of God*, trans. Emma Gurney Salter (New York: Frederick Ungar, 1960), pp. 43-44.

11 Cirlot points out that the tree often denotes the "life of the cosmos," its roots in the earth, its horizontal axes, and its branches reaching to the sky, all contributing to the symbolism of unity (pp. 328-32). See also Eliade, *Rites and Symbols of Initiation: The Mysteries of Birth and Rebirth*, trans. Willard Trask (New York: Harper & Row, 1958), p. 78; Campbell, p. 41.

12 Joseph Allen Bryant, Jr., notes that in the final scene Mrs. Larkin "[finds] herself . . . identified with the daemon of the chinaberry tree—or at any rate a similar daemon—as inexplicably she stands behind her kneeling Negro helper and threatens him with an upraised hoe." However, Bryant's emphasis is on the continuing mystery of "the purposes of the nonhuman world," rather than on the revelation of a pattern of wholeness (*Eudora Welty*, p. 12). Vande Kieft similarly sees an absence of "transcendental knowledge here"; in her view the only message received by Mrs. Larkin is that "chance is blind and irrational" (*Eudora Welty*, 1987, p. 196). St. George Tucker Arnold sees Mrs. Larkin at the end in "tragic and complete psychic return to pre-infancy," having "entered the stage of growth of the subhuman life around her" ("The Rain-cloud and the Garden: Psychic Regression as Tragedy in Eudora Welty's 'A Curtain of Green,' *South Atlantic Bulletin*, 44 [January 1979], 59). My reading agrees with Michael Kreyling's, p. 14.

[13] Eliade, *Rites and Symbols*, p. 65.

[14] For a discussion of the implications of this exchange of identities, see Lowry Pei, "Dreaming the Other in *The Golden Apples*," *Modern Fiction Studies*, 28 (Autumn 1982), 415-33.

[15] See Michael Kreyling on Nina's being barred from penetrating the mystery by "her own too-conscious thought" (pp. 87-91).

[16] In "Sleeping Beauty" (the Grimms' "Briar-rose," no. 50), a hedge of thorns cuts the castle off from the world, while everyone inside sleeps.

[17] Joseph Campbell distinguishes between judgment in the "field of time" (or the "field of action") and judgment as a metaphysical observer, in *Power of Myth*, where he refers to Heraclitus' belief that "for God all things are good and right and just, but for man some things are right and others are not" (p. 66).

[18] *The Golden Apples* (New York: Harcourt, Brace, 1949), p. 192.

[19] Eliade, *Rites and Symbols*, p. xiii.

[20] Alun Jones suggests that travelling in general creates "a disembodied kind of existence somewhere between time and space" and speaks of the two characters of this story as entering "that strange order of reality that exists on the edge of being . . ." ("A Frail Travelling Coincidence: Three Later Stories of Eudora Welty," in Turner and Harding, eds., *Critical Essays on Eudora Welty*, pp. 184, 187).

[21] Eliade points out the universal role of heat in initiation ceremonies, explaining that "access to sacrality is manifested, among other things, by a prodigious increase in heat" (*Rites and Symbols*, p. 86).

[22] "Looking Back at the First Story," *Georgia Review*, 33 (Winter 1979), 754.

[23] In her study of the capacity of the female consciousness to accommodate dichotomies in *The Golden Apples*, Elaine Pugh points out other instances of the unity of apparent opposites: for example, when Eugene sees a photograph of Madame Blatvatsky, mystic and leader of the London Theosophical Society, he sees in her features the face of his wife, Emma, "who in her bourgeois aspect," Pugh writes, "is surely far removed from Madame Blavatsky." In addition Pugh points out that the Spaniard seemed to Eugene "a stranger and yet not a stranger" ("The Duality of Morgana: The Making of Virgie's Vision, the Vision of *The Golden Apples*," 446).

[24] See, for example, "Asphodel," p. 206.

IV

"The Way Home through the Wilderness":
The Robber Bridegroom

The nature and purpose of the relationship between fairy tale and reality in Eudora Welty's *The Robber Bridegroom* (1942) has been discussed since the earliest reviews.[1] In one of the most penetrating critical responses to the work, Michael Kreyling has seen in the mixture of fairy tale and history an expression of the conflict between pastoral dream and capitalistic reality in America.[2] It is possible, however, to view the work in a larger metaphysical scheme. In this reading, we can see the collision of history and fairy tale as rising out of the human impulse to simplify life, to explain it in either-or terms, while life's insistent complexity keeps demanding a way of looking at reality that transcends both fairy tale and history.[3]

The folk fairy tale that Welty incorporated into her story is grounded on the child's need for simplicity. As Bruno Bettelheim writes:

> The figures in fairy tales are not ambivalent—not good and bad at the same time, as we are in reality. But since polarization dominates the child's mind, it also dominates fairy tales. A person is either good or bad, nothing in between. One brother is stupid, the other is clever. One sister is virtuous and industrious . . . [etc.].[4]

The child cannot handle the grandmother's crabby moments, so she sees the testy grandmother as the wolf, while the grandmother in her nice moods becomes the object of Red Ridinghood's charitable visit. The child avoids direct confrontation with her own double nature in stories such as "Sister and Brother," in which her undisciplined self, projected as her brother-companion, is turned into a fawn.[5] In *The Robber Bride-groom*, the characters attempt to sustain the child's simple vision of human nature, while life works inexorably to intro-duce them to its doubleness. In this way, Welty's novel is about the lesson needed to move us from the child's world to the adult's, from a fairy-tale vision of life to a philosophically, psy-chologically, historically, and metaphysically corrected outlook.[6]

Clement Musgrove's journey from his blissful home in Kentucky into the Mississippi wilderness is itself a trip from fairy tale to reality. Anthony Steven's analysis of the expulsion from the Garden of Eden applies to Clement's move: the loss of paradise, Stevens says, is "a parable of the emergence of ego-consciousness, and the replacement of harmonious unity with the conflicts born of awareness of opposing categories of experi-ence (e.g., good and evil, love and hate, pleasure and pain)."[7] However, Welty's characters will learn a lesson opposite to Adam and Eve's. While life in Eden was possible only in the presence of one of the paired opposites (good, love, pleasure), in the world Welty describes, life can be lived fully only with the acknowledgement of the harmony to be found in the co-existence of the contraries.

The natural world in *The Robber Bridegroom* (as in the initiation stories) bears witness to the cosmic reality of unified opposites, contrasting vividly with the human desire to see ev-erything in either-or terms. When Jamie Lockhart (the gallant who is also the robber) leaves Clement Musgrove's house after he has failed to recognize in Clement's daughter Rosamond the girl who attracted him in the woods, he enters a natural world whose complexity adumbrates the reality that he avoids. He rides "in the *confusion* of the moonlight, under the *twining* branches of trees . . ." (emphasis added).[8]

The next day when Rosamond, who has likewise failed to recognize in Jamie the bandit she found so charming, sets out to join her highwayman, she enters the same forest, that old liter-ary symbol for a mind on the threshold of self-knowledge—and, hence, knowledge of the reality into which that self fits. On the *silva* image, Bruno Bettelheim writes:

> Finding oneself in a dark, impenetrable forest is an
> ancient literary image for man in need of gaining self-
> knowledge. Dante evoked it at the beginning of the
> *Divine Comedy*, but long before him, it served as image
> of man in search of himself, of man caught in a moral
> crisis, of man having to meet a developmental impasse

as he wishes to move from a lower to a higher level of
self-consciousness.[9]

Although Rosamond does not realize it at the time, the
perceptual confusion she experiences as she penetrates the forest
(mistaking the gentle for the cruel, the animal for the human,
the predator for the defenseless) hints of the overlapping and in-
tertwining nature of reality:

> On and on she went, deeper and deeper into the
> forest, and its sound was all around. She heard
> something behind her, but it was only a woodpecker
> pecking with his ivory bill. She thought there was a
> savage there, but it was a deer which was looking so
> hard at her. Once she thought she heard a baby crying,
> but it was a wildcat down in the cane. (p. 77)

By the end of the tale she will have learned that other categories
that she had also thought to be mutually exclusive are, after all,
not so clearcut.

Jamie Lockhart experiences a similar illumination. He is
The Robber Bridegroom's best exemplar both of the human impulse to simplify one's sense of self and one's responses to
others, as well as of the need to move toward acceptance of the
self's polar reality. Jamie's first conversations with Clement reveal his desire for a life without complications. When Clement
confesses his own perpetual guilt before his second wife Salome,
Jamie replies: "Guilt is a burdensome thing to carry about in the
heart. . . . I would never bother with it." To this Clement
replies: "Then you are a man of action, . . . a man of the times, a
pioneer and a free agent. There is no one to come to you saying
'I want' what you do not want" (p. 27).

Things will change for Jamie in the course of Welty's
story. But at its start, he has tried neatly to partition his life, seeing himself as alternately the bandit or the gentleman, never
admitting that his reality includes simultaneously both identities. When, at their first formal meeting, he fails to recognize
Rosamond as the same beautiful girl he met in the woods, it is
not only because she is now ragged and dirty, but also because his
either-or vision interferes with perception of the real: ". . . it was
either love or business that traveled on his mind, never both at
once, and this night it was business" (p. 69).

However, when Clement offers his daughter as a reward if
Jamie captures the bandit who stole her clothes, Jamie is repulsed by the dirty, stupid young woman Clement presents to

him (Rosamond in her own disguise). In spite of the attraction of the dowry that is an unspoken part of the deal, this "man of enterprise" actually incarnates (without being aware of it) human *concordia discors*, combining within himself the contradictory qualities of the romantic and the materialist. Welty writes that "in his heart" Jamie "carried nothing less than a dream of true love—something of gossamer and roses, though on this topic he never held conversation with himself, or let the information pass to a soul . . ." (p. 74). Later, when his robber band chides him for staying with the beautiful Rosamond during the daytime (he had always before confined romance to night and devoted the day to banditry), he halfway draws his dirk in self-defensive protest: "For he thought he had it all divisioned off into time and place, and that many things were for later and for further away, and that now the world had just begun" (p. 87).

Jamie's challenge is to bring into conversation the two sides of himself, accepting his complex reality. Ironically, the innocent Clement voices most clearly the truth of this polarity, in his by-now familiar declaration to Rosamond when she visits him after her "marriage" to Jamie:

> "If being a bandit were his breadth and scope, I should find him and kill him for sure. . . . But since in addition he loves my daughter, he must be not the one man, but two, and I should be afraid of killing the second. For all things are double, and this should keep us from taking liberties with the outside world, and acting too quickly to finish things off." (p. 126)

It is strangely appropriate in a world where apparent opposites meet that kind-hearted Clement shares this awareness of doubleness with the villains of the piece. In fact, while the innocent planter has an abstract and non-specific intuition about the mingled identity of Rosamond's robber lover, the evil Salome and the Little Harp have specific evidence that Jamie Lockhart and the outlaw are one. The distinction is probably significant: Salome's and Little Harp's knowledge of doubleness exists only on the rational level; it is not a lived experience, illuminating their own lives and actions as it does Clement's. They *see* but do not *feel* the reality they have encountered.

It is probably worth recalling that Marshall McLuhan and Walter Ong have located in the movement toward vision as the primary sensory source for an understanding of reality the historical cause of the shift, in Western society, from a holistic sense of self-in-world to a self-world dualism. When seeing becomes the way to "truth," truth becomes defined as objectified knowledge, which is possible only when the seer is separated from the object to be known.[10] Recent studies of feminist epistemology, such as that of Evelyn Fox Keller and Christine R. Grontkowski, have associated patriarchialism with "the pervasive reliance on a visual metaphor [that] marks Western philosophy." Keller and Grontkowski point out that "vision is that sense which places the world at greatest remove. . . ." To think of knowledge as something acquired through "the mind's eye," they suggest, conveys the idea of the mind as a camera, passively registering images of a reality from which it is totally disengaged.[11] Mary Field Belenky and others have suggested that women, on the other hand, tend "to ground their epistemological premises in metaphors suggesting speaking and listening" (and, other scholars would add, touching).[12]

Appropriately then, at their first meeting, the stone-hearted, rational, stereotypically masculine Salome *sees* the berry stains behind Jamie Lockhart's ear (p. 75); the equally stony and equally greed-driven Little Harp *sees* Jamie with only a partially stained face after Jamie, interrupted as he began to disguise himself, runs to aid Goat's sister, whom Little Harp had decided to kill instead of marry. Little Harp gloats: "Aha, but I know who you are too. . . . Your name is Jamie Lockhart and you are the bandit in the woods, for you have your two faces on together and I see you both" (p. 112). (Later, Rosamond will make the mistake of thinking that she will learn her lover's true identity if she can but see beneath his disguise.)

Salome and Little Harp on the one hand and Clement on the other also demonstrate two responses to an awareness of human complexity. Clement shows that an appreciation of the full instead of the partial human being can lead to compassion and to patience with life's unfolding. He shows, too, that understanding the doubleness of others can illuminate dark areas of one's own life. His speech about Jamie's doubleness includes this startling bit of self-examination:

> "All things are divided in half—night and day, the soul and body, and sorrow and joy and youth and age, and sometimes I wonder if even my own wife has not been the one person all the time, and I loved her beauty so at the beginning that it is only now that the ugliness has struck through to beset me like a madness." (p. 126)

The trick in human relationships that Clement senses that he has not applied to his own wife and that Jamie and Rosamond must discover is to see the "sides" of personalities simultaneously (or in close sequence), not, as in the fairy tale, viewing as totally separate the good and the bad.

For Salome and Little Harp, however, seeing Jamie's dual self leads neither to compassion nor to self-perception. Their knowledge is completely objectified, and their relations to others have their own kind of simplicity: they use them. The information they have about Jamie becomes the basis of their powerplay over Rosamond and Jamie. That Rosamond and Jamie—both of whom deny one side of their nature—are such easy victims implies the vulnerability that accompanies attempted retreats to a simple identity. Paradoxically, however, that very vulnerability contains the seeds for human growth: it forces Rosamond and Jamie to confront their duplex identities, making possible their experience of life's fullness of sorrow and joy.

On the other hand, Salome and Little Harp illustrate the self-destruction that accompanies inviolate one-sidedness. If Clement is right that Salome is really the other side of his first wife Amalie (their names are practically anagrams), ugly now and hardened since the murder of their son by Indians, Salome has denied so totally the gentle, loving side of her self that she has become virtually inhuman. Her only passion now is for the acquisition of more and more possessions. Clement muses that even "in her times of love Salome was immeasurably calculating and just so, almost clocklike, in the way of the great Spanish automaton in the iron skirt in the New Orleans bazaar, which could play and beat a man at chess" (pp. 26-27). At one point Welty writes: " . . . Rosamond did not think the trickery went so deep in her stepmother that it did not come to an end, but made her solid like an image of stone in the garden . . ." (p. 123). Her end is also described with an appropriate metaphor: she falls over "stone dead" (p. 163).

The singlemindedness that negates Salome's humanity also leads to her capture by the Indians: " . . . her eye, from thinking of golden glitter, had possibly gotten too bright to see the dark that was close around her now" (pp. 144-45). The eye, depended upon too exclusively, is once more shown to have its limitations. Salome's coldly determined self-sufficiency leads to her destruction. When Goat, who has come to free her from the Indians, asks why she is crying, she screams: "I am not crying! . . . Be gone! I need no one!" (p. 152). And so he leaves her.

Brought before the Indians, she claims the power to command the sun. "Shaking both her fists in the smoky air," she proclaims: "No one is to have power over me! . . . . No man, and none of the elements! I am by myself in the world" (pp. 160-61). And she dances to her death, alone, ordering the sun to retire.

Little Harp also demonstrates that nothing is potentially so destructive as viewing self or other through a single lens. Having reduced himself merely to the violent outlaw—the shadow self of Jamie Lockhart's bandit persona—Little Harp dies when he declares the death of both Big Harp and the bandit Jamie Lockhart. (His plan was to keep the reward offered for Big Harp's head when it was mistaken for Jamie's.) Little Harp, like Salome, asserts that he alone is in control, bragging to Jamie: " . . . the Little Harp rules now. And for the proof of everything, I'm killing you now with my own two hands" (p. 157). Instead, of course, Jamie kills him. Only in death does Little Harp reveal the other, feeling, side of himself that he had denied in life: "The Little Harp, with a wound in his heart, heaved a deep sigh and a tear came out of his eye, for he hated to give up his life as badly as the deer in the woods" (p. 158).

However, while Little Harp's death, like Salome's, implies the deadness even in life of those who develop and recognize only one part of the self, the central significance of Little Harp's murder seems to lie in its symbolizing the death of Jamie's bandit self. Yet even this is not as simple as it first appears. We recognize as clearly as Jamie does that Little Harp represents the violent, outlaw side of Rosamond's handsome lover. While we, like Rosamond, actually see in action only the dashing Lochinvar-Robin Hood part of Jamie's persona, Welty is careful to remind us of the more somber business of his profession. The first intimation takes the comic form of Mike Fink's obvious fear of Jamie (p. 12): whoever can bring a tremor to that he-bull, he-rattlesnake, he-alligator of a flatboatman must be some sort of a he-terror himself. When Mike Fink's ominously croaking raven sits easily on Jamie's finger "as though there it belonged" (p. 19), we assume Jamie is at home, too, with Mike Fink's grimmer activities. (Fink has, after all, just had a hearty go at beating Jamie and Clement to death with a floorboard.)

Less laughter accompanies the next clue to the reality of Jamie's life as an outlaw, one he himself furnishes when he broadly hints to Clement—almost as if he wished to give himself away—about the parallels between the Indians robbing Clement and Jamie's own banditry (p. 22). Further inside the

nested boxes of *The Robber Bridegroom* are even darker reminders of the non-fairytale quality of robbers' lives. When
Jamie first encounters Little Harp and tries to kill him, he in-
stinctively recognizes their shared identity. Welty writes:

> He half pulled out his little dirk to kill the Little
> Harp then and there. But his little dirk, not unstained
> with blood, held back and would not touch the feeble
> creature. Something seemed to speak to Jamie that
> said, "This is to be your burden, and so you might as
> well take it." (p. 112)

So the Little Harp moves into Jamie's hideout, raping and
killing the Indian girl in the same house where Jamie lives with
Rosamond, whom he had abducted, too (though, in a fairy-tale
layer of the story, with her loving compliance). In the death of
the Indian girl we are about as far as we can get from light-
hearted innocence and from gay, soaring dreams without
nightmares.[13] And Jamie's character is here revealed as far from
the fairy-tale Prince Charming. To Jamie's outlaw band, Little
Harp declares: " . . . your chief belongs to me! . . . . He is bound
over to me body and soul . . ." (p. 130). Although Jamie throws
him out, he knows that "he'll be back with me tomorrow"
(p. 133). Even Rosamond comes close to acknowledging the real
life of her lover when she admits to Salome that Jamie still
brings her fine dresses and petticoats—obviously from other
women he has accosted and possibly raped (p. 118).

As the book moves away from its dark center, Jamie re-
solves comically the problems that have been generated by his
keeping the two parts of his self in isolation. However, the solution is not actually the death of his robber side, as the killing of
Little Harp may seem at first to imply. To think that the robber
in Jamie dies completely is to miss the whole point of the theme
of doubleness, of the necessary and valuable reality of human
psychological polarity. It is also to miss a good joke. Jamie becomes a rich merchant, the perfect way to be both a gentleman
and a highwayman. As Welty's narrator tells us: " . . . the outward transfer from bandit to merchant had been almost too easy
to count it a change at all, and he was enjoying all the same success he had ever had" (p. 184). Thus the death of Little Harp signals, not the death of Jamie's robber self, but his acceptance of
the integration of the two poles of self into one whole.

New Orleans is an appropriate setting for this integration,
since it too brings into concord apparent opposites: "Beauty and

vice and every delight possible to the soul and body stood hospitably, and usually together, in every doorway and beneath every palmetto by day and lighted torch by night. A shutter opened, and a flower bloomed" (p. 182). Here, Jamie—now a man of feeling as well as a man of action, and no longer quite so free of the wants of others—lives the wisdom he has come to, his heroic vision: "But now in his heart Jamie knew that he was a hero and had always been one, only with the power to look both ways and to see a thing from all sides" (p. 185). In Welty's moral scheme the willingness to take this Janus-like perspective is itself heroic.

Jamie is not the only character with two faces in *The Robber Bridegroom*. Writing about this work in "Fairy Tale of the Natchez Trace," Welty underlined the importance of this motif to her narrative: "There's a doubleness in respect to identity that runs in a strong thread through all wild happenings—indeed, this thread is their connection and everything that happens hangs upon it."[14] Almost everyone has either a double identity or a personality made up of contradictory elements, making it difficult for us easily to pass judgment on or, in Clement's words, to finish anyone off. The "evil" characters seem evil precisely because—and to the extent that—they refuse to acknowledge their complexity, a refusal that reduces them to one-dimensional fairy-tale villains in their evaluations of themselves and in their relationship to others.

But Welty insists that the reader not participate in this reductionism, leading us instead to detect worth even in the villains. So the Little Harp turns out in his death to have human feelings; so Salome and Amalie are two halves of an unrecognized whole. The loud-mouthed, murderous Mike Fink of the first part of the tale is also the timorous, ghost-bedeviled mail rider of the conclusion (and even in the opening scene he has such a queasy stomach that he covers his eyes and feels rather than looks at the ruin he thinks he has brought Clement and Jamie, a comic introduction to Welty's idea that all people are double). Later, we discover the stupid Goat moved to tears by Rosamond's song and the pitiless Indians feeling pity for Clement. We end up feeling strangely ambivalent even about Salome, whose defiance of all in heaven or on earth demands a kind of admiration as well as scorn.

However, next to Jamie, the character whose doubleness is most fully developed is Rosamond. She is both the spoiled daughter of a rich planter and the self-sacrificing lover of the bandit of the woods. While she has the fairy-tale attributes of Gretel, Cinderella, and Snow White (her name, Rose of the World, parallels the generic naming of fairy tales[15]), she is unlike them in being far from the one-sided, virtuous, long-suffering, passive maiden of fairy tales. She is "a great liar" from whose mouth untruths fall as naturally as jewels from the lips of fairy princesses (p. 38). She is also as sexually awakened as Snow White is innocent of all conscious sexuality. Rosamond has had fantasies of abduction and is coolly self-possessed when she is accosted by the outlaw Jamie ("... Rosamond ... had sometimes imagined such a thing happening, and knew what to say" [p. 48]).

In fact, it seems to be Rosamond who entices Jamie in their first encounter: "Well, then, I suppose I must give you the dress ... but not a thing further" (p. 47). When Jamie takes even her petticoats, she spends no time worrying about the precarious state of her virtue, but instead wonders "how ever she might look without a stitch on her" (p. 50). And when Jamie offers her a choice between being killed and going home naked, she shows no stupid fairy-tale preference for honor over life, asserting: "Why, sir, life is sweet ... and before I would die on the point of your sword, I would go home naked any day" (p. 50). Back home, she acquiesces to Salome's orders that she work like a scullery maid, finding in her subservience freedom from others' pleasures and plans for her—a neat instance of the harmony of opposites in personal relations. The next day, she returns to the forest of her own free will, giving Jamie the opportunity to take what he had left her the day before—a step that will lead to the very unfairytale-like predicament of her pregnancy.

After she begins to live with her robber lover, her psychological state also bears witness to the real-life adult's need for the state of tension created by the simultaneity of apparent contraries. In the robber's cottage, she is perfectly happy, we are told, except that "she had never seen her lover's face. But then the heart cannot live without something to sorrow and be curious over" (p. 88). So even the happiness of love is incomplete without sorrow, which passes in the world of the simple as totally alien to love.

Rosamond's doubleness is even more complexly present in her difference from and similarity to Salome. At first the two seem absolute opposites. An early description establishes their contrast: "For if Rosamond was as beautiful as the day, Salome was as ugly as the night ..." (p. 33). But as in the case of the yin-yang principle, Salome and Rosamond share points of contact and dynamic exchange. Like so many opposites in Welty's fiction, these two begin to reveal their similarities, especially after Rosamond is initiated into love, that business so likely to introduce us to life's complicated reality.

It is probably not so much ironic as appropriate in a world where opposites meet that the place where Jamie first made love to Rosamond is the same place where Clement had married Salome: " . . . there under the meeting trees at the edge" (p. 105). When Rosamond tells her father and stepmother of her marriage to the bandit, Salome senses her kinship with Rosamond: " . . . at that moment the stepmother gave Rosamond a look of true friendship, as if Rosamond too had got her man by unholy means" (p. 122). And when Salome voices the doubts that Rosamond feels about her lover's identity, "Salome drew so close to Rosamond that they could look down the well and see one shadow, and whispered in her ear . . ." (p. 123). She is as surely Rosamond's shadow self as the Little Harp is Jamie's. Thus it is fitting that Salome die when Rosamond moves toward integration of the parts of her self, just as Little Harp does when Jamie starts on a similar path.

The attitude toward life conveyed by The Robber Bridegroom is as double as Jamie's and Rosamond's identities are. It parallels the splicing of the fairy-tale tone to the real horrors of murder, rape, and other savage doings that fill the story. In The Robber Bridegroom Welty has given us a story about which we could say precisely what she said in summarizing the message of Chekhov's fiction:

> . . . "Life is terrible and marvelous, and so, however terrible a story you tell . . . however you embroider it with nests of robbers, long knives and such marvels, it always finds an echo of reality in the soul of the listener. . . . [Real life] was of itself so marvelous and terrible that the fantastic stories of legend and fairy tale were pale and blended with life."[16]

Terrible and marvelous—that is the estimation of life Welty gives us in The Robber Bridegroom. "Life is sweet," Rosamond has said, even as she is being robbed; her name, "rose of the world," implies in the old image of flower and thorns both the beauty and pain of life. And the horror is very much acknowledged, even in this tale so widely read as light-hearted entertainment. The undertone of horror accompanying the wonder of life is introduced early in the story. The first paragraph ends with the declaration, "the way home through the wilderness was beset with dangers," creating a sense of the threats that surround and (if we remember the symbolism of the wilderness) live within the human psyche. The theme of human cruelty to other humans is introduced in the first chapter. The first two innkeepers Clement encounters have lost ears for horse stealing and cock-fighting. While their cropped ears seem funny at the outset, deeper inside the tale we realize that the mutilation of criminals is but a societally sanctioned version of the mutilation of the Indian girl by Little Harp. Then, after the slapstick attempt by Mike Fink to kill Clement and Jamie, we are chilled with the sickening tale of the treatment of Clement's party by their Indian captors. Humiliation, torture, and murder have left Clement with "less than nothing" (p. 23). The story of Clement's experiences is doubly hard for readers to bear because we know that every act of cruelty detailed there actually has been perpetrated by one human on another, again and again, around the world, throughout history.[17]

Indeed, for all the rolicking gaiety of its surface, The Robber Bridegroom presents one of Welty's darkest visions of reality, a darkness intensified by Clement's perception of a cosmic horror in which humans appear as "little mice" in a life seen as "a maze without end" (pp. 23, 103). Psychological forces are as mysterious as the powers of nature. Clement cannot even remember why he came into the wilderness; all he knows is that "there was a great tug at the whole world, to go down over the edge, . . . and our hearts and our own lonely will may have had nothing to do with it" (p. 21). Just as frightening as the mystery of causality is the uncontrollable domino effect of human actions (yet another expression of the tangled nature of reality). Jamie determines to rescue Rosamond, saying, " . . . when I went off and left her, I had no idea what a big thing would come of it" (p. 164).

In spite of this recognition, however, human will is ineffectual in fighting life's horror. It is not Jamie who rescues Rosamond, but the stupid Goat. And when Clement, uncharacteristically moved from passivity, determines to rescue his daughter himself, he ends up wrestling all night with a monster that turns out to be a willow tree. If this were not a comedy, protected by its fairy-tale wrappings, a character like Clement would surely be driven mad by the cruel, senseless, and overpowering forces of life that assail him. Hearing that the gentleman he trusted to rescue his daughter is the bandit who stole her clothes, her honor, and her heart, he forgets his own wisdom about life's doubleness and retreats into the forest (the appropriate place for encounters with horrors within and without), demanding exactness from a world that will not furnish it:

> "What exactly is this now?
> . . . .
> "Wrath and love burn only like campfires. And even the appearance of a hero is no longer a single and majestic event like that of a star in the heavens, but a wandering fire soon lost. A journey is forever lonely and parallel to death, but the two watch each other, the traveler and the bandit, through the trees. Like will-o-the-wisps the little blazes burn on the rafts all night, unsteady beside the shore. Where are they even so soon as tomorrow? Massacre is hard to tell from the performance of other rites, in the great silence where the wanderer is coming. Murder is as soundless as a spout of blood, as regular and rhythmic as sleep. Many find a skull and a little branching of bones between two floors of leaves. In the sky is the perpetual wheel of buzzards. A circle of bandits counts out the gold, with bending shoulders more slaves mount the block and go down, a planter makes a gesture of abundance with his riding whip, a flatboatman falls back from the tavern door to the river below with scarcely time for a splash, a rope descends from a tree and curls into a noose. And all around again are the Indians.
> "Yet no one can laugh or cry so savagely in this wilderness as to be heard by the nearest traveler or remembered the next year. A fiddle played in a finished hut in a clearing is as vagrant as the swamp breeze. What will the seasons be, when we are lost and dead? The dreadful heat and cold—no more than the shooting star." (pp. 141, 143-44)

Love and wrath, massacres and mysteries, bandits and slave-owners, music and a swamp breeze—all become equal in insignificance before the rolling seasons, and the only solace seems to be a recognition of the transience and insignificance of everything. Clement could be the prophet of Ecclesiastes crying out on the vanity of life. As he watches Salome going to her death, he looks at the faces of the surrounding Indians and thinks: "The savages have only come the sooner to their end; we will come to ours too. Why have I built my house, and added to it? The planter will go after the hunter, and the merchant after the planter, all having their day" (p. 161).

The monstrous, self-devouring quality of life is captured in Clement's musings, but clearly this is only the dark center of Welty's tale. For while Clement's thoughts imply the question, "If this is what life is like, why go on?", go on he does. And he can go on, and Rosamond and Jamie can too, because they glimpse something of the whole of Welty's insight. Her story unites a confrontation with the monstrousness of life with a recognition of its wonder. This evaluation of life is very similar to that reflected in the Hindu legend about the god Shiva. Confronted by a demon demanding that Shiva hand over his wife, the world-goddess Parvati, Shiva hit the earth with lightning and created a new demon which he commanded to eat the first. The first demon threw himself on Shiva's mercy and was forgiven. Bound by the god's original order, the second demon asked, "What shall I eat now?" To which Shiva replied, "Well, let's see: why not eat yourself." And so the demon began, eating its own feet, belly, chest, neck. Joseph Campbell, who tells the story charmingly, continues:

> And the god, thereupon, was enchanted. For here at last was a perfect image of the monstrous thing that is life, which lives on itself. And to that sunlike mask, which was now all that was left of that lionlike vision of hunger, Shiva said, exulting, "I shall call you 'Face of Glory,' Kirttimukha, and you shall shine above the doors to all my temples. No one who refuses to honor and worship you will come ever to knowledge of me."
>
> The obvious lesson of all of which is that the first step to the knowledge of the highest divine symbol of the wonder and mystery of life is in the recognition of the monstrous nature of life and its glory in that character: the realization that this is just how it is and that it cannot and will not be changed. . . . So if you really want to help this world, what you will have to teach is how to live in it. And that no one can do who has not himself learned how to live in it the joyful sorrow and sorrowful joy of the knowledge of life as it is.[18]

It is in teaching how to live in such a world that Welty's tale offers help for travellers in life's wilderness, alive as it is with Indians, outlaws, and wild animals. She has no secret to make the threats go away, but she knows what will help us live with the horrors surrounding us. Surely part of that help comes from the recognition of the doubleness of life that the book reveals, an awareness of its marvelous as well as its terrible side.

The second part of Welty's strategy for survival is the old one: to have someone to love may make the world seem less terrifying, even if it does nothing to change objective reality. Clement suggests the power of love when he laments: "My wife will build a tower to overlook the boundaries of her land, while I ride its woods and know it to be a maze without end, for my love is lost in it" (p. 103). It is the lost love that makes the world seem a maze.

However, Welty makes clear that the mere physical presence of the loved one is not enough for sustained solace. Even though Rosamond lies by Jamie's side, "she would look out the window and see a cloud put up a mask over the secret face of the moon, and she would hear the pitiful cries of the night creatures. Then it was enough to make her afraid, as if the whole world were circled by a band of Indian savages . . ." (pp. 84-85). And her fear all wells from the fact that, in spite of her study of Jamie's face, "she did not know the language it was written in" (p. 84). For love to alleviate the night terrors of existence, it must be love of a whole self by a whole self. That full attainment of this lies beyond human power is life's eternal tragedy. However, the closer we approach it, the more effective will be love's protection. Rosamond and Jamie have physically consummated their love, but each recognizes only half of the other's identity. This is what makes theirs a false marriage, not just the drunken priest who performed the ceremony.

The desire to push beyond the view of life as *simplex*, into knowledge of its real multiplicity Welty herself identified as the motivation behind the plot in *The Robber Bridegroom*. The truth in the story, she wrote, lies in the need "to find out what we all wish to find out, exactly who we are, and who the other fellow is, and what we are doing here all together."[19] Yet, oddly enough, in the same essay Welty says that in washing off Jamie's disguise Rosamond is making "the classic mistake."[20] So which is it? Is the desire to know others a way to mitigate the pain of life or is it an unforgivable trespass? To an extent, Welty's answer is a perverse Yes—it is both.

More precisely, the novel suggests that there are right and wrong reasons for trying to fathom another's identity—and right and wrong ways to go about it. The story opens with a focus on the wrong reason. Mike Fink threatens to reveal the other part of Jamie's identity in order to have power over him. In silencing Mike Fink, Jamie makes an important distinction: "Say *who* I am forever, but dare to say *what* I am, and that will be the last breath of any man" (p. 13). Later Clement asks Jamie's name so he can express his gratitude, but he does not ask "*what* you may be" (p. 16). The problem with having handy names or labels for the multiple parts of a human identity is that they can fool us into thinking that we have psychological understanding or "control" of the other person, that we have reduced the mystery of his or her full selfhood.[21]

While it is natural to want protection from the reduction of self symbolized by the threats of Mike Fink and Little Harp to reveal what Jamie is, Welty reiterates in her essays and stories the view that the most pitiful life is one that has been made invulnerable. Certainly the outcome of *The Robber Bridegroom* seems to justify Rosamond's attempt to discover Jamie's identity. As a result of her act, Jamie's dual selves are integrated, and he and Rosamond are truly married. However, the initial consequence of Rosamond's penetration of Jamie's disguise is the rupture of their relationship, because at first she too asks for a label, not for an introduction to Jamie's fuller self. Furthermore, she thinks she will know him by merely *seeing* beneath his disguise.

The cause of Rosamond's growing need to know Jamie's identity is significant. As long as their life together is blissful (that is, as long as it has fairy-tale perfection), she can accept the mystery. However, with the arrival of Little Harp in their cabin and the death of the Indian girl, the simple happiness she and Jamie shared is threatened. The threat comes from the insidious invasion of her own awareness of Jamie's shadow self—a self she cannot accept and that she, in the form of the psychologically projected Indian maiden, finds terrifying:

> . . . she was torn as she had never been before with an anguish to know his name and his true appearance. For the coming of death and danger had only driven her into her own heart, and it was no matter what he had told her, she could wait no longer to learn the identity of her true love. (p. 134)

Multiplex reality has displaced fairy tale simplicity; Rosamond has entered the world we inhabit. Unfortunately, her reaction to her discovery that her bandit is also Jamie Lockhart does not lead her immediately away from isolation into union with another. Instead of understanding and accepting the sad and joyous human mystery, she retreats to simplistic labelling, and Jamie responds in kind:

> "You are Jamie Lockhart!" she said.
> "And you are Clement Musgrove's silly daughter!"
> said he.
> "Good-by," he said. "For you did not trust me, and
> did not love me, for you wanted only to know who I am.
> Now I cannot stay in the house with you." (p. 134)

We recall that Jamie was willing for Mike Fink to declare *who* he was, but not *what* he was. By seeking merely his name, Rosamond has chosen the least important part of Jamie's identity (one available even to his enemies), condemning herself to superficial knowledge of Jamie.

And yet Rosamond's impulse is not entirely wrong. Jamie, in hiding part of himself from the one who loves him, is endangering their love. Rosamond sounds at least partially right when she cries, after Jamie has left her: "My husband was a robber and not a bridegroom. . . . He brought me his love under a mask, and kept all the truth hidden from me, and never called anything by its true name, even his name or mine, and what I would have given him he liked better to steal" (p. 146). What she learns, however, is that "names were nothing and untied no knots" (p. 150). She has to move past the stage where she can assert: " . . . I already know everything and can learn nothing new" (p. 137). Goat's reply to that declaration ("Do not be so sad as all that . . .") is not the non sequitur it seems. Few states, Welty believes, are sadder than thinking we have figured out all life's mysteries—especially the mysteries about other people. When we get beyond the labels of "Jamie Lockhart" or "robber" or "Clement's silly daughter"—to appreciate the complex humanity on the other side of the name—that is when the universal search for "who we are and who the other fellow is" might pay off.

In Welty's story as in folk fairy tales, the woman is the one who pushes for integration. The message that Rosamond sends Jamie "out of the future"—from their twins to be born next week (p. 177)—makes very real the power of the female suasion to unification.[22] Rosamond's role is much like that ascribed by Bettelheim to the women in other tales who suspect they are married to beastly bridegrooms:

> One very significant feature of the animal-groom
> cycle . . . [is that] the groom is absent during the day
> and present only in the darkness of night; he is believed
> to be animal during the day and to become human only
> in bed; in short, he keeps his day and night existences

> separate from each other: . . . [H]e wishes to keep his
> sex life separated from all else he is doing. The female
> . . . is unwilling to accept the separation and isolation
> of purely sexual aspects of life from the rest of it. She
> tries to force their unification. But once Psyche embarks
> on trying to wed the aspects of sex, love, and life into a
> unity, she does not falter, and in the end she wins.[23]

Like Psyche, Rosamond does not falter. She does her penance
for asking the wrong questions about her lover's identity. Following Jamie's path through the tangled wilderness of the
Natchez Trace, she is "tattered and torn, and tired from sleeping
in hollow trees and keeping awake in the woods" (pp. 168-69).
The imagery here implies both enlightment and acceptance of
her unity with apparent opposites (in this case, human unity
with the natural world).

In the final chapter we feel the book's emerging from its
dark inner core (where we watched the deaths of the Indian girl,
the robber band, Little Harp, and Salome), its returning to the
realm of fairy tale. Mike Fink joins Rosamond now as he did
Jamie in the beginning. (But even he is chastened and im-
proved, shaken from his blustering self-importance by his encounters with what he takes to be Jamie's ghost.) The idyllic life
Jamie and Rosamond establish in New Orleans is our best hint
that a fairy-tale version of reality dominates as the novella ends.

Yet even in this conclusion Welty reminds her readers of
the doubleness of reality that Rosamond and Jamie fail to perceive—in spite of their personal integration (or, perhaps, because
of the protection it offers from life's darker side). Describing
their life to her father, Rosamond sketches a happy-ever-after
world, complete with beautiful twins (appropriate in a world
where "all things are double"), a stately house, a boat, servants,
and rich friends. For the moment their eyes are not on the
wilderness that still surrounds them or the Indians that inhabit
it. Nevertheless, Welty's concluding references to Rosamond
and Jamie's "hundred slaves" and to the pirates' galleons they
sail out to watch, as well as to Clement's return to the wilderness, remind us that evil (social and individual) is closer than
they may be aware—"with us, within us." Thus, while Jamie
and Rosamond have returned to life in a fairy tale, the reader
carries away a now corrected vision of the joyful sorrow and
sorrowful joy of life as it is.

Notes

[1] See, for example, "Briefly Noted Fiction," *The New Yorker*, XVIII (October 24, 1942), 82; Alfred Kazin, "An Enchanted World in America," *New York Herald Tribune Books*, October 25, 1942, p. 19; Nathan Rothman, "The Lost Realm," *The Saturday Review of Literature*, XXV (November 14, 1942), 16; Lionel Trilling, "American Fairy Tale," *The Nation*, CLV (December 19, 1942), 686-87; Katherine Gauss Jackson, "In Brief: Fiction," *Harper's Magazine*, CLXXXVI (December 1942), n.p.

[2] Kreyling, pp. 32-51. Floyd C. Watkins also focuses on "the doubleness of wonder and reality, fairy tale and novel," as well as the blend of "joy and violence" which he believes "coexisted in the spirit and adventures of the time" in which *The Robber Bridegroom* is set ("Eudora Welty's Natchez Trace in the New World," *The Southern Review*, 22 [October 1986], 709-10). Cf. Eunice Glenn, "Fantasy in the Fiction of Eudora Welty," *A Southern Vanguard*, ed. Allen Tate (New York: Prentice-Hall, 1947), pp. 78-91. Glenn sees in the "dualistic nature" of Jamie Lockhart "the conflict between idealism and realism, the neuroses that result from modern man's inability to attain his ideals. . . . The convincing force of the story is in the juxtaposition of the rough-and-tumble and grotesque life in the wilderness with the conventional, the real; and the harmonizing of the two." For other discussions of the general theme of doubleness in *The Robber Bridegroom*, see Bryant, *Eudora Welty*, pp. 18-20; Gordon E. Slethaug, "Initiation in Eudora Welty's *The Robber Bridegroom*," *Southern Humanities Review*, 7 (Winter 1973), 77-87; and French, "'All Things are Double': Eudora Welty as a Civilized Writer" in Prenshaw, ed., *Eudora Welty: Critical Essays*, pp. 179-88.

[3] Marilyn Arnold makes a number of similar points, analyzing *The Robber Bridegroom* as "a parody of the fairy tale" in "Eudora Welty's Parody," *Notes on Mississippi Writers*, 11 (Spring 1978), 15-22; rpt. in Turner and Emling, eds. *Critical Essays on Eudora Welty*, pp. 32-38. Ruth Vande Kieft says that *The Robber Bridegroom* "reveals the child's unabashed delight in the world of fantasy and legendary history, but in its hints of satire . . . we see the adult's critical intelligence" (1962, p. 86).

[4] Bettelheim, *The Uses of Enchantment: The Meaning and Importance of Fairy Tales* (Harmondsworth, England: Penguin Books, 1978), p. 9.

[5] *The Uses of Enchantment*, pp. 66, 78-83. This is not, of course, to deny that fairy tales are suspended on a fabric of nightmare. As Bettelheim has reminded us, the fairy tale confronts such major existential problems as separation from loving and protecting parents, death, aging, and the limits of mortality. The serene rescue from life's horror that characterizes fairy tales is accomplished only after the characters have been taken "to the very edge of the abyss" (Bettelheim, *The Uses of Enchantment*, 8, 11, *et passim*; Bruno Bettelheim, "Fairy Tales as Ways of Knowing" in *Fairy Tales as Ways of Knowing: Essays on Märchen in Psychology, Society, and Literature*, ed. Michael M. Metzger and Katharina Mommsen [Bern: Peter Lang, 1981], pp. 11-12).

[6] In its exploration of life's complexity, Welty's story is closer to the literary fairy tale (Kunstmärchen) than to the Grimms' Volksmärchen. Lawrence O. Frye has pointed out in "Making a Märchen: The Trying Test of Romantic Art, Magic, and Imagination" that Kunstmärchen tend to attribute a dualistic structure to the world (Frye uses "dualistic" to refer to a state of coex-

isting opposites; "polar" would more accurately express this idea), not only because of "a double perspective of how and where things happen" (the story belongs both to everyday reality and to a magical one), but also because characters in literary Märchen, unlike those in folk Märchen, are allowed to change, and even their heroes may be less than perfect. The Kunstmärchen present "an ambiguous universe within a single narrative" with the result of "more relativity and uncertainty." As Frye says: " . . . life is harder in the Kunstmärchen, for it often takes more than wishing or a magic object to work magic" (in *Fairy Tales as Ways of Knowing*, pp. 138-39).

7 Stevens, p. 94.

8 *The Robber Bridegroom* (Garden City, NY: Doubleday, Doran, 1942), p. 75. Hereafter, references to this edition will be given in the text of this chapter.

9 *Fairy Tales as Ways of Knowing*, pp. 14-15.

10 Marshall McLuhan, *The Gutenberg Galaxy: The Making of Typographic Man* (Toronto: University of Toronto Press, 1962); Walter Ong, *Orality and Literacy: The Technologizing of the Word* (London: Methuen, 1982); discussed in Craige, pp. 4-14. McLuhan and Ong associate the elevation of objectified knowledge with the development of the printing press.

11 Evelyn Fox Keller and Christine R. Grontkowski, "The Mind's Eye" in Harding and Hintikka, eds., *Discovering Reality*, pp. 207-24.

12 Belenky et al., p. 18.

13 *The New Yorker* review of *The Robber Bridegroom* included this evaluation: "If this *is* a dream it is one of the gay, soaring kind, without a breath of nightmare . . ." ("Briefly Noted Fiction," XVIII [October 24, 1942], 82).

14 *The Eye of the Story*, p. 310.

15 Her story will remind us that the world is not all fairy-tale rosey— another possible ironic implication of her name.

16 "Reality in Chekhov's Stories" in *The Eye of the Story*, p. 62. Welty spoke of the kinship she feels with Chekhov in her 1972 *Paris Review* interview with Linda Kuehl (Prenshaw, ed. *Conversations*, pp. 74-75).

17 This is a significant contrast to fairy tales. Even a child knows that on the literal level the fairy tale is not true and cannot possibly be true: there are no witches; people do not chop off bits of their feet, even to fit them into glass slippers; dead horse heads do not talk, even as a response to murder and usurpation. See Linda Dégh, "Grimm's *Household Tales* and Its Place in the Household: The Social Relevance of a Controversial Classic" in *Fairy Tales as Ways of Knowing*, p. 39.

18 Joseph Campbell, *Myths to Live By* (New York: Viking, 1972), pp. 103-4.

19 "Fairy Tale of the Natchez Trace" in *The Eye of the Story*, p. 311.

20 "Fairy Tale of the Natchez Trace" in *The Eye of the Story*, p. 308.

21 Later Mike Fink tries to protect himself in a fashion similar to Jamie's, refusing at the end of the story to give his name to Rosamond, who rejoins: "Too much of this secrecy goes on in the world for my happiness . . ." (p. 174). She makes him tell her his real name so that she knows whom to thank (pp. 178-79), parallelling Clement's request for Jamie's name so that he can express his gratitude.

[22] This also accords rather neatly with recent studies concerning the significance of relationship in women's lives. See, for example, Chodorow and Gilligan.

[23] Bettelheim, *The Uses of Enchantment*, p. 294.

V

A Truer Thing than Thought: *Delta Wedding*

"You sure don't know much"; " . . . you don't know anything"; "I don't know"; "Didn't you know . . . ?"; "Nobody
knew!"; " . . . she could not know"; "She wondered if she would
ever know. . . . What could she know now?" Such taunts, con-
versational tags, confessions, and questions jump repeatedly
from the pages of *Delta Wedding* (1946).[1] A kind of high point
for this pattern is reached near the middle of the novel when
Aunt Tempe and Ellen Fairchild accumulate eleven *know's* in a
little over a page of conversation (pp. 106-7). *Delta Wedding* is,
in fact, a novel in which almost everyone is concerned in one
way or another with questions of knowing: what kind of knowing is most humanly fulfilling? how can this knowing be
achieved—or avoided (for its attainment, like all things in
Welty's world, is double-edged)? what barriers interfere with
such knowing? what is a person like who truly knows? how
does that person affect others?

While both the initiation stories and *The Robber Bridegroom* were also concerned with the truth to which the enlightened consciousness comes, none of those showed the initiated
self reintegrated into daily life. (Jamie and Rosamond's life in
New Orleans in *The Robber Bridegroom* belongs too much to
the fairy tale world to have much to do with living as we experience it.) *Delta Wedding*, on the other hand, for all of its concern
with the privileged planter class, is anchored very much in reality, teaming with children and servants, relatives and friends,
with curtains that must be washed and lamps that can be broken,
with guns and ice picks that can really do injury. Against this
background, Welty explores how the holistic insights belonging
to initiates can survive the demands of routine, dualistic life.

Of the different varieties of knowing the novel examines, Troy Flavin's represents the simplistic, pragmatic approach that Welty suggests will give only a partial or a distorted version of reality. Troy has learned to see the similarities between the Delta and his home hill country, but in detecting likenesses, he has overlooked the simultaneous truth of differences. He also sees the most useful knowledge as knowing how to use, to manipulate—a relationship between the knower and the known that insists on separation of subject and object. Troy declares: "By now, I can't tell a bit of difference between me and any Delta people you name. There's nothing easy about the Delta either, but it's just a matter of knowing how to handle your Negroes" (p. 95).

Ellen Fairchild—who, in the course of the novel, approaches Welty's ideal of human knowing—cautions Troy: "Well, Troy, you know, if it was that at first, I believe there's more to it, and you'll be seeing there's a lot of life here yet that will take its time working out. . . ." When Troy asks, patronizingly, "What would it be?", Ellen replies "mysteriously": "The Delta's just like everywhere," but she means something quite other than Troy's declaration of there being not a bit of difference between Shellmound and Tishomingo County. For Ellen what unites everything is the mystery itself, our very inability to know it all. Indeed, Welty suggests that the first lesson in truly knowing is the recognition that we can't *know* in any final, complete, simplistic, rational way—indeed, in any way reducible to words. (Later Ellen will also redefine "knowing," revealing that there is a way to *experience* reality that lies outside traditional epistemology.)

Two minor characters suggest an extreme on the side opposite to Troy, an approach to knowledge that recognizes mystery, but one that Welty herself seems unwilling to pursue. Pinchy, the servant girl, is trying "to come through" to a state of religious awareness whose content has nothing to do with the world of pragmatism. With no apparently conscious effort, abstracted out of herself, she is "giving up every moment to seeking" (p. 32). The focus of her vision is opposite Troy's : " . . . her eyes were glassy. . . . Her eyes were wild but held a motionless gaze on the white fields and white glaring sky and the dancing, distant black rim of the river trees" (p. 147).[2]

Partheny, the old cook, claims access to another way of knowing (part of which involves a voodoo-like knowledge of how to make love-potion cakes). During a "spell," she has an out-of-body experience in which she is "transported" to the Yazoo River bridge. "I were mindless," she declares, defying her namesake, Athena Parthenos (p. 78). Welty introduces such experiences and then draws back, perhaps because, as Ruth Vande Kieft has said, Welty is not concerned with the "divine 'surround.'"[3] Pinchy's and Partheny's experiences belong to a way of knowing unavailable to Welty's main characters. She tells us of them, but then turns to explore the knowing that can serve everyday life without taking one from it, the knowing that acknowledges, cherishes, and springs from a view of life as intense, mysterious, polar, and dynamic.

But the book that will explore such a way of knowing so unusual to us, begins firmly rooted in the most comfortable and practical kind of knowledge, conveyed in direct, factual sentences:

> The nickname of the train was the Yellow Dog. Its real name was the Yazoo-Delta. It was a mixed train. The day was the 10th of September, 1923—afternoon. Laura McRaven, who was nine years old, was on her first journey alone. She was going up from Jackson to visit her mother's people, the Fairchilds, at the plantation named Shellmound, at Fairchilds, Mississippi.

Crammed with names of people and places, dates, numbers, and relationships, the first paragraph continues with the fact of Laura's mother's funeral in the winter, the fact of her cousin Dabney's coming wedding, and then concludes: "Of these facts the one most persistent in Laura's mind was the most intimate one: that her age was nine."

Laura, the "arriver" in this land (p. 5), is our surrogate learner ("At any moment she might expose her ignorance—at any moment she might learn everything" [p. 14]). Caught up in the lively chaos of the Fairchild family, she, who had been so sure of so many things on her train ride, quickly becomes sure of almost nothing (her cousin Orrin even tells her that "Marmion" is not her doll, but the place where he was born [p. 6]). This new vulnerability, this withdrawal of all secure knowledge, makes Laura ready to explore in a childish fashion the question of a better way to come to terms with—to know—this world. Nevertheless, when she thinks, shortly after her arrival, of *how* she wants to know, she is like most of us: "she would know the answer to the heart's pull, just as it would come to her in school why the apple was pulled down on Newton's head" (p. 76). She mistakenly thinks that knowing will be as clear as an equation,

as impersonal and as direct as $f=ma$. Like most of us, "Laura . . .
loved all kinds of boxes and bottles, all objects that could keep
and hold things" (p. 136). Learning that most precious things
can neither be boxed, bottled, nor fit into an equation is a difficult lesson.

The opening paragraph of *Delta Wedding* is stylistically
very unlike the beginnings of Welty's other novels in its insistence on facts, its avoidance of metaphor or exaggeration of any
kind. But the language quickly shifts in the following paragraphs, suggesting that reality cannot be captured so easily in the
factual. Laura's early responses to the land through which she
travels prefigure the way of knowing available to the sensitive
person in this world. In the second paragraph, the first figure of
speech in the novel ("the train . . . seemed to be racing with a
butterfly") reminds us that there is a good deal of reality that
language can only approximate and that the mind can approach
only through suggestions of similarities, even while being aware
of differences that deny the very identity suggested. The second
paragraph ends with the first confessions of not-knowing.
When the train stops in an open field, for no practical reason at
all, Laura sees "the engineer, Mr. Doolittle, go out and pick some
especially fine goldenrod—for whom, she could not know."
And then the cry of a thousand "unseen locusts" ring urgently at
the train windows. Mystery—human and natural—has entered
Laura's world. It has been there all along, of course, without her
knowing it, in the train she rides on, the Yazoo-Delta—named
for the river of Death, as India later tells her. Here is the greatest
mystery of all, cause (train and threat of death) of the family's
mysterious responses to the incident on the railroad trestle that
she will shortly be introduced to.

The metaphorical language increases in the following
paragraphs. The land, which appears so "perfectly flat and
level"—so straight-forward—, is also shimmery "like the wing
of a lighted dragonfly. It seems strummed, as though it were an
instrument and something had touched it" (p. 4). Dimensions,
directions, colors, names of owners, lists of crops—none of these
facts will contain the reality of such a landscape, which does not
just lie there, but shouts of mystery resident even in what seems
so neatly and cleanly laid out. Laura's response to this world is
significant: "Thoughts went out of her head and the landscape
filled it" (p. 4). Here is a knowing that has nothing to do with
reason, but instead rises out of the union of what in a dualistic
system would be termed the knower and the known. In this way

of knowing, however, knower and known cease to be separate. Tellingly, Laura, who had before closed her eyes to the soot, now stretches her arm out the window and lets the soot sprinkle it.

While these early paragraphs introduce us to the sense of mystery that must be part of any real knowing, they also hint of the union of contraries that underlies that mystery. As the Yazoo-Delta approaches Fairchild station, Laura suddenly sees that "the sky, the field, the little track, and the bayou, over and over—all that had been bright or dark—was now one color" (p. 5). Throughout the novel, characters with the keenest insight experience moments of perceptual change just like Laura's here. In those moments, reality will seem to shift for them as surely as it does for us when we look at the profiles-vase drawing: at one moment they see the unity; in the next they are struck by diversity and individuality. Welty's most sensitive characters keep both visions, as they would access to two languages, switching back and forth between the two as needed—perhaps the closest human approach to the mystic's (and the artist's) simultaneous vision of contraries.[4]

Delta Wedding makes clear, however, that such knowing is not without penalty. In the train Laura "sat leaning at the window, the light and the sooty air trying to make her close her eyes" (p. 3). Many of the adults in the novel seem (at least to other characters who view *themselves* as more feeling and more perceptive) to respond in precisely this way to life's persistent combining of vision with pain: they close off their "vision," not necessarily to physical reality, but to truths that cannot be detected with the eyes.[5] Unwilling to accept life's sooty darkness, they seem to miss the illumination as well. Indeed, the Fairchild family as a whole—when it operates as a family characterized by "Fairchild" traits—is presented by the various narrative sentient centers of the novel as a vigorous enemy of true knowing; that is, knowledge of the other in its fullness.

Ironically, the source of the family's opposition to an understanding that goes beneath surface appearance is its capacity to love. And theirs *is* a loving family, indisputably filled with good-will and good humor, endowed with a capacity to give and to take care of each other. However, their love unites and separates in one stroke.[6] Caring for each other as they do, they cannot stand the thought of a family member having his or her feelings hurt, much less suffering deeply. Ready at any moment to respond to each other's practical needs, they are at a loss in dealing with emotional requirements.

When Dabney needs crooks for her wedding, handmade mitts for her bridesmaids, cornucopias or mints or flowers for the reception, even an old house renovated and made ready as her new home in three days, the family will move heaven and earth to see that she gets it. What they will not do is ask how she truly feels or tell her how they feel. During her engagement visit to her Aunts Primrose and Jim Allen, we see at work what may be thought of as the Southern code of polite conversation (don't talk about religion, politics—or anything that might make anyone uncomfortable[7]). The aunts reprimand nine-year-old India when she asks Dabney about her honeymoon plans ("Little girls don't talk about honeymoons. . . . They don't ask their sisters questions, it's not a bit nice" [p. 46]). While even readers do not know for sure, Welty gives several hints that Dabney is rushing to marriage because she is pregnant.[8] The aunts, however, no doubt unwilling to hurt Dabney's feelings or to deal with their own feelings if they had to face this situation, get nowhere near that possibility.

India feels their conscious evasion ("They're never going to ask Dabney the questions, India meditated" [p. 48]). Dabney herself seems to want to break down the wall that their love and politeness have erected, but she also bends to the code:

> They don't make me say if I love Troy or if I don't, Dabney was thinking, clicking her heels in the pantry. But by the time she came back to the porch, the flowers in a Mason jar of water, she knew she would never say anything about love after all, if they didn't want her to. Suppose they were afraid to ask her, little old aunts. She thought of how they both drew back to see her holding their night light. They would give her anything, but they wouldn't touch it again now for the world. (p. 48)

It is probably Dabney's desire to shatter the wall of polite love separating her from her aunts (who, in typical Fairchild fashion, give without touching) that leads her to say loudly, "I hope I have a baby right away . . ." (p. 48). But the aunts merely "looked at nothing, as ladies do in church" (p. 49). Looking at nothing, they apparently manage to see nothing of the life beneath the surface in this happy Fairchild world.

Dabney believes this evasion characterizes her whole family:

> Now that she was so soon to be married, she could see
> her whole family being impelled to speak to her, to say
> one last thing before she waved good-bye. She would
> long to stretch out her arms to them, every one. But
> they simply never looked deeper than the flat surface
> of any tremendous thing, that was all there was to it.
> They didn't try to understand *her* at all, her love,
> which they were free, welcome to challenge and
> question. In fact, here these two old aunts were
> actually *forgiving* it. All the Fairchilds were
> indulgent—indulgence was what she couldn't stand!
> (p. 47)

One of the reasons the family fails to know each other as
individuals ("to understand *her*") is that they are so conscious of
each other as part of the family. We are told that Laura

> was a child too familiar, too like all her cousins, too
> much one of them (as they all were to one another a
> part of their very own continuousness at times) ever to
> get the attention she begged for. By Aunt Shannon in
> particular, the members of the family were always
> looked on with that general tenderness and love out of
> which the single personality does not come bolting and
> clamorous, but just as easily emerges gently, like a star
> when it is time, into the sky and by simply emerging
> drifts back into the general view and belongs to the
> multitudinous heavens. All were dear, all were
> unfathomable, all were constantly speaking, as the
> stars would ever twinkle, imploringly or not—so far, so
> far away. (p. 63)

Robbie puts her finger on this reason for the Fairchilds'
incapacity to know each other when she ponders the family's attitude toward her husband George: "Well, the comfort they took
in him—all the family—and that he held dear, was a far cry
from *knowing* him. . . . The Fairchilds were always seeing him
by a gusty lamp—exaggerating, then blinding—by the lamp of
their own indulgence" (p. 191). Earlier she had exclaimed to
Ellen:

> "I think you are already the same as what you love. . . .
> You'[re] just loving yourselves in each other—your-
> selves over and over again!" She flung the small brown
> hand at the paintings of melons and grapes that had
> been trembling on the wall from the commotion in the
> house, forgetting that they were not portraits of
> Fairchilds in this room, and with a circle of her arm in-

cluding the two live old ladies too. "You still love
them, and they still love you! No matter what you've
all done to each other! You don't need to know how
to love anybody else. Why, you couldn't love *me*!"
(p. 165)

In Robbie's analysis, the Fairchilds see each other not as
individuals, but as representatives of Fairchildness. Loving a
member of the family is thus an expression of self-love. Consequently, love, which like knowledge is usually thought of as
shattering barriers, ends up erecting them. It is a love that en-
closes and excludes—and thus protects its own; but it also refuses
to acknowledge variation, in effect destroying the particularity of
the individual—at least as far as the perception of the loving one
is concerned. *Philia* becomes *thanatos* from the nicest of moti-
vations.

And, indeed, some of the Fairchilds—Great Aunts Mac
and Shannon, for example—are much more comfortable with
the dead loved ones than with the living. The dead they *know*.
The dead ask no questions, make no revelations, beg for no surprising pity or understanding. But Mac's and Shannon's age and
past suffering make their preference for such emotional simplicity excusable. More disturbing is the ease of the next generation
of Fairchilds with the dead, because of what this says about their
relations with the living. When Aunt Tempe declares categori-
cally that she *knows* her brother Denis' spirit haunts the woods,
Dabney muses that Tempe "looked pleased . . . as if she were
mollified that Denis was dead if his spirit haunted just where
she knew. Not at large, not in transit anymore, as in life, but
fixed—tied to a tree" (p. 117). Tempe—and indeed all the
aunts—take much the same tack with the living, declaring that
they know just what they are like. They especially direct that certainty toward their brother George, the family hero, with the result that they know little at all about the one they pride themselves on knowing so well.

Certainty brings a kind of death to the knower and the
known, denying as it does life's dynamic, alternating quality,
denying also the possibility of real knowing—that is, a true connection—between subject and object. It is appropriate that
Dabney think of the portrait of the long-ago Fairchild, Mary
Shannon: "How sure and how alone she looked . . ." (p. 41). Certainty, loneliness, and death are three parts of a finished whole.

In *Delta Wedding*, Battle Fairchild represents the strongest
inclination toward this kind of love, all the while apparently

oblivious to its consequences. A kind and generous man who, Ellen says, "can't stand anybody to be ugly and cruel" to him (p. 106), Battle also cannot stand to see anyone he loves less than happy. Driven by the "protective serenity" of the Fairchild men (p. 162), he—like all Fairchilds when they are acting in the Fairchild mode—runs from trouble, whether it is Robbie's pain or Ellen's fainting. (Ellen thinks of the family's relief in dashing away to chase the bird Robbie brought into the house: "It was not anything but pure distaste that made them run; there was real trouble in Robbie's face, and the Fairchilds simply shied away from trouble as children would do" [p. 159].9)

Basing his vision of himself and his family on the Fairchild legend of happiness ("The Fairchilds are the happiest people!"), Battle can brook no challenges to that vision. Over and over at Dabney's wedding he keeps asking, "Are you happy, Dabney?" (p. 222). The other family legend is the changelessness of the Fairchilds ("Laura from her earliest memory had heard how they 'never seemed to change at all'" [p. 15]), and he does his best to fight life's dynamism too—or at least to avoid seeing changes. His discouraging his children from reading alone is but an expression of his war with introspection in general—that source of differences and dissatisfactions.

Battle's way of responding to his family was to love them, not as individuals, but "by the bunch," as Shelley says, "which makes him a more cheerful man" (p. 84). But in his desire not to have to know what Shelley is really thinking, not to know how Dabney feels in her love of Troy, not to know Ellen's or Robbie's or even Laura's sorrow, Battle misses much—perhaps most of all the depth of love and knowing that Ellen could have brought him had he not opted for a child's security (as if committed to being perpetually the fair child of his last name), evading the dark side of knowing and loving.

This is the "separating thrust of Fairchild love" with which "they eluded whatever they feared, sometimes the very things they really desired . . ." (p. 149). To protect themselves and their loved ones from confronting pain, the Fairchilds cut themselves off from that deeper love that comes from knowing and sharing the painful secrets, the mysteries of the other. Taking all as "a bunch," they have created the opposite: individuals closed in little shells of selfhood, "all more lonely than private," as Shelley confides in her journal, and most private "just when things are most crowded" (pp. 84-85). Ellen sees the tragedy, even while recognizing the comfort (and, no doubt, also, in this

large and potentially overwhelming family, the practical necessity) of this loving and not-knowing. Looking out at her family
just before the wedding rehearsal, Ellen thinks: "Here they sat . . .
their truest selves, like their truest aberrations and truest vir-
tues, not tampered with. Here in the closest intimacy the
greatest anonymity lay . . ." (p. 188). They have retreated to the
sanctuary of imperviousness Welty warned of in "Writing and
Analyzing a Story."

Ellen perceives that the mentally deficient Maureen epitomizes the family's obliviousness to a larger reality. Ellen is
thinking specifically of George's and Maureen's escape from the
Yellow Dog: "Here in the long run so like them all, the mindless
child could not, as they would not, understand a miracle. How
could Maureen, poor child, see the purity and dullness of *fact*, of
outside-world fact? Of something happening? Which was miracle" (p. 188). Ellen's is a knowing that can see dull fact and miracle as one, that can ask to know more about the people she
loves, and that can accept the penalty and rewards of such knowing. It is a way of knowing that she shares with George Fairchild,
a way that Welty points to as an alternative to the typical
Fairchild's approach to reality.

Ellen and George are both, to an extent, strangers in the
Fairchild world. Ellen, a Virginian, "the opposite of a Fairchild"
in appearance and manner, "had never had a child take after
herself" (pp. 20, 22). George alone of all the Fairchilds remained
left-handed (we would see that today as a hint of his right-brain
dominance), while Battle conscientiously broke all his children
of that trait as Ellen trembled secretly. Dabney senses George's
difference from the family:

> It was actually Uncle George who had shown her
> that there was another way to be—something else. . . .
> Uncle George, the youngest of the older ones, who stood
> in—who was—the very heart of the family, who was
> like them . . . —he was different somehow. Perhaps
> the heart always was made of different stuff and had a
> different life from the rest of the body. (pp. 33-34)

While we learn that George and Ellen know more than
any of the others,[10] they say less, knowing first of all the incom-
municability in words of real knowing. Repeatedly both Ellen
and George are described as centers of quiet in the chaotic
Fairchild household. Of Ellen, Welty writes:

> She walked into the roomful of family without imme-
> diately telling them anything. She was more restful
> than the Fairchilds. Her brown hair and her dark-blue
> eyes seemed part of her quietness—like the colors of
> water, reflective. Her Virginia voice, while no softer
> or lighter than theirs, was a less questioning, a never
> teasing one. It was a voice to speak to the one child or
> the one man her eyes would go to. They all watched
> her with soft eyes, but distractedly. (p. 20)

George brings a similar quietness. Entering a room full of
children and sisters and aunts, he is described as the unmoved
center. We are told, for example, that "George walked through,
and the children all swept around him. Tempe took hold of
him. Caught in their momentum, he looked out at Ellen
perfectly still, as if from a train window" (p. 125), and still later,
"in the midst of the room's commotion he stood by the mantel
as if at rest" (p. 186). At those moments his eyes catch Ellen's,
and we know that he knows—or is striving to know—something that is beyond words. In her turn, Ellen senses George's
knowing and knows him too (the word used—twice in the
passage below—is actually "felt" rather than "knew," to distin-
guish this knowing from our ordinary, rational apprehension).
The inadequacy of words to express what she perceives about
him is clear in her yoking of the opposites "passion" and "indif-
ference" when she tries to describe it to herself:

> It seemed to Ellen at moments that George regarded
> them, and regarded things—just things, in the outside
> world—with a passion which held him so still that it
> resembled indifference. Perhaps it *was* indifference—
> as though they, having given him this astonishing
> feeling, might for a time float away and he not care. It
> was not love or passion itself that stirred him, neces-
> sarily, she felt—for instance Dabney's marriage
> seemed not to have affected him greatly, or Robbie's
> anguish. But little Ranny, a flower, a horse running, a
> color, a terrible story listened to in the store in
> Fairchilds, or a common song, and yes, shock, physical
> danger, as Robbie had discovered, roused something in
> him that was immense contemplation, motionless pity,
> indifference. . . . Ellen had always felt this in George
> and now there was something of surprising kinship in
> the feeling; perhaps she had fainted in the way he
> was driven to detachment. (p. 186)

George's is a knowing that is "vision" in the deepest sense. (Welty repeatedly underscores his standing "perfectly still," his always looking quietly, "intently," or with "penetration," often without regard to what is being said.[11]) At the heart of his vision is the capacity to see the lines disappear between himself and what he is regarding: he takes into himself what he truly, feelingly perceives.   He is clearly another of Welty's characters who fit Michael Polanyi's profile of the possessor of "personal knowledge": "the passionate participation of the knower in the act of knowing."[12]   Dabney is aware of this ability of George's:

> She saw Uncle George lying on his arm on a picnic, smiling to hear what someone was telling, with a butterfly going across his gaze, a way to make her imagine all at once that in that moment he erected an entire, complicated house for the butterfly inside his sleepy body. . . . She had then known something he knew all along, it seemed then—that when you felt, touched, heard, looked at things in the world, and found their fragrances, they themselves made a sort of house within you which filled with life to hold them, filled with knowledge all by itself, and all else, the other ways to know, seemed calculating and tyranny. (p. 34)

The knowledge that deals only with facts; the knowledge that aims at control and manipulation; the knowledge that puts things and people into boxes and bottles and categories—this is tyrannical knowledge, and it is the way of knowing that most people settle for. George's knowing is different. He "could have lifted a finger and touched, held the butterfly, but he did not" (p. 37): without possessing the butterfly—and thus perhaps killing it—he makes it part of himself.

Probably both consequence and cause of George's capacity to know in this way is his acceptance of life's mystery. Strangely enough, because of this "George was not surprised" by life. Expecting "things to amount to more than you bargain for," accepting human weaknesses also as "just other ways that things are going to come to us," he is able to face life with a strength denied his brother Battle (pp. 85-86). For example, immediately after recalling the scene with the butterfly, Dabney remembers George's stepping into the middle of a knife fight between two black boys: "What things did he know of? There were surprising things in the world which did not surprise him. Wonderfully, he had reached up and caught the knife in the air. Disgracefully, he had taken two little black devils against his side" (p. 36). The juxtaposing of George's connection with the butterfly and his response to the fighting boys is evidence that his special kind of knowing does not incapacitate him from dealing effectively with everyday life. He can shift back and forth between the vision of wholeness in which he unites with the other, exercising no control in a manipulative sense, and the vision of a dualistic world which demands distinctions between self and other, even at times domination of the other by self.

Yet for George "wonderful" and "disgraceful" (Dabney's words) are not two mutually exclusive categories. He carries over into his everyday dealings something of the sense of mystery and union that his other experience of reality has given him. Out of this acknowledgement of life's mysterious wholeness comes George's respect and love for all. While Uncle Denis walked away from the fight in a typical Fairchild evasion, George ended up kneeling and embracing the two weeping black boys, even asking their names before releasing them. When he turned to Dabney after this, he looked "like a man who had stepped outside" (p. 36), as indeed he had stepped outside himself—that is, his Fairchild self—to care for strangers, to participate in other lives.

Just as Dabney is repulsed by what she feels is a rejection of the Fairchilds in George's connection with the youths with knives, so later the family is amazed and troubled that his love can extend even to the railroad engineer, Mr. Doolittle.[13] Laura senses that what George feels is more than mere kindness: " . . . it was a waiting, a withholding, as if he could see a fire or a light when he saw a human being—regardless of who it was, kin or not . . ." (p. 75). Ellen declares George "a human being and a complex man" (p. 64); he seems ready to discover such human complexity in everyone else as well.

George's feelings for others are also evidenced by the fact that he never turns the stories of their lives into "a facile thing or . . . make[s] a travesty out of human beings," as the other Fairchilds do with their tales, protecting themselves from the potential seriousness of past events by transforming the events into great jokes on themselves.[14] Ellen thinks: "Only George left the world she knew as pure—in spite of his fierce energies, even heresies—as he found it; still real, still bad, still fleeting and mysterious and hopelessly alluring to her" (p. 80). We recall Welty's commendation of E. B. White's presentation of the components of life as "varied, but not opposites; . . . the real thing." Ellen sees that George, too, confronts the real thing.

In George's vision, all exclusive, absolute categories seem to blur. When he asks Laura the old riddle of St. Ives, eliciting her answer, "One . . . you. You were going to St. Ives, all by yourself," George responds in amazement "as if he expected anything in the world to happen—a new answer to the riddle, which she, Laura, had not given him" (p. 57). We begin to wonder, too, if "one," really *is* the answer here—or if there is a single answer even to such a time-worn riddle as this.

Perhaps it is George's desire to share with Ellen his awareness of life's mysterious polarity, including its coexistent darkness and light, that leads to his telling her—with a smile that has both "gratification" and "regret" in it—that he had slept with the runaway girl she had met in the woods (p. 79). Ellen senses that "it was as if he had known life could not go on without this thing—now, like a crash, a fall, it had come" (p. 79). The same recognition—that the full life is created only out of the tension of the union of opposites—seems to be behind his wish, even after making up with Robbie, that "it might yet be intensified" (p. 189)—in spite of all the pain inherent in their conflict.

George's vision of life's wholeness extends even to an open-eyed confrontation with death, when he stands on the trestle trying to get Maureen's foot out of the track while the Yazoo-Delta train bears down on them. This central incident in *Delta Wedding* is one of the most puzzling parts of the novel (its causes and consequences puzzling the novel's characters; its thematic significance initially puzzling its readers). The encounter with the Yazoo-Delta provoked Robbie into leaving George; it seems to have led to Dabney's engagement to Troy; it certainly contributed to Shelley's late-adolescent angst; it may have stimulated Pinchy's "seeking." In a way typical of the Fairchilds, India turns the near-tragedy into an entertaining tale. Only Ellen knows that George's facing of the "Yellow Dog" is a "miracle" at the heart of his secret self (p. 188). The rest of the Fairchilds are constantly blinking before the reality of death that the Yazoo-Delta represents. The Yazoo River—the river of Death—is practically at the back door of the Fairchilds, yet they have run from the river as they do from death itself. The family had moved out of Marmion, the estate located on the river banks, when its builder (Battle's father) was killed in a duel and his wife died broken-hearted shortly after. ("Marmion was too heart-breaking" [p. 120].) For all their ease in speaking of the dead, they seem unwilling to confront the painful reality of death. They domesticate death (keeping about them the mementoes of the departed, speaking without discomfort of Annie Laurie's preference for the gizzard, for example), but we never see them mourn. When a bird flies into the house (a sign of death, as Roxie says), they run about in terror.

But Ellen knows that George is different, because "of course he saw death on its way, if they did not" (p. 188). Facing down the Yellow Dog is both a literal and figurative expression of this part of his vision of reality. And its consequence is the ultimate freedom: accepting the fact that death is inevitable ("a fate whose dealing out to him he would not contest" [p. 221]), he can yet assert his will: "I'm damned if I wasn't going to stand on that track if I wanted to! Or will again" (p. 187). In this response to death, he creates a self more complete, more alive than that of any of his kin.

And because of his own intense liveliness (he seems perpetually young [p. 75]), George is able to intensify the lives of those around him. It is this that has made him the heart of the family, though Robbie realizes that a better metaphor might be the eye of the family. He, the one with the knowing vision, is the eye with which the family sees itself:

> George was not the one they all looked at . . . as he was always declared to be, but the eye that saw them, from right in their midst. He was sensitive to all they asked of life itself. Long ago they had seized on that. He was to be all in one their lover and protector and dreaming, forgetful conscience. From Aunt Shannon on down, he was to be always looking through them as well as to the left and right of them. . . . (p. 212)

The intensity of George's vision has another consequence as well: for others who are particularly sensitive, it can lead to intensification of their own ability to see truly. Laura experiences this when she comes upon George in the library:

> There was nothing at all abstract in Uncle George's look, like the abstraction of painted people, of most interrupted real people. There was only penetration in his look, and it reached to her. So serious was it that she backed away, out of the library, into the hall, and backwards out the screen door. Outside, she picked up a striped kitten that was stalking through the grass-blades, and held him to her, pressing against the tumult in her fingers and in his body. The willful little

> face was like a question close to hers, and the small
> stems of its breath came up and tickled her nose like
> flowers. In front of her eyes the cardinals were flying
> hard at their reflections in the car, drawn up in the
> yard now. . . . A lady cardinal was in the rosebush,
> singing so hard that she throbbed between her shoulder
> blades. Laura could see herself in the car door too,
> holding the kitten whose little foot stretched out. She
> stood looking at herself reflected there—as if she had
> gotten along so far like an adventurer in an invisible
> coat, as magical as it was unsuspected by her. Now she
> felt visible to everything. (p. 56)

It is as if George's seeing her—knowing her—not only empowered her to see vividly (the kitten, the bird, herself), but also
made her feel her own selfhood.

Shelley also is empowered by George. The insistence on
choice, on individual will, that Ellen had detected in George's
stand in front of the Yazoo-Delta, Shelley sees even in the way
George crosses the dance floor, and she appropriates it for herself: "She followed, she herself had a vision of choice, or its
premonition, for she was much like George." And with that
recognition, she accepts the complexity of life, ceasing to demand
simplicity and happiness of it as she had earlier:

> . . . she might not be happy either, wholly, and she
> would live in waiting, sometimes in terror. But Dab-
> ney's marriage, ceasing to shock, was like a door closing
> to her now. . . . It shut a door in their faces. Behind the
> closed door, what? Shelley's desire fled, or danced se-
> riously, to an open place—not from one room to another
> room with its door, but to an opening wood, with
> weather—with change, beauty. . . . (p. 220)

The willingness to enter the dark wood is characteristic of
those with the capacity for vision. George goes literally into the
woods, and so does Ellen—that other stranger among the
Fairchilds who sees and knows more than she says. This is not
to say that Ellen cannot behave just like a Fairchild. Like a bilin-
gual person, she knows the language of surface relationships as
well as the inexpressible communication of a deeper union. So
she can regale the wedding party with the story of Shelley's birth,
turning potential trouble into hilarity just as India did with the
tale of the Yazoo-Delta. And she who knows so well that nothing is really simple can speak the language of reductionism
(motivated by the Fairchild desire not to hurt or trouble some-

one she cares for). Ellen sounds just like Aunt Tempe or Aunt Primrose when she tells Robbie: " . . . we all love Georgie, no matter how we act or he acts. . . . And isn't that all there is to it?" Yet we know of Ellen what we don't know of Tempe or Primrose: that she recognizes life's complexity even while talking of its simplicity. After her assurances to Robbie "all of a sudden, [Ellen] felt tired. She was never surer that all loving Georgie was not the end of it; but to hold back hurt and trouble, shouldn't it just now be enough? She had said so, anyway—as if she were sure" (p. 162).

Ellen's introduction to life's mysterious doubleness had come early, back at Mitchem Corners when she was Laura's age. Her mother had run off with a man and lived with him in England three years before returning to her household in Virginia, where her life went on just as it had before, with no questions asked. As a consequence, "Ellen had grown up not especially trusting appearances." However, as a young woman, she had not begun to suspect

> that other people's presence and absences were . . . the least complicated elements of what went on underneath. Not her young life with her serene mother, with Battle, but her middle life . . . had shown her how deep were the complexities of the everyday, of the family, what caves were in the mountains, what blocked chambers, and what crystal rivers that had not yet seen light. (p. 157)

Ellen's capacity for a knowledge beyond the factual and analytical is hinted of in a number of ways. She is the keeper of the family keys, the "heaviest and most keys in the world," although Ellen admits that "some of them are to things I'll never be able to think of or never will see again" (p. 182). Not a linear person, Ellen finds it difficult to keep track of time. She is not quite sure whether the wedding rehearsal is tonight or tomorrow night. Yet, like Dilsey in *The Sound and the Fury*, she is tuned in to another temporal scheme: when the clock strikes two, she knows it is eight. She tells Mr. Rondo that she can read Robbie and George's happiness in their faces. And, while her older children laugh at her, she trusts the insights that come to her in her dreams, sharing them with her youngest child, the one least touched by society's rules for finding truth. Through those dreams she has detected mistakes in accounts and payrolls, discovered the overseer's cheating, learned of relatives or tenants in need, and located things lost. The demands of everyday life keep her from knowing of these things in any other way: "She was too busy when she was awake to know if a thing was lost or not—she had to dream it" (p. 65).

The novel speaks also of Ellen's "darker instinct of a woman" (p. 221), suggesting an intuitive knowledge that Welty may be connecting with her role as "mother to the world" (p. 70).[15] Welty emphasizes the link between Ellen's response to life's mystery and her motherhood, when she writes: "All the mystery of looks moved her, for she was with child once more" (p. 22). Certainly there is no implication that this deeper knowledge is limited to women—George is evidence of that. Perhaps what is implied is the inherent link between knowing and generativity. To know truly is a creative act, as we saw in George's effect on others, particularly in his giving them—or helping them see—themselves. A further symbolic implication of the connection of true knowing with motherhood may lie in the association of such insight with death, which Ellen faces in each childbirth: perhaps knowledge of life's intense wholeness can emerge only at the interface between life and death.

What Welty clearly wants us to see is that Ellen, who does not deal with life's truly important matters through reason, *knows*. Ellen herself recognizes this near the end of the book, sitting at Battle's side on the way to the picnic welcoming Dabney and Troy home and bidding farewell to George and Robbie:

> The repeating fields, the repeating cycles of season and her own life—there was something in the monotony itself that was beautiful, rewarding—perhaps to what was womanly within her. No, she had never had time—much time at all, to contemplate . . . but she knew. Well, one moment told you the great things, one moment was enough for you to know the greatest thing. (p. 240)

One reason Ellen comes to know is her willingness to step out of the sanctuary of extremes. Unlike Battle, she does not demand a changelessly happy life for herself or her family. Ellen's commitment to exposure to life's fullness is symbolized by her movement deep into the woods, where "many little paths crisscrossed and disappeared," where "moss from the cypresses hung deep overhead," and "water vines like pediments and arches reached from one tree to the next," where cypress trunks grow four feet thick, and old spider webs impede her way. Another of Welty's arenas of initiation, this *axis mundi* beside the Yazoo (the chillingly named river, another symbol of Ellen's facing death) strikes Ellen quite rightly as "an ancient place" (pp. 68-69).

It is here that "a whole mystery of life open[s] up" to Ellen in the beautiful young girl she discovers in the deepest part of the woods (p. 70). In fact, in Ellen's (and George's) meeting with this girl and in Ellen's surprising acceptance (and even celebration) of George's sexual encounter with the girl, the strange young woman seems not so much realistic as an embodiment of the mystery of the woods that both George and Ellen are willing to enter. In her first response to the girl, Ellen, troubled by her confrontation with a stranger, speaks as a Fairchild, telling her to "Stand still," warning her of the mistakes she might bring on herself "way out here in the woods!" (pp. 70-71). Then Ellen draws back from her Fairchild voice, even while she says, "'I ought to turn you around and send you back . . .'" (p. 71). Later she half admits to herself the resentment (and, we imagine, something of envy) she feels for the young woman's plans to run away to Memphis, "the old Delta synonym for pleasure, trouble, and shame"—a life totally foreign to Ellen's (p. 72). Responding to the ambiguity and mystery that the girl embodies, Ellen drops the girl's hand, letting go any attempt at control.

Suddenly, she and the mysterious young woman share a moment of unity. Welty's description of that instant is remarkable in its ability to convey the union and the creativity of the moment (suggested in the grape, symbolic—through its Dionysian associations—of renewal of life, of vitality, of growth) and also the simultaneous loss of that union: "In the stillness a muscadine fell from a high place into the leaves under their feet, burying itself, and like the falling grape the moment of comfort seemed visible to them and dividing them, and to be then, itself, lost" (p. 71). Fallen to the ground, the grape, unseen by Ellen and the girl, will release its seed to generate itself anew. Similarly, this moment of affective union, even though now the union itself is past, will become a seed for further illumination for Ellen.

That comes when she finds that George, too, has been in the woods and has met the stranger: "Then [Ellen] was speechless. It was a thing she had never learned in her life, to expect that what has come to you, come in dignity to yourself in loneliness, will yet be shared, the secret never intact" (p. 79). If willingness to venture from safety has its perils—including the possibility that one will learn something startling about oneself—it also has its compensations, including the possibility of a union in knowledge with others who also venture into the unknown.

George's telling her that he has slept with the girl re-enforces for Ellen the lesson of human mystery, by offering further evidence of his own complex self. And Ellen responds to the evidence of George's multiplicity first by "let[ting] go in her whole body, and [standing] languidly still under her star a moment"—accepting, not fighting this new knowledge of George (p. 79). Then she experiences her own ability to be at ease with—to embrace the union of—opposite emotions: she is "bitterly glad" (p. 80).

If Ellen's willingness to step out of the safety of comfortable knowledge contributes to her superior insight, so too does her standing at ease with not knowing. And because she does not claim clear and full knowledge of everything, she is sometimes struck with a new vision of old realities. The narrator tells us: "She was often a little confused about her keys, and sometimes would ask Dabney, 'What was I going for? Why am I here?'" Yet sometimes "she would look over the room . . . and it would be as if she had never before seen anything at all of this room. . . . At that moment a whisper might have said Look! to her, and the dining-room curtains might have traveled back on their rings, and there *they* were" (p. 21).

The ability to see people as new, as constantly changing, as *unsolved* means that they live freely and as whole selves for Ellen. For her, love means not reducing the other to easy formulae. In thinking of George's happiness,

> she could be diligent and still not wholly sure—never wholly. She loved George too dearly herself to seek her knowledge of him through the family attitude, keen and subtle as that was—just as she loved Dabney too much to see her prospect without its risks, now family-deplored, around it, the happiness covered with danger. (p. 26)

Love for Ellen means acknowledging and even wishing for the loved one all of life's fullness, including its risks and pains. Ellen becomes most conscious of this when, just before she faints, she "giv[es] George an imploring look in which she seemed to commit herself even further to him and even more deeply by wishing worse predicaments, darker passion, upon all their lives" (p. 166). She knows as George does—as he telegraphed her in his revelation about his relation with the girl, as he reveals to us in his desire that his relation with Robbie intensify—that life's fullness is created out of the dynamic tension between darkness and light, pain and joy. And she welcomes the fullness that she senses Battle cannot face.

Such knowing has its burdens. Battle *will* be more cheerful than she. When Ellen looked at George and Robbie in their moment of Edenic happiness, wet, almost naked, lying on the sweetpea vines after George carried Robbie from the river during a family picnic, she saw not merely joy, but also vulnerability. In their happiness, Ellen felt they were "almost—somehow—threatening" (p. 25). The narrator reminds us of the double reality to which Ellen is responding when we are told that India sprinkled the couple with pomegranate flowers and handfuls of grass, emblems both of life and of mortality. Ellen confronts this ultimate union of opposites in her own life during the taking of the wedding picture. Just as Ellen is remembering herself as a young girl of Mitchem Corners, the photographer reveals that the girl she had met in the woods had been killed by the Yazoo-Delta. When the photographer takes a second picture, youth and death form a montage in Ellen's mind (pp. 217-18).

Ellen's treasuring of life's polarity is symbolized in her response to her gardener's declaration that he wishes "there wasn't no such thing as roses. If I had my way, wouldn't be a rose in de world. Catch your shirt and stick you and prick you and grab you. Got thorns." Battle and the Fairchild aunts seem similarly to wish away the thorns of the world—and with them the roses. But Ellen is left trembling at such a possibility (p. 226).

Because of her willingness to venture beyond the surface, to expose herself to the pain that can come with such a vision, Ellen knows her children in a way Battle, it seems, never will. While Battle, according to Shelley, sees them only in bunches, "under [Ellen's] gaze her family, as they had a trick of doing, seemed to separate one from another like islands being created out of a land in the sea that had sprawled conglomerate too long" (p. 188). Later, the imagery Welty uses to describe Ellen's differentiating vision—the beam of light broken into a prism of colors—underscores the simultaneous reality of both similarity and difference. Ellen is looking for her daughters at the wedding dance:

> It was the year—wasn't it every year?—when they all looked alike. . . . It was too the season of changeless weather, of the changeless world, in a land without hill or valley. How could she ever know anything of her own daughters, how find them, like this? Then . . . as if a bar of light had broken a glass into a rainbow

> she saw the dancers become the McLeoud bridesmaid,
> Mary Lamar Mackey . . . , become Robbie, and her own
> daughter Shelley, each different face bright and
> burning as sparks of fire to her now, more different and
> further apart than the stars. (p. 221)

During this dance, too, she experiences her closest union
with George. Initially she had wanted to talk with him, but she
realizes that she never really has time to talk "in any civilized
way"—and, besides, George is a little drunk (p. 221). What happens instead is beyond words. Giving up a need to know all the
specifics about George, she has insight into George himself, in a
vision replete of mystery and the union of opposites:

> As he looked in her direction, all at once she saw
> into his mind as if he had come dancing out of it leaving
> it unlocked, laughingly inviting her to the unexpected
> intimacy. She saw his mind—as if it too were
> inversely lighted up by the failing paper lanterns—
> lucid and tortuous. . . .
>   . . . . She did not need to know each little thing
> about him any more—to be a mother to him any more.
> She recognized him as far from kin to her, scarcely tol-
> erant of her understanding, never dependent on hers or
> anyone's, or on compassion (how merciless that could
> be!). He appeared, as he made his way alone now and
> smiling through the dancing couples, infinitely simple
> and infinitely complex, stretching the opposite ways
> the self stretches and the selves of the ones we love
> (except our children) may stretch; but at the same time
> he appeared very finite in that he was wholly singular
> and dear. . . . (pp. 221-22)

Her response to this insight demonstrates her ease in living a life at the axis of polarities. She loves George; she wonders
if, had they met at a different time, she could have been the one
who "relieved [his] heart's overflow"; but she has not one regret
for her life with Battle. Thinking thus of George and Battle, she
notices the perfect emblem for her relationship to both: "There
was the mistletoe in the tree. It was like a tree, too—a tree within a tree" (p. 223). Ellen lives in a similar doubleness—in the
everyday world and in the hidden world of the visionary; she
sees life's wholeness, and, seeing that, she is herself whole.[16]
    Resistance to seeing the tree within the tree, to penetrat-
ing the surface layer of reality has been the charge against the
Fairchilds throughout *Delta Wedding*. Yet early in the novel
Dabney (asked to carry to her aunts a sack of onion bulbs—or hy-

acinths, as she thinks), introduces the idea that "people are mostly layers of violence and tenderness—wrapped like bulbs . . . I don't know what makes them onions or hyacinths" (p. 42). We have already seen that George's vision triggered new visions of themselves and of reality for Shelley, Dabney, and Laura. Indeed, for a family that is characterized repeatedly as content to live on the surface of every tremendous fact, the Fairchilds have a surprising number of people who make forays beneath the surface layer.[17] Dabney, for example, sees her Fairchild identity as just one layer of her self:

> Sometimes Dabney was not so sure she was a Fairchild—sometimes she did not care, that was it. There were moments of life when it did not matter who she was—even where. Something, happiness—with Troy, but not necessarily, even the happiness of a fine day—seemed to leap away from identity as if it were an old skin, and that she was one of the Fairchilds was of no more need to her than the locust shells now hanging to the trees everywhere were to the singing locusts. What she felt, nobody knew! It would kill her father—of course for her to be a Fairchild was an inescapable thing, to him. (pp. 32-33)

Her older sister Shelley also comes to see life's dynamic complexity, in contradiction of Battle's desire for stasis and for an existence eternally one-dimensional, protected, unchanging, serene. Shelley thinks: "Life was too easy—too easily holy, too easily not. It could change in a moment. Life was not ever inviolate . . . " (p. 193). This insight, at first the cause of despair, she comes to terms with when she drives across the path of the Yazoo-Delta. She also recognizes the fallacy of that dare-devilish act: it is contrived, whereas the real disasters of life come unbidden. However, it symbolizes her willingness to meet all of life, to evade nothing: "It had struck her all at once as so fine to drive without pondering a moment onto disaster's edge—she would not always jump away!" (p. 234)

The third sister is also curiously endowed with ways of knowing independent of concrete evidence, penetrating surface appearances. We are told that India knows "what everybody was doing at all times, which she knew though she herself, as now, might be cutting paper dolls . . . she seemed truly the only one who knew" (p. 124). Ellen muses: "I can't imagine how India finds out things. . . . It's just like magic" (p. 105). During the final picnic in the novel, India intones (in an echo of the biblical prophecy "And his name shall be Emmanuel"): "I'm going to have another little brother before long, and his name shall be Denis Fairchild" (p. 241). And on the last page, in a vision in which distinctions between terrible and marvelous blur, she is described as standing "showily, hands on hips, as if she saw certain things, neither marvelous nor terrible, but simply certain, come by in the Yazoo River" (p. 247).

Laura, surrogate for us as an arriver in this land, has travelled all sorts of avenues of knowing since that first fact-filled page—from her early experience when she realizes that she "knew in her fingers the thready pattern of red roses in the carpet on the stairs" (p. 8);[18] to her learning that even without "seeing the others [her cousins] anywhere, . . . she had them everyone separate in her head" (p. 75); to her own insight into humanity's onion/hyacinth nature:

> People that she might even hate danced so sweetly just at the last minute, going around the turn, they made her despair. She felt she could never be able to hate anybody that hurt her in secret and in confidence, and that she was Maureen's secret the way Maureen was hers. Maureen! Dabney! Aunt Ellen! Uncle George! She almost called them, all—pleading. There was too much secrecy, too much pity at the stairs, she could not get by. (p. 102)

She has even seen the bees—marvelously double creatures with their stings and their honey—fly out of Aunt Studney's mysterious sack.[19]

Such transcendence of the Fairchild superficiality is not limited to George and Ellen and the younger generation. Aunt Jim Allen, for all her unwillingness to face Dabney's feelings, has, during the picnic at the end of the novel, a momentary vision of life's being larger than simple either-or categories when "for the first time" she becomes "quite aware that her brother was married—not hopelessly, like the dead Denis, but problematically, not promisingly!" (p. 246). Even Tempe, usually so sure of her facts about everyone, so committed to reducing life to certainties, finally concedes during the same picnic, " . . . I don't understand George at all" (p. 246). And earlier, looking at little Ranny, Tempe "experienced not a thought exactly but a truer thing, a suspicion, that what she loved was not gone with Denis, but was, perhaps, perennial" (p. 190).

And even of the oldest Fairchild generation, now so apparently walled off from life, enclosed in a protective shell that no pain can penetrate, we learn something surprising. We are told of Aunt Shannon:

> In her the Fairchild oblivion to the member of the fam-
> ily standing alone was most developed; just as in years
> past its opposite, the Fairchild sense of emergency, a
> dramatic instinct, was in its ascendancy, and she had
> torn herself to pieces over Denis's drinking and Denis's
> getting killed. (pp. 62-63)

Two insights are important here. One is that we should never assume we have seen the whole until we take into account patterns of polarity in which a rhythm is created by alternating extremes. The other is the dynamic quality of that wholeness. No doubt the very intensity of Shannon's involvement, in times past, with the pain of others led to her retreat in the present from such union with other. In the same way, Dabney's and Shelley's response to the isolation they have experienced as a consequence of the Fairchild oblivion to the other compels them to move to the opposite pole.

Indeed, on close reading, we see that this novel, filled with people protesting that everyone else is living on the surface, aware only of facts reducible to words, is actually filled with characters who at least occasionally experience a truer thing than thought. In such an apparent contradiction of the first reading, *Delta Wedding* does not destroy its own meaning or "deconstruct." Instead, leading her reader through such ostensible contradictions, Welty helps us experience our own encounter with the mystery and polarity of reality. Sure at first—because that is all we are shown from the external perspective of other character's evaluations—that all Fairchilds are *X*, we come to see first Ellen, then Dabney, then George, then Shelley, separate themselves from such a simple definition. Before our eyes the vase changes into the profiles. By the end of the novel, as we have noted, even Jim Allen and Tempe, shatter the box into which we (or the other characters through whose eyes we have seen them) had tucked them.

What then *can* we be sure of by the end of the novel? Certainly not that the remaining characters are different from those whose consciousnesses we have seen into. What layers might there not be beneath Battle's evasive serenity? (We recall that even Ellen talks like a Fairchild and is dismissed by Tempe as such "a very innocent woman" that "there were things you simply could not tell her" [p. 190]—a far cry from what we know of the Ellen who accepts with bitter gladness the revelation that George had slept with the girl in the woods.) As readers, we reach the point where we, too, have to make our peace with ambiguity, resting at ease with not knowing for sure—about Battle and Aunt Mac and Aunt Primrose and all the other Fairchilds into whose minds we have not seen. Our relationship to them, indeed, mirrors our relationship with most people in this world. To acknowledge that we do not know, to sense that here is mystery, to suspect that in everyone there are layers of onions and hyacinths—these are the first steps toward the kind of knowing that the novel illuminates. If we began the novel, like Laura, with our attention on facts, we may, by the end, arrive at a willingness to embrace another kind of truth (including the darkness that generates light), arrived at by a path other than reason: in the final line of the novel Laura stands with "both arms held out to the radiant night."

Notes

[1] See, for example, *Delta Wedding* (New York: Harcourt Brace & World, 1946), pp. 4, 33, 36, 42, 90, 111, 112, 174, 179, 240. Future references to this edition will be given in the text of this chapter. For an early discussion of *Delta Wedding*'s focus on "the single, illuminating, still act of private perception," see John Edward Hardy, "*Delta Wedding* as Region and Symbol," *Sewanee Review*, 60 (July-September 1952), 397-417.

[2] Having "come through," Pinchy suggests her own encounter with the reality where opposites unite. At Dabney's wedding she is described as looking "wild and subdued together now in that snowiness with her blue-black" (p. 211). (Louise Westling interprets Pinchy's "coming through" as a movement from puberty to womanhood [*Eudora Welty* (Totowa, NJ: Barnes and Noble Books, 1989), p. 108, and *Sacred Groves and Ravaged Gardens*, p. 84]. I believe, however, that a spiritual, rather than physical change is indicated by the quest imagery associated with Pinchy's transition, as well as by her apparently new white garb, once favored by black women church members on special ritual occasions (see Welty's photographs in *One Time, One Place* [New York: Random House, 1971], pp. 82, 83, 86).

[3] *Eudora Welty*, 1962, p. 33.

[4] Richard Gray also analyzes the description of Laura's view from the train window, developing another thesis, but one that also suggests the human hunger for holism ("A Dance to the Music of Order: Eudora Welty" In *The Literature of Memory: Modern Writers of the American South* [Baltimore: Johns Hopkins University Press, 1977], pp. 174-85). Gray sees the fact that in these early paragraphs "things are constantly melting into one another or dividing their identity between different levels of experience" as evidence that *Delta Wedding* is the best example of Welty's dealing with the human vacillation

between fixity and change, between "the energies of their personal being . . . and the fixities and definites of their environment" (p. 178).

[5] For a discussion of how "*Delta Wedding* provides images of how to *be* which are directly related with those of how to *see*," see Ruth M. Vande Kieft, "The Vision of Eudora Welty," *Mississippi Quarterly*, 26 (Fall 1973), 517-42.

[6] Robbie becomes aware of the separating power of love, too, musing: "What do you ask for when you love? . . . so much did she love George, that that much the less did she know the right answer" (p. 146).

[7] Battle makes Laura wash her mouth out for using the word "fool"; Aunt Mac chides Robbie for saying "hate": "You're in Shellmound now . . . " (pp. 151, 163).

[8] For example, Dabney folds her hands across herself in imitation of the "good defiant pose" in the portrait of her Great-Grandmother Mary Shannon: "Dabney thought that Mary folded her arms because she would soon have her first child" (pp. 41-42). In addition, Aunt Jim Allen, in thinking of all the champagne George will bring to the wedding, exclaims, "*That* will show people," making us wonder why the leading family in the area need worry about showing anyone at all (p. 47).

[9] For other references to the tendency of Fairchild men to run from trouble, see pp. 103, 162. The Fairchild men are not alone in their childishness. Aunt Tempe's evasion of reality is expressed in a similar fashion. Considering her aunt, Dabney thinks: "You never had to grow up if you were spoiled enough. It *was* comforting, if things turned out not to be what you thought . . ." (p. 185). Never sharing her feelings with her sister, Shelley evaluates the family trait this way: " . . . men were no better than little children. . . . Women . . . did know a *little* better—though everything they knew they would have to keep to themselves . . . oh, forever!" (p. 196).

[10] Vande Kieft locates their superiority in their balance of "inward and outward vision" ("The Vision of Eudora Welty," 529-30).

[11] See, for example, pp. 50, 125, 126.

[12] Quoted in Belenky, p. 141.

[13] Robbie sees that he "cherish[es] the whole world" without forfeiting anything of himself (p. 213).

[14] Shelley describes her family as one that "cherishes its weaknesses and belittles its strengths" through such tales (p. 85).

[15] When Ellen is first introduced in the novel, she is also described as "the mother of them all" (p. 10).

[16] Albert J. Devlin approaches the theme of holism in *Delta Wedding* from a different angle, writing: "In their mutual address—their 'confluence,' to use that 'wonderful word' of *The Optimist's Daughter*—George and Ellen Fairchild reconcile the claims of vision and feeling, of the contemplative and social, to form an image of psychic wholeness. It is an image too . . . of the artist striving to integrate vision, and passion, with the uses of common life" ("Meeting the World in *Delta Wedding*," in Turner and Harding, eds., *Critical Essays on Eudora Welty*, p. 98). Dorothy G. Griffin, who focuses on the architecture of *Delta Wedding* as symbolic of a Jungian aspiration to "psychic wholeness," sees George as "a figure of potential release and synthesis, of achieved wholeness" in her essay, "The House as Container: Architecture and Myth in *Delta Wedding*," in Devlin, ed., *Welty: A Life in Literature*, pp. 98-107.

[17] For a discussion of the "voyages" of initiation made by the women of the novel, see Jane L. Hinton, pp. 120-31.

[18] Cf. "Laura remembered everything, with the fragrance and the song. She looked up the steps through the porch, where there was a wooden scroll on the screen door that her finger knew how to trace, and lifted her eyes to an old fanlight, now reflecting a skyey light as of a past summer . . . (p. 7).

[19] For an intriguing discussion of the relation between Aunt Studney's sack and "a whole vision," see Carol Moore, "Aunt Studney's Sack," *The Southern Review*, 16 (Summer 1980), 591-96.

VI

In the Heart of Clay: *The Ponder Heart*

Eudora Welty's *The Ponder Heart* (1954) has been read as a comic re-enactment of the Dionysian-Apollonian conflict. In this analysis, Uncle Daniel is seen as the admirable center of the work, the Dionysian life force, engaged in a struggle with his niece Edna Earle, the "funny and pathetic" Apollonian advocate of order, reason, self-denial, and society's values.[1] However, while there is something in Welty's story of Dionysus and Apollo's old battle, the combatants are other than this reading suggests. The representative of the side of reason actually turns out to be not Edna Earle, but Grandpa Ponder, and as a life force Uncle Daniel turns out to be strangely lifeless. The values suggested by the work are also not as they first appear: what has been viewed as Uncle Daniel's admirable Dionysianism actually has as many flaws as Grandpa Ponder's Apollonianism. And the outcome of the battle is other than has been suggested: Edna Earle emerges not as the shrewish proponent of the old, orderly, rational ways, but as the life-engaged, dynamic balancer of reason and feeling, either of which in isolation is deadly to humanness.

From their extreme positions, both Grandpa and Uncle Daniel approach life dualistically, as an either-or proposition, acting, in Jung's words, "as if we were *simplex* and not *duplex*."[2] Not at all the static character she has been taken to be, Edna Earle does not so much blend the two extremes of reason and feeling as perform a breathtaking—both because it is admirable and exhausting—balancing act, now combining the two approaches, now running between the two sides (both literally and figuratively). She has no safety in retreat to one position, but is constantly at risk from both. Because of this, in Welty's scheme, while always vulnerable and often in error, she has constantly the potential for growth and for extension of her humanity.

Welty gives us a broad visual hint that one of the themes of *The Ponder Heart* is achievement of a synthesis of contraries (and involvement in life's complexities) in the coat-of-arms painted for the Ponder family by Eva Sistrunk and hung up over the clock. Hitting upon the pun *pond + deer*, Eva came up with a device featuring three deer, in honor of the surviving Ponders. The dear/deer/hart/heart is a triumph of circular punning, echoed in Edna Earle's frequent exclamation of "dear heart!" when she is talking to Uncle Daniel. If Eva gave the harts the usual heraldic placement for triads of one-over-two or two-over-one, she also gave the perfect image of the thesis-antithesis-synthesis pattern that underlies the work. The reader's job is to determine which h(e)art represents the synthesis.

The first sentence of the work establishes one of the extremes between which Edna Earle moves: "My Uncle Daniel's just like your uncle, if you've got one—only he has one weakness. He loves society and gets carried away."[3] Two paragraphs later Edna Earle introduces the second pole: "Grandpa Ponder (in his grave now) might have any fine day waked up to find himself in too pretty a fix to get out of, but he had too much character" (p. 8). That in her vocabulary "character" suggests emotionless self-sufficiency is made clear when Edna Earle says that Grandpa "regarded getting married as a show of weakness of character" (p. 26).[4] Edna Earle lays out the motif of extremes in geographical terms and introduces the idea of a balancing middle point associated with herself when she gives advice to Uncle Daniel after he "gave the girl at the bank a trip to Lookout Mountain and Rock City Cave, and then was going along with her to watch her enjoy both." She cajoles Daniel (on leave from the mental hospital in Jackson to which Grandpa had committed him): "Dear heart, *I* know the asylum's no place for you, but neither is the top of a real high mountain or a cave in the cold dark ground. Here's the place" (p. 16). The place she means is the Beulah Hotel that she manages. Topographically in between the cave and the mountain, it is a point of balance sociologically as well. At one extreme away from the Beulah is the wide world where the drug salesman, Mr. Springer, roams ("I told Mr. Springer at the time, about straying too far from where you're known and all—having too wide a territory" [p. 20]) and where Grandpa is locked up in the asylum instead of Uncle Daniel because no one knows his name. Out there are too many people, not a community, but a conglomerate.

Metaphorically on the other side of the Beulah and its shadowy mirror ("almost exactly the same size," but with no city lights [p. 54]) is the Ponder Place, Grandpa Ponder's farm, "miles from anywhere" (p. 44). It is the externalization of Grandpa's character. He chose the isolated setting because he "despised" society (p. 12); the hilltop location, because, needing always to *know*, to be in control, he wanted to "see all around him and if anybody was coming" (p. 43). Even his aesthetics is based on competition rather than feeling: he crams his house with furniture, trims it elaborately, paints it "bright as a railroad station"— "Anything to outdo the Beulah Hotel" (p. 44). The very hoot-owls filling his woods create the picture of a man of reason unbreachably surrounded by Athena's birds. And the roof of his house he "sprinkled . . . with lightning rods the way Grandma would sprinkle coconut on a cake" (p. 44). In Welty's moral scheme, Grandpa was probably justified in fearing heaven's fury. That the spiny metallic protectors against bolts of light from above were later transferred to the courthouse, that other locus of rational order (and simplistic, unenlightened judgment), makes her joke even funnier.

The complexity of Welty's fun here is heightened by our recognizing Grandma Ponder's role. When Edna Earle says that her grandparents were "evenly matched" (p. 44), the metaphor that is equally applicable to prize fights and to pieces of plaid or teams of animals conveys both the conflict and the dynamic harmony of their relationship, a harmony that comes from the tension between opposites, not from the conquest of one opposite by the other. Grandma's metier was coconut cake (sweets made for sharing), not lightning rods, which she "never could stand" (p. 118). While almost as smart as Grandpa, Grandma loved people (being "in the thick of things") as well (p. 67). She was, indeed, Edna Earle's predecessor as a uniter of extremes. And *her* place was the Beulah Hotel.

The name "Beulah" perfectly evokes the idea of harmoniously linked opposites, implying as it does the union of the earthly and the celestial.[5] In spirituals Beulah Land was another word for heaven; in *Pilgrim's Progress* it was the celestial antechamber, but in the Old Testament it was simply a name for the earthly Israel or Jerusalem, literally meaning "married" (to God). The Beulah Hotel is the symbol of the marriage of opposites, seen first in Grandma and then in Edna Earle, the Beulah's present owner: not the angelic perfection of Uncle Daniel or the dark, even comically demonic misanthropy of Grandpa, but the best that humans can hope for. This comic, secular paradise sits "right in the heart of Clay" (p. 13)—the perfect name for the county and for the Beulah's position at the symbolic heart of clay-made humankind.[6] It is one of Welty's many points of intersection between the higher and lower realms, threatened constantly by both, open always to energy from either. In the Beulah Hotel, "life goes on on all sides" (p. 66).[7]

Grandpa, however, preferred life to come at him from one side only. Plato, the Stoics, Descartes, even Freud might have commended Grandpa as one in whom Reason ruled as the imperial governor. Jung would likely have judged that he suffered from tyranny of the left hemisphere. Welty signals her agreement with the latter judgment by making Grandpa comic in his rigid adherence to one part of the truth as if it were the whole. He *is* comic, not evil, of course, loving his son enough to bring him to town each Saturday in spite of his own hatred of society, praying over Daniel for years before committing him to Jackson. He simply is totally baffled by Daniel, because each lives at a different pole of the human world. A ponderer worthy of his family name, Grandpa's concern is the "realm of reason" (p. 14). His approach to people is as mathematical (he wants them "to measure up" [p. 8]) as his choice of pastimes (dominoes, that game of addition). While Edna Earle delights in Uncle Daniel's riotous tales of life in the asylum, declaring, "It didn't matter if you didn't know the people . . ." (p. 16), Grandpa's response is that of the rational reporter hungry just for facts: "Who?—What, Daniel?—When?" (p. 17).

Even in matters of the heart, Grandpa is all mind. An anti-Eros, he sounds a lot like a comic version of Miss Sabina of Welty's "Asphodel": "Grandpa would be a lot more willing to stalk up on a wedding and stop it, than to encourage one to go on, yours, mine, or the Queen of Sheba's" (p. 26). When he decides that Uncle Daniel should marry, it is not a concession to love or to passion, but presumably to stifle his son's feelings and control his developing interest in the other sex, demonstrated in Daniel's attraction to the "girls" in the Escapade side-show, with "their come-on dance" (p 23). Then only after "debating" does Grandpa "come to [the] conclusion" that he will have to "fork up a good wife" (p. 24). (That the wife turns out to be Teacake Magee completes the nice gastronomic objectification.)

However, even that scheme doesn't succeed in controlling Daniel—and, like the Freudian Superego, Grandpa is obsessed with the need for control, especially control of forces that smack of the undisciplined Id. Underscoring the extremity of Grandpa's response, Edna Earle says that he goes "too far with *discipline*" (p. 36). Using the language of the reasonable school master, Sam Ponder puts his son in the insane asylum—"to teach [him] a lesson" (p. 14).[8] Grandpa's temporary confinement, because of mistaken identity, in the same asylum (reserved for those not able to function in society) implies the weakness of both Grandpa's and Uncle Daniel's relation to the world.

On the day Grandpa is led off into the asylum, leaving reason temporarily in abeyance, Uncle Daniel marries Bonnie Dee Peacock. Learning of the marriage, Grandpa dies not because of the Ponder heart (as Edna Earle originally thinks), but, according to the doctor, because of a popped blood vessel (a stroke); that is, a failure in his head. However, both Edna Earle's and Dr. Ewbanks' diagnoses were metaphorically correct. All Grandpa's intellectual systems had finally broken down in the face of Daniel's totally irrational marriage to the little clerk he had met at Woolworth's that day—and his heart had been too weak to cope when his mind had failed.

Edna Earle says it is the Ponder head that is distinctive— "large, of course" (p. 11). But she exclaims equally over "the Ponder heart!" (p. 24). The battle of the extremes is, of course, at work (or play) in these anatomical references. While Uncle Daniel's hatsize is enormous, his intellect is pea-sized; but his heart is overworked ("racing") Dr. Ewbanks says, as he warns Daniel to "use more judgment around here" (p. 61). In both Grandpa and Uncle Daniel, the Ponder heart of the title is in an unhealthy condition, Grandpa's weak from disuse; Daniel's, from overuse. Either extreme, Welty seems to warn with a smile, is likely to do you in.

The extremity of Daniel's good-heartedness is indicated by his angelic nature. The possessor of "everlasting springs" (p. 8), he is willing to give away everything he owns. However, just as an angel would be among us, he is incapacitated for life on this middle plane. He must, literally, be housed, fed, barbered, and transported by others. And, like an angel, he has no traffic with the pangs of mortality: " . . . he hates sickness and death. . . . He can't abide funerals" (p. 41). Having no awareness of death, his experience of life is circumscribed. He is too pure, too unself-conscious, too "young"—that is, too ungrown. He suffers too little. His heart of gold really does not teach us ordinary humans very much. This is no Dionysus. That god's colors were the green and purple of the vine, which does fade and die, not the saintly and spooky emptiness of Uncle Daniel's white.

Indeed, outside of comedy, Daniel would horrify. He has no capacity to act, even in order to get back the bride whose loss he mourns every evening in stories. What he does do, Uncle Daniel seems not to be responsible for. Striking us as not a human force, but as a chaotic, supernatural impulse, he is equally uncontrollable by others—Grandpa, DeYancey, or the Judge crying, "Order!" at his trial.

Oddly enough for one who generates such chaos, Uncle Daniel has a childlike need for order—another challenge to the view that Uncle Daniel is the Dionysian advocate of spontaneous life against Edna Earle's obsession with stasis. In its various phases, his life follows rigid patterns: the weekly trip to town in the old days; then during Bonnie Dee's absence, the ritual of the same meal, the same plaint, the same obsessed tale, night after night. Like a child, he expects constancy in people as well. Both Bonnie Dee's death and Edna Earle's self-sacrificial lie on the witness stand (to save him) he sees as personal betrayals, violations of the fragile stability of his existence.

Uncle Daniel makes us uncomfortable, too, because he is not in touch with everyday reality. The Tom Thumb wedding of his childhood is as real to him as his marriages to Teacake Magee and Bonnie Dee. In fact, his equation of the fantasy wedding with the actual marriages gives us a clue to what makes us most uneasy about him. Since he likes everyone—and values every event in his life—equally (he has "a remarkable affection for everybody and everything in creation," Edna Earle says [p. 27])—, he can feel nothing with any special intensity. Edna Earle exclaims: "He loved being happy! He loved happiness like I love tea" (p. 14). Indeed.

Actually, Uncle Daniel, the man who is thought to be so full of feeling, trivializes feeling. Daniel likes Elsie Fleming pretty much the same as he does Bonnie Dee, and he liked Miss Teacake, too—he just could not abide the sound of her spool-heels on the floor. This kind of emotional egalitarianism might at first seem saintly. However, from the human point of view it is evidence of a person doomed to miss not only love's intensity, but any real experience of self or of other.[9] He cannot truly love, because Bonnie Dee is never a real person in his eyes, a being separate from himself. (That is the main reason it never occurs to him to give her money—until Edna Earle makes him.)

As evidence of how extremes have a way of meeting in Welty's world (in this case, by showing their essential similarity), Daniel objectifies Bonnie Dee much as Grandpa did Teacake when he decided to "fork her over." When Bonnie Dee returns, Daniel crows: "Oh, my bride has come back to me. Pretty as a picture. . . . Edna Earle got her back for me, you all, and Judge Tip Clanahan sewed it up. It's a court order, everybody. . . . She's perched out there on the sofa till I get home tonight. I'll hug her and kiss her and I'll give her twenty-five dollars in her little hand" (pp. 62-63). To Uncle Daniel she is always "pretty as a doll" (pp. 42, 51, 77, 133)—or a picture—and that is how he treats her. He wants her at home, while he goes off to the Beulah Hotel, looking for an audience for his stories *about* her.

Only the person possessed of a self (a person with a sense of his or her individual distinction from others) can recognize the independent selfhood of others. Welty herself made a similar point in a discussion of the relationship between individual and family in *Losing Battles*. In an interview with Charles T. Bunting, Welty declared: " . . . you can't really conceive of the whole unless you are an identity. Unless you are very real in yourself, you don't know what it means to support others or to join with them or to help them."[10] Daniel can regard others as only part of his own undifferentiated being. He treats Edna Earle as generously as everyone else, giving her the hotel just as he gave Mr. Springer's brother-in-law's sister a major operation, but in his scheme of things (much like that of an infant), she exists mainly for his comfort and protection. He has no sense of what she suffers for him. As Edna Earle says, it would never occur to him that *she* has a story to tell too (p. 70).

A further paradox of Daniel's selflessness is that, since he has no independent sense of self, he can get a feeling of selfhood only from others. From this perspective, he is absolutely other-directed. When, for example, Bonnie Dee's sister, Johnnie Ree, refuses Uncle Daniel's invitation to go riding, "he just stood still in the bright sun, like the cake of ice that was melting there that day" (p. 152). When he cannot make people happy—by giving away a car ride, or his love, or a brooder and incubator, or his stories—and see himself in people's joyous reaction to him, he, in effect, ceases to exist. No doubt, this need accounts for his obsessive giveaway at the end of the novel: unable to tell his story, he begins desperately to scatter his money around, hoping to regain the joy and the selfhood that come when he is created anew in the grateful eyes of the recipients.

One of the great ironies of *The Ponder Heart* is the disastrous result on the rare occasion when Uncle Daniel assumes the role of adult. Always "mortally afraid" of lightning (p. 140)—in fact, this experience of fear is one of his few mortal qualities— Uncle Daniel overcomes his own fear in order to play "creep mousie," hoping to make Bonnie Dee stop crying in her terror. For once he is the adult, tickling the child. Why should death be the consequence of Daniel's single grown-up act? Perhaps it is a reminder of the adult's inevitable involvement in mortality. Perhaps it suggests the unavoidable muddle of cause and effect, intention and responsibility that the mature person confronts. Perhaps, however, all we can actually conclude about this episode is best summarized by Edna Earle: "Maybe what's hard to believe about the truth is who it happens to" (p. 143). It does not seem fair that this should happen to Uncle Daniel, but there it is.

For whatever reason, when Uncle Daniel responds to his wife's distress and reaches out from the safety of his own angelic or childish sanctuary, his plan misfires in the worst possible way. Bonnie Dee dies, and Uncle Daniel retreats once more into his oblivious self, never again, we surmise, to take a chance at human risk and human growth. At Bonnie Dee's funeral we hear his return to the old refrain as he tells Mrs. Peacock that her daughter is "pretty as a doll." The fact of Bonnie Dee's death seems lost on him.

Of course, in the rollicking comedy of *The Ponder Heart* we do not waste many tears on Bonnie Dee either. One reason Welty can get away with killing Bonnie Dee off is that she has never struck us as being particularly alive anyway. In fact, she is just about the perfect wife for Daniel (after all, she stays married to him for something like seven years). Like Daniel, she is not fully human, but for different reasons. In this study of extremes, Bonnie Dee serves as a kind of negative synthesis, *lacking* the dominant qualities of *both* Grandpa and Uncle Daniel. Certainly none of Grandpa's reason is hers. Bonnie Dee knows how to make change and cut hair, but otherwise she does not have enough sense "to get alarmed about" (pp. 41, 121). On the other hand (this sounds like the old joke: she may be stupid, but she sure is homely), she possesses none of Uncle Daniel's overflowing feelings for others. On the day of their wedding, only a bribe makes her listen to his request that she get out of the car so he can show her off.

Her death from heart failure neatly balances Grandpa's aneurism. Gladney may well ask, "What makes the heart fail?" (p. 108), but we have had hints of the answer all along—and not just in her shortness of breath. Whereas Uncle Daniel gives away, she accumulates (six years of *Movie Mirror* magazines—an appropriate publication in a story shimmering with mirror imagery), a washing machine, clothes, a telephone that never rings. " . . . *things* began to pour into that house," Edna Earle says (p. 67), balancing the novel's second paragraph with its tally of "things . . . [Uncle Daniel has] given away" (p. 8).

Just as Uncle Daniel's giving is a sign of his selflessness (in the literal sense of the word), Bonnie Dee's accumulation reveals a similar absence of independent human selfhood. Like Uncle Daniel, too, she doesn't know how to fight (p. 49), a skill most humans acquire early as evidence of a defined sense of self and of other. Like him, she never grows, so she never ages. At her death she still looks seventeen, just as on the day of her marriage.

However, while Uncle Daniel seems inhuman because he is angelically above us, Bonnie Dee, in the exaggerated imagery of comedy, strikes us as belonging to the realms below us. Criticism almost always seems heavy-handed when it deals with comedy—which should make us all aware of its difference from the art it describes. It is important to recall in studying the novel what we cannot miss in reading it: that Bonnie Dee is not evil any more than Grandpa is. She simply never develops past the stage of a child playing jacks or dress-up with Narciss. (Her relationship with the symbolically named Narciss tells us that her self-involvement is as complete as Daniel's. Narciss' going in the back door of the Beulah while Bonnie Dee and Uncle Daniel go in the front completes this bit of doubly mirrored narcissistic imagery.) Edna Earle makes clear that Bonnie Dee had potential that was not developed when she exclaims about the dead Bonnie Dee: "When you saw her there, it looked like she could have loved *somebody*!" (p. 77). Bonnie Dee's putting in a telephone that never rings implies an inchoate desire for connection with others. Nevertheless, in the comic imagery of the novel, she remains less than human.

A collector of "things," she is herself repeatedly described as "a little thing" (pp. 29, 42) or even less than a thing—a pretty cover for nothingness (her downy yellow hair reminds Edna Earle of those "dandelion puff balls you can blow and tell the time by," having "not a grain beneath" [p. 34]). Other images reiterate her lack of human qualities: she is a doll and a picture; she has coon eyes. When Dr. Ewbanks pushes back "that yellow fluff," he asks, "You don't mean she's flew the coop?", transforming the dead Bonnie Dee Peacock into the bird that her last name suggests (p. 143). Like a cat, she yawns all the time, never smiling because "she didn't know how" (p. 42). If the human being is defined as the smiling animal, Bonnie Dee doesn't make the cut-off. When she dies laughing, Edna Earle realizes that her laughter was only a physiological response, not the result of human connectedness and communication that a smile represents: "I could have shaken her for it. She'd never laughed for Uncle Daniel before in her life. And even if she had, that's not the same thing as smiling; you may think it is, but I don't" (p. 141).

That Bonnie Dee dies laughing is, of course, the central joke of the book. To analyze any joke is risky business, but in terms of the theme of the unity of extremes this episode is worth a closer look. The question of why tickling produces laughter has long stumped scientists and students of humor alike. (Darwin wrote of it in terms of a defense-reaction, the withdrawal of the tickled part.[11]) Arthur Koestler's comments on babies' responses to tickling seem germane to Bonnie Dee's response:

> [A child] will laugh only—and this is the crux of the matter—when it perceives tickling as a *mock attack*, a caress in mildly aggressive disguise.
> . . . .
> The rule of the game [with babies] is: "Let me be just a little frightened so that I can enjoy the relief."
> Thus the tickler is impersonating an aggressor, but simultaneously known not to be one; this is probably the first situation in life which makes the infant live on two planes at once. . . .[12]

Perhaps it is also the child's foretaste of the Janus-faced comedy and horror of life itself. To put it heavily, Bonnie Dee—shrieking from Uncle Daniel's tickling as much as from the thunder—is unable to balance on two planes at once. She cannot see that love can come in the form of its apparent opposite, aggression. She is incapable of the double vision that Welty sees as the basis of a risking, erring, growing human life.

It is this vision that Edna Earle has—Edna Earle, who is Bonnie Dee's mirror on the side of positive synthesis. Welty underscores the mirror relationship between Edna Earle and Bonnie Dee when, on Bonnie Dee's death, Edna Earle runs into the bathroom to get ammonia for Uncle Daniel: "In the bathroom I glanced in the mirror, to see how I was taking it, and got the fright of my life. Edna Earle, I said, you look as old as the hills! It was a different mirror, was the secret—it magnified my face by a thousand times—something Bonnie Dee had sent off for and it had come" (p. 142). Mirrors in art and literature frequently reveal the self that a person, Medusa-like, resists confronting.[13] Throughout her narration, Edna Earle has coyly been suppressing acknowledgement of her age. For example, while she is only slightly younger than Uncle Daniel—who is "up in his fifties now" (p. 11)—she speaks of the poem she is saving to show her grandchildren and bristles when DeYancey calls her "Ma'am" (pp. 59, 110). Seeing herself as old as the hills is a brutal collision with reality.

For us, however, it is evidence of her humanity. She does not stand outside of time as do Bonnie Dee and Uncle Daniel, whose unetched countenances tell us that life has scarcely touched them. Because she truly lives—making mistakes, feeling anger and frustration, knowing unfulfilled love, having to find substitutes for the romance she craves—her appearance shows it. She has earned her face. She has no everlasting springs like the ones she attributes to Uncle Daniel, but her declaration that she looks "as old as the hills" implies her rugged, earthly strength. The spring she does have is a very human one: Mr. Ovid Springer—if only slightly true to his name, still the frail source of her hope for romance and for a metamorphosis from the routine of her present life. We feel that deep-down Edna Earle knows that her reason has been dulled by the drug salesman who has courted her all these years, but she chooses to hang on anyway to her dream that someday he will propose. After a fashion, she is her own spring of hope, giving another punning meaning to the *Pond* in her name.

In Edna Earle, the dominant traits of Grandpa and Uncle Daniel meet, in a very fault-filled, but human way. She is as smart as Grandpa (when she passed Uncle Daniel in the seventh grade, people said she ought to be the teacher) and at times as scientific in her approach to life (she echoes Archimedes' "Eureka!" when she decides that Teacake is the one to be forked over to Uncle Daniel; she "keep[s] tabs" on Bonnie Dee's allowance [pp. 25, 134]; she neatly categorizes people, from the "country" Dorris Gladney to the "nice" family which included a murderer [p. 80]). But, in her, Grandpa's capacity for action and Uncle Daniel's for feeling combine. She can account for the hotel with Grandpa's mathematical accuracy ("twelve bedrooms, two bathrooms, two staircases, five porches, lobby, dining room, pantry and kitchen. . . . And two Negroes. . . . And that plant . . .") and "still be out here looking pretty," ready to go riding with Mr. Springer, should he come tearing through town (p. 10).

One of the most important characteristics of Edna Earle's mediation between the extremes represented by Grandpa and Uncle Daniel is the dynamic quality of that mediation. Edna Earle does not represent a static synthesis: a little bit of reason, a little bit of feeling. The union of opposites we find here is like the energy-generating union of the positive and negative poles of a magnet or battery. Balanced as she is between extremes, Edna Earle has created a life not of peace, but of vitality. Although she is actually doing nothing but talking during the narration of the novel, we picture her in action—sailing back and forth between two homes, running rummage sales for African missionaries, feeding the crowds from court and highway. While Uncle Daniel and Grandpa respond to human multiplicity by ignoring it, giving all their allegiance to one part of human nature, Edna Earle does not try to eliminate either side of her self. She arrives instead at a reciprocal harmony between the superior intelligence that characterizes Grandpa and the unrestrained feelings of Uncle Daniel. The thinking and feeling one, she is the real possessor of the pondering and ponderous heart of the title.

Just as she has managed to salvage strengths from both extremes, she has suffered from both sides, too. She asks no one to cry for her, as Uncle Daniel does, and she wastes little pity on herself. Grandpa and Uncle Daniel both in their own ways (in another meeting of extremes) have been the enemies of romance in Edna Earle's life, but she has managed to fulfill her duties while hanging on to the dream at least of love—of "step[ping] off with, say, Mr. Springer" and appeasing Grandpa by naming the first child Ponder Springer (p. 26).

Our laughter is mixed with a kind of admiration for Edna Earle when she says, "The day I don't rate a pinch of some kind from a Clanahan, I'll know I'm past redemption—an old maid" (p. 84). We know that is precisely what she is, but her own ever-hopeful attitude will not allow us to categorize her this way. Besides, no simple category like "old maid" can contain all the humanity that Edna Earle *is*. If love fails her (and she does suspect that true love is just a "castle in the sky" [p. 50]), she has the flexibility to consider company as a substitute—or maybe she will direct her energies toward a chinchilla farm: "Don't think about it, Edna Earle, I say. So I just cut out a little ad about a booklet that you send off for, and put it away in a drawer—I forget where" (p. 44).

One of the most convincing measures of the superiority of Edna Earle's heart is her capacity to suffer, not just for self (Daniel's suffering is of this variety), but for others, too. What makes that suffering as close to heroism as we are likely to find in comedy is that it comes from acts of will, from consciously accepted responsibility, and from rational awareness of consequences. For all his altruism, Uncle Daniel seems largely unconscious of the significance of his acts. Since he places no value on possessions, his gifts cost him nothing. However, because Edna Earle is aware of the serious consequences of her decision,[14] her willingness to let Daniel give away all the money that she one day would have inherited must be seen as an act of loving courage.

Her lying for Daniel at the trial is of the same mettle. She says: "I never lied in my life before, that I know of, by either saying or holding back, but I flatter myself that when the time came, I was equal to either one" (p. 143). She *is* equal to life's challenges from whichever quarter. And she allows herself to be vulnerable to both extremes: her lie exposes her not only to the penalties of perjury from the law's rational side, but also to the possibility of rejection by the feeling Uncle Daniel, who "looked at me like he never saw me before in his life" (p. 120). What greater measure of self-sacrifice can there be than this: taking the chance that in saving a loved one you may lose that love? And Edna Earle is equal even to this.

In a novel with lightning at the center, Edna Earle, for all her lapses in perception, is the enlightened one. Because Grandpa refused to install electricity, she learned "to read in the dark" (at Uncle Daniel's place she reads "for the thousandth time" the imagistically apt *The House of a Thousand Candles* [pp. 54-56]). Her repeated tag line "Lo and behold," preceding her descriptions of various unexpected events throws the clarification that periodically illuminates her life into contrast with Uncle Daniel's imperceptive parody and imagistic inversion of the phrase: "Low-in-the-hole."

Her insights are far-ranging. In her maturity, she recognizes that Grandpa's expectation of "correcting" the childish Uncle Daniel by consigning him to an asylum is itself "child-foolishness" (pp. 15, 37). She, not Uncle Daniel, is actually the champion of a life fully and freely lived. Whereas Grandpa is miserable without control—of Uncle Daniel or of the heavens—

and Uncle Daniel needs the protection of a rigid routine, Edna Earle (who "abhors the asylum" [p. 15]) has learned the paradoxical power that comes from letting go. The Miss Ouida Simpson plant that she once toted annually to the County Fair competition she now just leaves alone; it still blooms now and then, she says (p. 10). She has come to a similar attitude toward people:

> I don't even try, myself, to make people happy the way they should be: they're so stubborn. I just try to give them what they think they want. Ask me to do you the most outlandish favor tomorrow, and I'll do it. Just don't come running to me afterwards and ask how come.
> (p. 57)

When she violates this principle—as, of course, she is bound to as a changeable human—the result can be disastrous. Even though Uncle Daniel seems satisfied with his life at the Beulah after Bonnie Dee throws him out, Edna Earle gives in to a bothersome conscience that says Uncle Daniel is not happy in the *right* way. (She is also just pure-D tired of listening to his tales.) Convincing Daniel to withhold his wife's allowance, she starts the chain of events leading to Bonnie Dee's death. Unlike Uncle Daniel, however, when Edna Earle becomes tangled in the uncontrollable consequences of human acts, she does not retreat from engagement in life.

Perhaps the most convincing sign of her enlightenment is her own notion of her position in relation to the poles of this world. For example, Edna Earle has some insight into her position between Uncle Daniel and Grandpa. She says: "I've got to get out there and stand up for both of them" (p. 40). Later, describing the trial, she tells us: "When somebody spoke to Uncle Daniel, I tried to answer for him too, if I could. I'm the go-between, that's what I am, between my family and the world" (p. 120). She is also the life-filled middle term between the white-clad, angelic Uncle Daniel and the death figure Gladney with his black coat, buzzard-like appearance, and "his old bony finger" (p. 134).

That Edna Earle is also privy to the truth of the coincidence of apparent opposites is seen in her acknowledgement that love itself may look and sound like its very opposite.[15] Consider her explanation of Uncle Daniel's message to Bonnie Dee on the day of her death ("I'm going to kill you dead, Miss Bonnie Dee, if y' don't take m' back" [p. 91]). According to Edna Earle, the words mean nothing "except love, of course. It's all in a way of speaking. . . . Putting it into words. With some people, it's little threats. With others, it's liable to be poems" (p. 117). She does not need a big-city linguist to tell her that words mean nothing separate from context, that the maps are not the territory. Edna Earle has also learned the *concordia discors* of affection and verbal violence from her predecessor in harmonizing opposites, Grandma Ponder—"the gentlest woman on the face of the earth," who nevertheless peppered her "perfectly normal household" with threats of mayhem and murder (pp. 110-11).

In her own life, Edna Earle demonstrates the truth of her insight into love's double nature, in her response to Bonnie Dee.[16] Like all polar combinations, this too seems to defy reason. Throughout her narration, Edna Earle has directed nothing but disparagement toward Bonnie Dee. Yet it is humanly convincing when, at the end of her story, she reveals her fondness for her niece-in-law: "And you know, Bonnie Dee Peacock, ordinary as she was and trial as she was to put up with—she's the kind of person you do miss. I don't know why—deliver me from giving you the *reason*" (p. 156). Only when we are delivered from reason, do her feelings make sense.

For Mr. Springer she can feel the same tension between censure and affection. The following passage, in fact, begins with a response of the mind and ends with the heart:

> Oh, I did well not to make up my mind too hastily about Ovid Springer. I congratulate myself still on that, every night of the world. Mr. Springer would not have hesitated to blacken Uncle Daniel's name before the world by driving sixty-five miles through the hot sun and handing him over a motive on a silver platter. Tired travelling man if you like—but when it came to a murder trial, he'd come running to be in on it. . . . Of course, he never had anybody to look after him. (p. 122)

One of the clearest marks of the functional superiority of Edna Earle's accommodation of the double poles of her human nature lies in her role as story-teller. Daniel, too, is a teller of tales, bringing joy to his listeners at the Beulah when he entertained them with the funny accounts about his asylum stay and creating a kind of community ritual with his poignant story of Bonnie Dee's running away. However, Daniel's problem as a creative spirit is his lack of self-control. In story-telling, he feels more intensely than at any other time. Edna Earle says: " . . . I don't think he could bring himself to believe the story till he'd heard himself tell it again" (p. 51). Fiction—that is, his lived reality transmuted by his gift of exaggeration—is more real than fact for the man who has so few anchors in day-to-day reality. And he experiences his story, not as a poet-creator, but as if he were reliving it: " . . . it was steadily breaking his heart" (p. 51). Unable to step back from his story to achieve some sort of objectivity, he cannot complete his act of creation: as his "tale of woe" approaches the part about Bonnie Dee's farewell note, "he broke down at the table and ruined it all" (p. 52). Because of his confinement at the pole of feeling, Daniel cannot truly represent the artist. As emotion without form or discipline, he is pure poetic potential (just as Grandpa was mere mechanistic prosaic impulse).[17]

Edna Earle is the real story-teller here, the model (comic, of course) of the creative self. Capable of feeling deeply, involved in her story, she can yet step back enough to tell the tale Daniel cannot complete. Certainly, her control is not perfect: she creates better and other than she knows. But the book itself, the record of her long narration, is the artifact attesting her ability to transmute suffering into art.[18]

Far from being the butt of the comedy in *The Ponder Heart*, Edna Earle is Welty's comic presentation of the whole human self. Speaking of Uncle Daniel's story-telling, Edna Earle exclaims: "Well, if *holding-forth* is the best way you can keep alive, then do it—if you're not outrageously *smart* to start with and don't have *things to do*" (emphasis added; p. 70). Feeling (and creating a story from those feelings), thinking, acting—Edna Earle does them all. And her dynamic, shifting, experimental combination of the qualities—with no static hierarchical ordering—is humanly superior to the rigid control of any one of the extremes. In Welty's world, the flexible heart of clay will beat the heart of gold every time.

Notes

[1] Kreyling, pp. 106-17.

[2] C. G. Jung, *Civilization in Transition*, p. 290.

[3] *The Ponder Heart* (New York: Harcourt Brace, 1954), p. 7. Subsequent references to this edition will be given in the text of this chapter.

[4] Edna Earle tells us that "weakness of character" was the major bane of Grandpa's life, followed by electricity (p. 54).

[5] *Beulah* is also the title of a novel by the popular writer Augusta

Evans (1835-1909), who created a character named Edna Earle in another work.

⁶ That Welty drew the name of Edna Earle's hometown from the real West Virginia town (and county) where Welty's maternal grandfather practiced law does not lessen its symbolic significance.

⁷ The mythical quality of the Beulah Hotel, making it a station on the *via vitae* is underlined when Edna Earle speaks of all the people who "come here, pass through this book [i.e., the hotel register], in and out, over the years" (p. 11).

⁸ Grandpa's need for control of the rampaging Id of the mentally deficient Daniel and Grandpa's subsequent "blood-purchase" of a car when he takes Daniel (coincidentally at Easter time) to the asylum after the marriage to Miss Teacake fails (and his sexuality is once more potentially on the loose) are intriguingly reminiscent of Jason in *The Sound and the Fury*.

⁹ John Allen concludes similarly that because his "almost total ignorance of reality so badly distorts his understanding of himself and of his relationships to others," Uncle Daniel's "feelings are, for useful purposes, null and void" (p. 25). Rachel Weiner has a similar evaluation of Uncle Daniel ("Eudora Welty's *The Ponder Heart*: The Judgment of Art," *Southern Studies*, 19 [Fall 1980], 264).

¹⁰ "'The Interior World': An Interview with Eudora Welty," Prenshaw, ed. *Conversations*, p. 49.

¹¹ Cited in Koestler, p. 125.

¹² Koestler, pp. 125-26.

¹³ Cf. Carl G. Jung, *Man and His Symbols*, p. 218.

¹⁴ John Edward Hardy, "Marrying Down in Eudora Welty's Novels," in Prenshaw, ed., *Eudora Welty: Critical Essays*, p. 103.

¹⁵ Kreyling believes that Edna Earle fails to see life "in a larger, more comic order that includes contradiction" (p. 117). Cf. Robert Y. Drake., Jr., "The Reasons of the Heart," *Georgia Review*, 11 (Winter 1957), 420-26.

¹⁶ Edna Earle sounds very much like her grandmother when she says: "I don't blame Bonnie Dee. . . . I could just beat her on the head, that's all" (p. 49).

¹⁷ The terms are Owen Barfield's, from his explanation of Coleridge's theory of the polar nature of artistic creativity (*Evolution of Consciousness: Studies in Polarity*, ed. Shirley Sugerman [Middletown, CT: Wesleyan University Press, 1976], p. xi). Barfield is discussing this passage from Coleridge: "Grant me a nature having two contrary forces, the one of which tends to expand infinitely while the other strives to apprehend or find itself in this infinity and I will cause the world of intelligences with the whole of their representations to rise before you."

¹⁸ Seeing her as the creative artist of this comedy suggests the significance of Edna Earle's given names. In *One Writer's Beginnings*, Welty points out that "Edna Earle" was a common name for southern girls in her day because of the wild popularity of Augusta Evans' tear-jerking *St. Elmo*, with its heroine of this name (p. 40). What Welty does not tell us is that Evans' Edna Earle become a writer, a fact pointed out to me by Elizabeth Moss (see her study of Southern domestic novelists, forthcoming from LSU Press).

VII

The Tie That Binds: *Losing Battles*

Losing Battles (1970) is Eudora Welty's most complex exploration of how metaphor and imagery can express the human experience of the coexistence of contraries in a way impossible through discursive language. The novel focuses on humanity's eternal involvement in what seem to be hopeless struggles against the same universal enemies: the battles are between people and nature, between generations, between the pull of family ties and the need for individuality, between ignorance and wisdom, between life and death.[1] These battles are almost certain to be lost (that is, the conflicts will never be settled permanently). Nevertheless, Welty's novel suggests, the paradoxical potential of victory exists: the possibility of acting heroically, of achieving a depth of feeling (compassion, love, courage), and of growing in understanding within the changeless struggles.

This double vision of coexisting victory and defeat is developed in *Losing Battles* by a group of four overlapping image patterns, within each of which is an apparent contradiction: mythological imagery suggesting heroic grandeur is used to describe simple hill folk of Mississippi in the Thirties; images of motion and of stasis are applied to the same events; circle imagery associated with enclosure and limitation seems contradicted by imagery of chains and spirals; and images of light and darkness describe the same object (indeed, at one point, darkness is explained in terms of light). Welty not only confronts the contradictions within each group, but also connects each group with the other, making *Losing Battles* not the sprawling, disjunctive novel early critics thought, but an astonishingly unified work.[2]

The underlying source of unity in *Losing Battles* derives primarily from Welty's use of mythology and archetypology.

Although *Losing Battles* is anchored in the specifics of Depression Mississippi, the novel is pervaded by a sense of timelessness. At the heart of *Losing Battles* is the image of the Wasteland. In Boone County, Mississippi, in the 1930's, people see themselves in a kind of desert east of Eden where the land itself has turned on them. What a fall this is from the past—at least as they like to remember it! Uncle Noah Webster tells his new bride: "Cleo, the old place here was plum stocked with squirrel when we was boys. It was overrun with quail. And if you never saw the deer running in here, I saw 'em. It was filled—it was filled!—with every kind of good thing, this old dwelling. . . . "[3]

But now the river is drying up; the well is low. Just a year before, Grandpa Vaughn, the mainstay of the family, had died, increasing the speed of the family's downhill slide. (That the decline in the family's fortune had begun long ago is indicated by the family name *Beecham*—a corruption of the aristocratic *Beauchamp*.) The head of the clan is now a timid little man, Ralph Renfro, whose every act seems to go awry: on his wedding day he had somehow managed to blow off a bit of his foot with dynamite, and he had later lost the store that had belonged to three generations of Renfros before him. The goat, pig, and cow are long gone; the Renfros have killed both rooster and chickens for the reunion feast in honor of Granny Vaughn's ninetieth birthday—and Jack, the favorite son, has been in prison for eighteen months for what his mother calls just plain "manfoolishness."

Yet Jack is also the embodiment of the family's hope for escape from the cycle of losing battles and the center of the heroic imagery in the novel. To his family Jack is the knight—or Welty's version of a comic Fisher King—returned to bring new life to the Wasteland. They fantasize that at Parchman Penitentiary "whatever he sticks in the ground, the Delta just grows it for him," while at home, one uncle says, "everything's going to dry up or burn up or blow up, one, without that boy" (p. 70). After Jack returns, Aunt Birdie voices the family's hope for their fertility god: " . . . when Jack jumps out in those fields tomorrow, he'll resurrect something out of nothing" (p. 326).

To the reader, Jack seems a sort of Jack the Giant Killer, a Disneyesque Paul Bunyan-Pecos Bill, a burlesque Hercules with a safe on his back, a would-be hero whose grand schemes all crash about him. But to his family Jack is their own private deity, the vessel of their hope. Only superlatives are worthy of him: he is "the sweetest and hardest-working boy in Banner and Boone

County and maybe in all Creation" (p. 62). At school, he was "the whole Banner School basketball team in one" (p. 37), as well as school-bus driver, flag-raiser, and killer of "all the summer flies" (p. 22). It is little wonder that when Jack finally does make his appearance, home at last from the pen, he arrives with a whirl and clash worthy of the announcement of the descent of a young Jupiter. A tablecloth flutters (an appropriate family banner); a sister screams; dogs "little and big" set up a frantic barking as they race to welcome their master; a pan bangs to the floor in the kitchen; the new tin roof shimmers, while "riding a wave of dogs, a nineteen-year-old boy leap[s] the steps to a halt on the front gallery. He crash[es] his hands together, then [swings] his arms wide" (p. 71).

Taking command of his kingdom, Jack declares: " . . . Banner is still my realm" (p. 141). And this realm itself is mythic country. Banner Road is the *via vitae*, crowded with humanity, along which pass the dead and the barely toddling, the great and the lowly. When Aunt Cleo asks the gathered reunion, "Where they all get here from?", she is answered, "Everywhere," making clear the symbolism of this road (p. 18). The nature of the territory Welty is exploring is suggested at the outset in the map printed before the text of the novel—a map drawn by Welty herself.[4] Shaped like a heart—not the symmetrical greeting-card variety, but the real organ—with Banner Road going through it like an arrow, the map prepares the reader for Miss Beulah's declaration that Banner is "the very heart" (p. 18)—of Boone County (she means), but also of humankind.

Here the preacher, Brother Bethune, fulfills his ministry by killing all the snakes in the county and warns of the possibility of "meeting with the Devil in Banner Road" (p. 187). "Funeral-crazy" (p. 406) Willy Trimble travels Banner Road too, the aptly named archetypal figure of death (the question mark he always places after his name makes us read it "Will-he Tremble?"). He finds at one end of the road the dead Julia Mortimer and at the other the ninety-year-old Granny Vaughn whom he claims as his "next girl," teasing her family: "If . . . you-all don't want her, send for me and I'll come back after her and have her for mine" (p. 350). But the road is also the path taken by the Banner school bus. Described as "bulging like the Ark" (p. 135), the bus, we realize, is like Noah's ark, the vessel preserving future generations.

In other hands, the treatment of life in Depression Mississippi in terms of heroic or archetypal mythology might have served only to reduce the significance of the combatants and the battles of the present, making the novel a mock heroic. And Welty does ridicule the diminished battles of the likes of Homer Champion—the ethically blind justice of the peace—and his adversary, Excell "Curly" Stovall. Welty laughs too at the bungling Jack. She sees the ridiculous even in Julia Percival Mortimer (her name evocative of the hero of the Grail), teaching on in the face of rising flood waters, throwing herself on the dictionary in defiance of a cyclone, sending hybrid peach trees to all her former students in a final desperate attempt to improve their lives. But true to her unifying vision, Welty perceives that Jack can be both foolish and heroic, that Julia Mortimer can be both ridiculous and admirable, that ordinary people can be petty and noble, vicious and altruistic.

A second major janusian image group unifying *Losing Battles* conveys the idea of the coexistence of stasis and flux. The novel is filled with descriptions of motion that is ultimately denied, of pell mell rushes that lead nowhere, of people running in place. The Judge's car hanging over the cliff, tires spinning furiously, is the central trope of movement arrested. Through most of the book, the Buick is in the background of our awareness, poised on the "jumping off place" (that name itself, in its suggestion of imminence, both asserting and denying action), held up by nothing but a sign warning, "Destruction Is At Hand." The balanced car becomes the symbol of the precarious state of everyone in the book. They, too, are involved in a cliffhanger, existing just on the edge of going over (or, as we usually say when speaking of economic situations, of going under). Judge Moody moans: "We're all holding on here now by the skin of our teeth!" (p. 390).

While the car on the cliff is the clearest image of arrested motion, the same idea is suggested throughout the novel in imagery of breathless suspension, alternating with descriptions of headlong dashes. Granny, for example, is introduced in such a kaleidoscopic passsage:

> For the length of a breath, everything stayed shadowless, as under a lifting hand, and then a passage showed, running through the house, right through the middle of it, and at the head of the passage, in the center of the front gallery, a figure was revealed, a very old lady seated in a rocking chair with head cocked, as though wild to be seen.
> Then Sunday light raced over the farm as fast as the chickens were flying. (p. 4)[5]

Even Granny's sitting in a *rocking* chair suggests the integration of opposites. When Beulah Renfro's young daughters follow Granny into the house, they "[make] up for going slowly by jumping all the way" (p. 5), as if vertical motion could compensate for lack of horizontal progress. Welty makes this paradoxical union of stillness and movement a constant part of the novel's background when she writes that on the day of the reunion not a breath of air stirs, "but all the heart-shaped leaves on the big bois d'arc tree by the house were as continually on the spin as if they were hung on threads" (p. 21).

Emerging from this motif is the idea that beneath the apparent sameness and calm of ordinary life is a constant shifting, a careening into literal darkness and into the unknown future. Welty captures the mystery of movement that includes stasis, and stasis that hides motion as she describes the family singing "Gathering Home" (with its promise of rest: "never to roam") while the dizzy movement of time and the threat of change (witnessed by Granny's age and approaching death) undercut the calm of the moment:

> As they sang, the tree over them, Billy Vaughn's Switch, with its ever-spinning leaves all light-points at this hour, looked bright as a river, and the tables might have been a little train of barges it was carrying with it, moving slowly downstream. Brother Bethune's gun, still resting against the truck, was travelling too, and nothing at all was unmovable, or empowered to hold the scene still fixed or stake the reunion there. (p. 223)

For all its apparent progress, humankind has remained essentially the same. Yet for all that sameness, every scene, every person is constantly changing. To think that a person could be simply and permanently labelled was one of the problems with Miss Julia Mortimer's approach to education. To her, Jack was summarized in Gloria's gradebook: "Scholastic average 72, attendance 60, and deportment 95 . . ." (p. 249). Miss Julia "had no use for a mystery" (p. 316); "she wanted everything brought out in the wide open, to see and be known. She wanted people to spread out their minds and their hearts to other people, so they could be read like books" (p. 432). (A little joke here is that the books Miss Julia had in mind couldn't be anything like the ones Eudora Welty writes—in which no one can be read "like a book.") In spite of all her education (or perhaps because it was an education in only one way of knowing), Miss Julia lacked the vision truly to see and understand the contradictory truths about human nature.

A variation on the motif of action suspended appears in all the episodes in which we wait for the other shoe to drop—for the car to go over the cliff, for Gloria's parentage to be revealed, for the dynamite Mr. Renfro planted to go off, for the human chain pulling on the Buick to snap. But even when the shoe is dropped, escape from suspense (from a resumption of another round of something-about-to-happen) is short-lived. When the rope finally breaks and the car falls back to the ridge, Judge Moody sighs: "It brings some relief. . . . Of course it's temporary" (p. 392).

The dynamite that Ralph Renfro uses so ineptly becomes an intriguing part of this image pattern, a symbol of human nature itself. (It is appropriate that the father of the family is the one "planting" the dynamite, from his wedding day down to the present.) Discussing the problems involved in the marriage of cousins, Judge Moody says that such a union "just aggravates whatever's already there, in human nature—the best and the worst. . . . And of course human nature is dynamite to start with" (p. 319). Earlier Jack and Gloria's baby, Lady May (who is for a while suspected of being the product of such an explosive union), is compared to "a little firecracker about to go off" (p. 223). That the members of the family take turns sitting on Mr. Renfro's keg of dynamite suggests the uneasy stability of human life in general. A variation on this motif appears toward the end of the novel when Captain Billy Bangs (his name itself a pun) recalls that Julia Mortimer had taught him that the "world's round and goes spinning." Captain Billy remembers: "'And if that's what it's doing, daughter,'" I says back to her, "'I'd hate to think there's a can of kerosene setting anywheres on it'" (p. 424). Welty's world is, of course, loaded with cans of kerosene.

One specific eruption constantly threatening (and one which Welty presents in terms of the imagery of combined motion and stasis) is the age-old rush of the individual away from the family, balanced against the family's eternal pull of that individual back into its control. This theme is introduced on the first page of the novel. The stillness of early morning is broken as eighteen-month-old Lady May Renfro bolts naked out of the house. Even when she is captured by her mother, her legs still work like a windmill. Lady May's arrested dash to freedom and her churning legs suggest the ceaselessness of the younger generation's attempts to escape, a pattern expressed decades before in the flight of Granny's daughter and son-in-law away from their family and to their deaths in the Bywy River. In the years since, Granny has seen grandson after grandson leave her. And those grandsons have watched *their* sons desert them. Yet accompanying all this movement away there is also the eternal return, the pull on the heart that leads them home, in their memories and in reality, every year at reunion time.

Of the Beecham children, only Beulah with her husband Ralph has stayed on at the old homesite. Mr. Renfro boasts: "Well . . . we was never going to move, me and Beulah. Granny's got us. And now, Jack and his family—we got them" (pp. 194-95). In the ambiguity of that "got" lies both the security and the entrapment of the family. To fight against its control has become the obsession of Jack's wife, Gloria. In a significant frozen tableau, while Mr. Renfro boasts about "having" Jack, Jack and Gloria, in the background, are pulling on a wishbone. Gloria, we know, is wishing for freedom from the family that Jack, with equal fervor, is committing himself to. But even while Gloria dreams of independence from the Renfro family, she says to her husband concerning their daughter, Lady May—who in her turn is constantly pulling away, running off, dashing under, and otherwise evading her parents: "She's our future . . ." (p. 358).

Since so much of the action of the novel reflects this pattern of repetition, and since the larger theme emphasizes that humanity as a whole is involved in retracing the steps of those gone before, it is appropriate that the third major image cluster in *Losing Battles* should involve circles, suggesting the cycles of life.[6] The book is filled with returns to starting points. In the background of the reunion conversation, children sing rounds— cyclical songs that give the sense of progression, but always return to their beginnings. The story of Beulah's mother's and father's deaths makes the family recall the wedding ring that Ella Fay gave to Curly, the gift that eventually led to Jack's imprisonment. "It's the same gold ring, and all the one sad story . . . ," Miss Beulah says (p. 219). When Gloria went to Banner to teach, she thought she was "going forth into the world. . . ." "Instead, you was coming right back to where you started from . . . ," Aunt Birdie tells her (p. 319). In another retraced circle, Gloria, we learn, was like her mother in "jumping the gun"—getting pregnant before marriage. When the Buick is nearly over the cliff and on sure ground, the engine dies and the car rolls back where it came from. Then when the limping car arrives in Banner, Mrs. Moody sees the shimmering water tower and exclaims: "Why, we're right back in mortal sight of *that*! . . . For all we've travelled!" (p. 410). The long-gone father of Jack's best friend turns up at the end of the book (to tow Jack's truck away), causing another character to declare: "Well, it just don't do any good to say good-bye to anybody . . ." (p. 415).

Circle imagery also appears in allusions to family unity. Welty makes clear the contradictory nature of that circle, with its potential for protection and for malice. Offended by Gloria's refusal to reveal her feelings to them and by her declaration that she wants to be an individual, one to herself, and not a Beecham (as she would be if it were proved that she was the daughter of Jack's uncle, Sam Dale), the aunts come "circling in" on Gloria (p. 268). They trap her in their arms (to the tune of "London Bridge"—that folk song of destruction and imprisonment), pin her flat, and shove a red hunk of watermelon down her throat. In its malicious assertion of power and violation of intactness, this is, of course, a symbolic rape (they "cram" the watermelon and its seeds down her "little red lane" while Gloria's sister-in-law warns that she is liable to grow a Tom Watson watermelon in her stomach [pp. 269-70]). It is also a forced sacrament of the family blood (she swallows not only the seeds, but the "blood heat" of the melon Mr. Renfro has produced). Afterwards the aunts exult in having reduced Gloria to their level. Aunt Beck says: "You're one of the family now, Gloria, tried and true. . . . You're just an old married woman, same as the rest of us now. So you don't have to answer to the outside any longer . . ." (p. 352).

But the terror of that vision of the family circle, bent on reducing everyone to its level, excluding as threats all outsiders or anyone who seems self-contained is balanced against another scene: the reunion closes with all the family holding hands in a circle, singing, "Blest Be the Tie."[7] The circle here not only symbolizes family unity, but also effects it. Just making the circle of hands, Beulah says, will sometimes bring running the one who is missing (p. 348). Indeed, it is the reconstruction of the family circle at the yearly reunion that brings Jack home from the penitentiary.

Shortly before the family makes the last circle of the day, someone chimes out, "And we're sitting here in the dark, ain't we?" (p. 312). Then "hard as pickaxe blows" the harsh, new electric lights "drove down from every ceiling and the roof of the passage, cutting the house and all in it away, leaving them an island now on black earth, afloat in night, and nowhere, with only each other" (p. 312). Significantly, it is in the glaring light—so often associated with the light of reason, with linear thinking—that they seem alone, the positive implications of that last phrase ("with only each other"), minimized. Yet the narrator reminds us of the janusian quality of the human condition: every face is "black with the lonesomeness *and* hilarity of survival." The same double evaluation extends to the family as a whole: the family circle isolates (they cannot understand why Judge Moody cares so much for Miss Julia if she is not a relative); it reenforces ignorance and prejudice; it encourages mediocrity. It has even led Nathan to commit murder (for his brother) and Jack to commit "aggravated battery" (for his sister). But as surely as it isolates, it insulates and protects: they are at least together on their island on the black earth.

The double evaluation of the family circle is reflected in *Losing Battles* in the contrast between Jack's and Gloria's views. Jack sees it always as a source of safety ("We're safe. . . . And never mind, sweetheart, we're a family. We've still got the whole reunion solid behind us" [p. 171]). For Gloria that family is a threat (" . . . everybody finds us. Living or dead" [p. 171]). Welty knows, of course, that Jack and Gloria are both right.

Just as Gloria had hoped to preserve her integrity in the face of the overwhelming family, so, too, she had hoped to preserve her baby's distinction, naming her, grandly, Lady May. She insists on protecting her from ordinary food by breastfeeding her, trying to keep her from eating at the family table—a symbol of human communion. Yet at the end of the novel (just after she has repeated her insistence that her baby is "speckless"), Gloria spies a freckle on Lady May, a sign of her belonging to the imperfect human family (p. 319).

In many ways, Gloria has tried to keep herself as speckless as Lady May. She is so scrupulously neat, we are told, that when she has put away her Bible, baby, writing tablet, and curling paper, she leaves no trace of herself in the Renfro home. Too spotless, too little connected with human frailties, she is in danger of losing her selfhood by having no effect on others. Yet by the end of the novel, Gloria has been humanized, too. Her once billowing wedding dress is dirty and trimmed of its excess fabric; her face is smeared with a mixture of her husband's blood and the clay of their home town. She has not given up her hope of eventually having a home of her own; but she has not given up

Jack either, and that means accommodating his family ties. Like most people, Gloria is learning to live with a hope that contradicts probability. In the last paragraph of the book, the family circle seems to close about her, both as protection and as threat. After Julia Mortimer's funeral, Jack, his arm around his wife, turns toward home, singing the old hymn of the lost being returned: "Bringing in the Sheaves." The end, with its movement home balances the beginning with Lady May's dash from the house, establishing another of those moments of frozen and balanced motion. Jack's love of his family and Gloria's love of Jack lead to a temporary stasis: she is returning with her husband, but her vow to continue to fight for their freedom from the encircling family lingers in the air.

Understanding both the flaws and the values of the family circle, Welty suggests the existence of other possibilities for human connectedness. Expanding the basic circle image (and contradicting its implications of exclusion), she introduces the possibility of the chain—circle and line combined when circles become linked and extended, no longer merely superimposed lines covering the same space, but through union creating new configurations. When the (circular) wheels on the Judge's Buick blow out, it is the chain that pulls the car back to town. Just so, it had been a human chain—made of people who were previously defined by their insular, merely familial concerns—who righted the car and prepared it for its lurching trip to Banner.

Although some, like Miss Lexie, refuse to join that effort, all are connected, willy-nilly, in another chain, the one linking them to the past and its dead. When Aunt Cleo laughs at Granny's ordering Beulah to take the long-dead Sam Dale "a generous slice of my cake," Beulah retorts: "She knows we're all part of it together, or ought to be!" (p. 346). While this suggests the presence of the dead among the living, in a reversed vision of this unity, Jack and Gloria, going through the graveyard, look at the plots where they will someday lie. Among the "army of tablets" memorializing dead Renfros, the living family members are described as "the skips" (p. 427).

The idea of the chain of human connections contributes to the imagery of alternating stasis and flux: not even the dead can be taken for granted, neatly labelled, and expected to stay unchanged throughout eternity. During the recital of the family history, dead people keep popping up in a new light, influencing the living in new ways, making new chains of connections. Is Sam Dale really Gloria's father; the fox-haired Rachel Sojourner, her mother? Does this mean that Beulah was not responsible for Sam Dale's impotence? And that rascal Dearman—did Miss Julia accept his attentions? Did he father Rachel's child? Did Uncle Nathan kill him for Sam Dale? When the family unrolls the picture of Beulah's wedding, the living and the dead all stand together.

But even the frozen art of the photographer cannot still the sense of eternal motion. Rachel, having turned her face during the picture-taking session, is a blur (motion made permanent—as elusive in the static photo as she is in Gloria's past). And the mischievous Sam Dale, by running behind the standing relatives as the panoramic camera rolled, managed to be at both the beginning and the end of the picture. Creating a practical joker's alpha and omega, Sam Dale makes himself into the perfect image of Welty's version of contraries united, not in God (as they were for Nicolas of Cusa), but within human experience. The past, Welty says, is ever present, ever changing, ever influential. The hope of possessing the past—reducing it to simple fact—is but another losing battle.

One explanation of Welty's title is that all the battles people engage in are bound to be lost, if for no other reason than that we are all fated to repeat universal cycles. No fight is won forever. Yet within this pattern of eternally retraced circles, Welty holds out the possibility of progress. Often, admittedly, it is merely the progress of leaving one cycle of battles for another. For Curly Stovall and Ella Fay Renfro, the battle that began as part of a family feud is transformed into the battle of courtship and promises to move on to the battles of marriage. Even the words with which Curly greets Ella Fay at the beginning of this new stage of their relationship are the same as those he had used at the beginning of the old (pp. 23, 411). Stasis and motion are once more combined.

Yet on occasion the circles that everyone seems caught in are actually transformed into spirals. Gloria holds out the hope that she and Jack will someday have children who will be both good and smart. (The Renfros have put a low valuation on learning: Beulah's idea of punishment is to make her daughter come home from school and tell something she's learned.) Yet there is already in the family one who promises to achieve this higher synthesis: Jack's brother, the ignored and maligned Vaughn (the archetypal younger son who engages in a symbolic cornstalk duel with his returning older brother, expressing in this sibling rivalry the union of the apparent opposites of love and conflict). Vaughn is an independent spirit (his mother complains that he does not mind if people criticize him), who quietly gets the farm work done while Jack engages in his fruitless heroics. There is ironic wisdom in Jack's advice to Vaughn as Jack hands over, for the return trip, the school bus he had commandeered: "Don't forget all you learned on the way down, and remember it's the opposite" (p. 408). Vaughn is levelheaded, hard-working, determined, and he loves school in a way foreign to all the other Renfros. He earned the position of bus driver not by being most popular—the basis of the choice in the past—but by being best speller. And he spends his savings on a new geography book, whose fresh pages ("dearer than the smell of new shoes" [p. 365]) he sniffs lovingly, a harbinger perhaps of his own future in the world beyond Banner.

Miss Julia had tried to bring the higher synthesis of goodness and wisdom to Banner in a stroke. In this battle with ignorance and complacency, she was vanquished, in a large measure by the insular family's entrenched resistance to change, a threat to their security and self-esteem. But Miss Julia was at fault too: she denied the complexity of the people whose lives she wanted to alter. Even more, her failure derived from the nature of human change itself. Perhaps, Welty suggests, if change comes in a world so apparently changeless, the spiral will not be created in a grand coup even by so valorous a hero as Julia Percival Mortimer, but will be effected slowly, coming sometimes from the most unexpected quarters.

There are spirals other than Vaughn's in the novel, other moments of personal progress, usually marked not so much by a change in action as by new self-awareness. One such moment comes to Beulah after the reunion. Behind her is a day of contained emotions spent attempting to gloss over the pain Jack has brought her. But, alone in her room with her husband, Beulah finally allows herself to admit: "I've got it to stand and I've got to stand it. . . . After they've all gone home, Ralph, and the children's in bed, that's what's left. Standing it" (p. 360). Nothing will change, but because of her enlarged vision everything will be different.

For Granny, too, the day marked the movement out of ordinary cycles and into new perceptions. During much of the reunion, she seems cut off, turned in on the blurred memories that haunt old age, an island in herself. Yet before the day is over, she emerges from that isolation to confront the ultimate fact about life. During Lexie's account of Miss Julia's struggle

with death (an account punctuated by the aunts' callous comments), Granny looks bewildered, as if the room were filled with
strangers. At the end of the recitation, she whispers: "I'm ready
to go home now." She asks for her presents and is told: "You've
already had every single one" (p. 287). She covers her eyes—
probably a symbol of her new inner vision. If she is fighting
insight, it comes anyway. She and Beulah look at each other
with grief-stricken faces. Everyone at the reunion knows, intellectually, that Granny will be the next to die. What Granny and
Beulah seem to have confronted is the awful emotional reality
of that coming emptiness. It is an understanding that carries
them above the others.

However, it is Judge Moody whose perceptions are most
marked by the pattern of the spiral. His experiences in Banner
shatter the legalistic callousness that he had displayed at Jack's
trial—the willingness to judge actions out of the context, seeing
"aggravated battery" in what was really ritual combat. Feelings
return to the crusty old man—first of all, feelings of bitterness
and despair, occasioned by what he hears concerning Miss Julia.
Coming face-to-face with his complicity in the matter of Julia
Mortimer's disappointed life and cruel death, he confesses that
he had stayed on resentfully in Boone County because Julia had
wanted him to practice law there. The Judge realizes now that
he "never fully forgave her." And when Beulah asks, "Who did
you take it out on?", his glance at his wife signals his answer
(p. 305).

The new self-awareness that comes to the Judge brings
with it finally a vision of reconciled opposites. The Judge is right
when he says of life (speaking specifically of Miss Julia's end):
"'It could make you cry'" (p. 306). However, by the close of the
day, he has learned that it can also evoke a number of other,
brighter emotions. He comes, for example, to unite recognition
of the essential inefficacy of Jack's heroics with gratitude for
Jack's good intentions and steadfast efforts. And as an expression of his new sense of realities in life that cannot be dealt with
simplistically, Judge Moody decides that he will not return Jack
to the pen, nor will he report the possible illegality of Jack and
Gloria's marriage—nor Uncle Nathan's murder of Dearman
(and his guilt in the hanging of an innocent man).

Clearly, acquiring this new perspective does not incapacitate the Judge for action (an answer to those who might predict
that the holistic vision's lack of simple answers will lead to para-
lytic indecision). Rather, Judge Moody is more fully than ever

engaged in life, making decisions now on his own and not just out of a law book. We also see his involvement in the human chain in actions outside his judicial role: at first, after his accident, he had wandered pathetically about looking for help; after the reunion, he takes charge of his fate, driving his own car up the cliff—that path itself suggesting a spiral.

While Welty's frequent use of circle imagery seems to justify our using the spiral to describe occasions in which characters transcend circularity, the images Welty herself most often turns to, to convey increased perceptions are related to light/sight, darkness/blindness—the fourth major image pattern of *Losing Battles*. In this novel, which begins at dawn and moves in the last paragraph to full noon of the following day, the imagistic emphasis on light is balanced throughout by an undercurrent of symbols suggesting darkness. Indeed, imagery of darkness appears in the very first sentences of each of the six parts of the novel:

Part One: "When the rooster crowed, the moon had still not left the world but was going down on flushed cheek, one day short of the full. . . . [T]he clay hills . . . stood in *darkness*" (p. 3).

Part Two: "The *dust* Uncle Homer had made still rolled the length of the home road, like a full red cotton shirtsleeve" (p. 97).

Part Three: "The *shade* had circled around to the front yard" (p. 175).

Part Four: "They sang for a while longer, still in their chairs but settled back, some of them singing with their *eyes closed*" (p. 227).

Part Five: "The substance fine as *dust* that began to sift down upon the world, to pick out the new roof, the running ghost of a dog, the metal bell, was moonlight" (p. 311).

Part Six: " . . . Mr. Renfro, the Renfro girls, Miss
              Lexie, and Uncle Nathan were eating
              breakfast *by lamplight*" (p. 371).

Of course, even in the passages above which seem to emphasize darkness, Welty's integration of opposites is evident in
the juxtaposing of darkness and an almost full moon in Part
One, of dust and a bright color in Part Two, of darkness and
lamplight in Part Six. Most astonishing of all, perhaps, is the
image at the beginning of Part Five in which moonlight is described in terms of the antithetical dust, a particularly odd
metaphor, since what is emphasized about this dusty moonlight
is that it is an aid to vision, helping the family "pick out" the details around them.[8]
    However, the vision that allows simultaneous perception
of opposites does not come for most characters in *Losing Battles*.
The literal darkness pointed to in the opening passages of each of
the novel's parts is paralleled by intellectual and emotional ob-
tuseness. Eyes are always being closed. The purpose of the new
tin roof is to "blind" Jack to the reality of the family's desperate
straits (p. 68). Gloria tells Jack: "You're so believing and blind"
when it comes to the family (p. 360). Uncle Homer complains
that Jack can never "look and see where he's headed" (p. 81).
Before that, Jack and Homer had blinded each other with buckets
of milk when Homer had come to cart Jack off to jail for assaulting Curly. Jack's eye swells shut after Lady May kicks him, and
he loses his truck "in the twinkling of an eye" when he's out
cold after Curly knocks him into a telephone pole (p. 418).
When Gloria speaks of her hope to move away with Jack, Welty
tells us that, because of the "blinding light," "beyond the bright
porch she couldn't see anything at all" (p. 320). And even
though Granny puts on Grandpa's glasses over her own when
she goes to her Bible for evidence about Gloria's past, the family
misinterprets her message.
    Indeed, except for the anguished, wide-eyed look Beulah
and Granny exchange at the moment they perceive Granny's
imminent death, the family is characterized mainly by the absence of vision and by their acceptance of darkness. (Welty's earlier works have prepared us to accept the futility of depending
on physical eyes and literal light to really see. We recall that
when the glaring electric lights are turned on at the Renfros'
house what is illuminated is their isolation—only half the
truth.) It is Judge Moody who more than anyone else grows in

enlightenment during this reunion day—and that enlightenment is signalled by his closing his eyes. After hearing Miss Julia's story, the Judge's face is "strained around the eyes" (p. 290);
he suffers the weariness that comes from insight painfully pursued: sitting in the school desk, he is once again a student, this
time not of law, but of human nature. As he moves toward a
higher wisdom, darkness itself paradoxically becomes an aid to
vision. When Judge Moody brings out the letter Miss Julia had
sent him, "the world had turned the hyacinth-blue that eyes see
behind their lids when closed against the sun" (p. 297). What he
perceives about himself and others leaves him "staring as if
aghast into the purple of first-dark" (p. 307).

Gazing into the darkness, Judge Moody achieves his enlightenment, a recognition of his own faults and of the cruelty
and heroism of human nature. He turns away from a cool, rational, legalistic approach to Jack and Gloria's marriage (the approach urged by Miss Julia). By closing his eyes to the law, he at-
tains compassion, a virtue beyond reason. He becomes, with
that act, the truly perceptive one, synthesizing what Miss Julia
had taught him long ago with what the common folk of Banner
had shown him that day.

The Judge, like Jamie Lockhart of *The Robber Bridegroom*,
has attained the heroic vision acknowledging the doubleness of
all things. This is the insight that Welty has led her readers to,
through the major image patterns of *Losing Battles*. Though set
in Mississippi in the Thirties, the novel describes people in
terms of heroic myths of the past. Though life in the novel
seems to be static from one perspective (repeating with almost
ritualistic regularity the old patterns of farm and family life), it is
also always subtly in motion or threatening change. Equally
true, that which seems to be moving dizzily is actually part of a
stable, unchanging whole. Action that is caught in an endless
circle may any moment be transformed into a spiral. The bright-
est tin roof may hide the darkest despair and at the same time
signal the most courageous hope. From the midst of darkness
may burst out the light of insight. And lost battles may also be
victories.

But a battle that is never completely won nor lost, a battle
without victors or vanquished is scarcely a battle at all. Consequently, by the end of the work, the title—apparently the product
of a blatantly dualistic view of life—has been subverted. A better
paradigm for life, Welty may be suggesting, is play, epitomized
in the ritual combat of Curly and Jack. No one in the Banner

community takes their battles seriously; it is the Judge's legalistic, dualistic mind that applies the terms of defendant and plaintiff, guilty and innocent to the game. Or better yet, life may be like a dance, a possibility hinted at by Granny's final precarious jig on the table in the face of death. For in a dance, pattern and freedom, convention and individualism, tension and harmony unite. As Alan Watts has written concerning the symbolism of dance in Eastern philosophy: "There emerges, then, a view of life which sees its worth and point not as a struggle for constant ascent but as a dance. Virtue and harmony consist, not in accentuating the positive, but in maintaining a dynamic balance."[9] And *that* is the very heart of Banner, Mississippi, and of Welty's *Losing Battles*.

Notes

[1] Michael Kreyling focuses on the battle between mythical consciousness and historical consciousness in *Losing Battles*, in *Eudora Welty's Achievement of Order*, pp. 140-52. Sheila Stroup points out other "well-matched foes" in the novel: "the oral tradition and the written word, the natural world and the civilized world, emotion and intellect, the enduring and the ephemeral—'love' and 'separateness,'" in "'We're All Part of It Together': Eudora Welty's Hopeful Vision in *Losing Battles*," *Southern Literary Journal*, 15 (Spring 1983), 46.

[2] For example, Christopher Lehmann-Haupt, "Too Slow and Not Terrific Enough," *New York Times Book Review* (April 10, 1970), 37; T. H. Landers, "More Trouble in Mississippi: Family vs. Anti-Family in Miss Welty's *Losing Battles*," *Sewanee Review*, LXXIX (Autumn 1971), 626-34. Even Ruth Vande Kieft has written that "because of the seemingly random quality of folk speech and the episodic nature of much comic action, *Losing Battles* does not appear to have the structural coherence of *Delta Wedding*, the unifying symbolism and dimensions of classical and Celtic mythology to be found in *The Golden Apples*." The rather loose unity Vande Kieft finds in the work she locates in theme ("the paradox suggested by the title"), in the action ("the celebration of reunion"), and in recurring references to Bible stories and gospel hymns (Vande Kieft, 1987, pp. 152-62).

[3] *Losing Battles* (New York: Random House, 1970), p. 193. All future references to this edition will be given in the text of this chapter.

[4] In an interview with Jean Todd Freeman in 1977 Welty said: "But maps—they're of the essence. I drew my own map for *Losing Battles*. I had to; I used it when I was working. I had to be sure just for one thing that I had people turning left or right correctly, when they charged up and down. To be sure I got all those routes right. Oh, it was just a delight. I loved being able to do my map" ("An Interview with Eudora Welty," Prenshaw, ed., *Conversations*, p. 180).

5 Welty spoke with Jean Todd Freeman about the care she took in revising this opening: " . . . I went back at the very end and rewrote that very beginning many, many times. It was the hardest thing in the world for me to lead into what had come out of it. . . . In the opening part that you're talking about, with all the similes and so on, I was trying to see if I could condense all that was ahead into just such terms, in a very concentrated way to give a picture" (pp. 181-82).

6 Cf. Michael Kreyling's interpretation of the circle/line imagery in the novel as part of the theme of the conflict between mythical consciousness and historical time (pp. xix, 140-52). See also Randisi, pp. 83ff.

7 That hymn, of course, has the same doubleness of comfort and threat as the song sung at Katie Rainey's funeral in "The Wanderers" from *The Golden Apples*: "O Love That Will Not Let Me Go."

8 For a quite different explanation of Welty's unconventional use of imagery of light and darkness in this novel, see Larry J. Reynolds, "Enlightening Darkness: Theme and Structure in Eudora Welty's *Losing Battles*," *Journal of Narrative Technique*, 8 (Spring 1978), 133-40. Reynolds traces the movement in the novel from the full brightness of the opening (which he sees as ironically associated with ignorance of reality) to gathering darkness (associated with the family's growing recognition of the truth). According to Reynolds, the family's "ignorance is essential to survival. . . . They nurture and defend their ignorance because to recognize the truth would bring unbearable loneliness and despair" (134-35).

9 Watts, p. 54.

VIII

Learning to See Bridges: *The Optimist's Daughter*

Welty herself seems to have thought of *The Optimist's Daughter* (1972) as a kind of culmination. Of that novel, Welty declared: "*The Optimist's Daughter* was very close to me personally. It meant a lot to me in a way that some of the others hadn't. . . ."[1] And on another occasion she said, tantalizingly: "It came to be a kind of essence of what I've been trying. . . . I was glad that I wrote it."[2] It is impossible to know just what "essence" Welty had in mind, but what we can see in *The Optimist's Daughter* is a resolution to a question repeatedly raised in earlier works. Throughout those writings, Welty had dealt with the relationship between life and death. She had explored again and again various attitudes of the living toward the dead, an inquiry that for Welty always raised the corollary question of whether the dividing line between those states is as absolute as we have been taught.

These are the enigmas driving Mrs. Larkin in "A Curtain of Green"; Clement Musgrove makes us ponder such questions in *A Robber Bridegroom* as we think of his response to the loss of his son and wife to the Indians. In trying to figure out their relationship with the dead (and their close family ties mean that their memories are full of those no longer living), the Fairchilds, for the most part, run from death in *Delta Wedding* or domesticate the dead to protect themselves from confronting the reality of their pain, anger, and loss in the face of that eternal Yellow Dog. The dead become heroes (like Denis) or subjects of fond memories like Annie Laurie (with her preference for the gizzard), in either case reduced in their full humanity and thus trivialized. The Renfro-Beecham clan in *Losing Battles* comes closer, in comedy, to a relationship with the dead that authorizes

the full range of human emotions. Even though they too turn
the dead (Sam Dale and Grandpa) into heroes, and send flowers
(and cake) to the family graves on reunion day, they do not run
as frantically from death's reality as the Fairchilds do. The family remembers its loss of Grandpa as real loss. Beulah and her
brothers have not canonized their parents, clearly suspecting
that they met their death running away from something, possibly their own children. And Beulah and Granny look levelly at
the horror of death, at least briefly.

The Optimist's Daughter (the novel Welty completed
while working on Losing Battles) extends and deepens this level
examination of death, through its focus on the changes experienced by its main character, Laurel Hand. Laurel moves out of
her own version of Fairchildish evasion of death's reality, to
confront and accept first her rage at death for what it has taken
from her. She moves finally to an understanding—more specific than in any of Welty's previous works—of the nature of the
connection between the dead and the living. Like Welty's first
novel, this one also involves a bird in the house, that symbol of
death. But while Laurel Hand runs from the literal bird just as
the Fairchilds did, her flight brings her to an understanding of
the meeting point of life and death, of the dynamic relation between the two—an understanding that the Fairchilds as a group
could not attain.

Near the end of The Optimist's Daughter, when the chimney swift somehow enters Laurel's childhood home, she retreats
in panic into the tiny room—cold and "all dark"—attached to
her dead parents' bedroom.[3] Laurel's flight from the sooty bird
and her experience in that little room adumbrate the novel's
theme. The small, cold, dark room Laurel enters is another
memento mori, a prophecy of the final chill and lightless
enclosure to which all are destined. Here Laurel, only two days
past her father's funeral, re-experiences the deaths of her mother
and husband. The room is also, however, a place of beginnings,
where Laurel had slept as an infant, next to the room of her
birth. Although the cubicle is dark and cold, Laurel's memory
floods it with "firelight and warmth," creating a place where
light and dark, warmth and cold, life and death, present and past
unite. Laurel emerges from the room, not paralyzed by her vision of death, but re-engaged in life. And this is precisely
Welty's point. The Optimist's Daughter is about a creative response to death—and not just to literal death, but to destroyers

of the human meaning of life and of love, like Fay McKelva in this novel.[4]

In Eden "the rind of one apple tasted" (as Milton said) introduced humanity to both death and birth. To transform her own responses to death into creativity, Laurel must arrive at just such an ontology acknowledging the inextricability of the two. Laurel has been no stranger to death. However, her previous responses to the deaths of her husband and her mother have led her to run from life as she does from the bird of death. In fact, those deaths have left Laurel half dead herself, suggesting her betrayal of the evergreen implication of her name. Now past the spring of her life, she is the unblooming beech tree "that had kept its last year's leaves"—a vision of herself seen in the window of the train as she goes home for her father's funeral (p. 45). At the beginning of *The Optimist's Daughter*, she appears perfectly self-contained, almost emotionless, sure that she has the one truth (for example, about her father's life). At her father's funeral, listening to all the tales about him, she cries: "What's happening isn't real" (p. 82). Her new encounter with death will enlarge her definition of reality.[5]

Perhaps this new response can be accounted for by an intensification of death's impact on Laurel's life. In her middle forties, she is herself, most likely, nearer to her own death than to her birth. Before the novel is one-fourth over, Laurel has been stripped by death of all her family. As the insensitive Mrs. Chisom pronounces: " . . . you ain't got father, mother, brother, sister, husband, chick nor child" (p. 69). In Mount Salus, she is reduced to the role of eternal visitor. Her old neighbor kindly offers: "Feel free, of course—but it was always my opinion that people don't really want visitors" (p. 112). Since she is cut off from the dead and the living, part of Laurel's test is to find a way to transcend the limits of her existence, to unite the dead and the living, and herself with both.

The novel begins in New Orleans in Carnival season, the perfect setting—because of its coalescence of bacchanalian celebration and anticipation of the sobriety of Lent—in which to introduce the theme of the union of apparent opposites. This motif is developed through an exploration of the contrasts—and (as is appropriate in Welty's world of polar unity) the similarities—between Laurel McKelva Hand, the daughter of Judge Clinton McKelva, and Fay Chisom McKelva, the Judge's second wife. The thematic relationship of Laurel and Fay is intimated in the opening paragraph when Judge McKelva, so near to death now, is described as sitting on a "raised, thronelike" examination chair, "flanked by Laurel on one side and Fay on the other."

Fay becomes the exemplum of the person with a single view of reality. Totally absorbed in self, Fay is incapable of experiencing her husband as other, as an individual with significance separate from her own existence. Consequently, his death passes right over her head, leaving her as out of touch with life as she was with death. Fay reminds one, indeed, of the story from the Grimm brothers of the boy who sets out on a quest for the capacity to shudder; that is, to fear. In his study *Psyche and Death*, Edgar Herzog explains the fairy tale this way:

> The boy who cannot shudder is still living in an undifferentiated state of the world. He is a part of the world with no individual destiny of his own, so that like the animals he is an unthinking expression of life and existence: that is why he cannot experience fear. He is not horrified by the dead lying in the churchyard, nor the spectre in the church tower at midnight, because he has not become aware of the existence of "the other" as other than himself. He is the child who "can make no differentiation." Everything is part of the same thing, which is himself—he is "identical" with everything, and everything is "identical" with him. When he is confronted by a hanged man he has no fear because he does not feel him as other than and different from himself.
>
> From one point of view the boy's inability to differentiate his environment from himself is pleasantly childish, but it is also inhuman.[6]

Fay is similarly childish and inhuman. (Her name— "fairy"—implies her alien nature.) Her response to her husband's description of the first symptom of his final illness is typical and symbolic of her inhumanity: she sounds "a single, high note, as derisive as a jay's" (p. 5). Fay's dialogue in the first five and a half pages of a novel that will be filled with imagery of sight and insight reveals that she has no vision. When she cries, "It's dark!" as the lights are turned off so that Dr. Courtland can examine her husband's eyes, she is describing her incapacity for understanding as well as the condition of the room. Concerning her husband's disturbed vision, she says: "I looked. I couldn't see anything had got in it" (p. 5). And then when she learns that the Judge must have immediate surgery, she wails: "I don't see why this had to happen to *me* . . ." (p. 8). We understand, of course, that she cannot see precisely because she sees everything as happening to her. Fay is so self-involved that she "never called anyone by name" (p. 27). Because for her all of the world is "Fay" and "things-that-will-affect-Fay," there is no possibility of her seeing anyone else. She breaks doctor's orders and shakes her immobilized husband because "I wanted him to get up out of there, and start paying a little attention to *me*, for a change" (p. 175).

After her husband dies (perhaps, at least in part, as a consequence of her actions), Fay makes her way by taxi through New Orleans streets on Mardi Gras night, encountering such grotesques as a man "dressed up like a skeleton and his date . . . in a long white dress, with snakes for hair, holding up a bunch of lilies! Coming down the steps of that house like they're just starting out!" In the face of such a masque of death, her husband only hours dead, she can only moan: "Nobody told me *this* was what was going to happen to me!" (pp. 43-44). And because she has no inkling of the meaning of her husband's death to him, she does not realize that this is exactly what will someday happen to her. Her absorption in self continues when she and Laurel return home to Mount Salus for the funeral. Seeing Laurel's bridesmaids waiting for the train, Fay says: "A lot of good her bridesmaids will ever do me." And of the women decorating the house before the funeral—friends of Laurel's mother— she asks: "What's Becky's Garden Club got to do with me?" (p. 53).

Fay is absolutely right when she whines: "I haven't got anybody to count on but me, myself, and I" (p. 54). Indeed, as if to make absolute her self-containment, Fay has done in her family with a lie, telling Laurel that all of her relatives are dead. And for all practical purposes they are, just as everyone is essentially dead to Fay. *The Optimist's Daughter* demonstrates that there are more ways than one to be dead in this world and more ways than one to be alive.

Yet the most important insight that Welty offers through Fay is that because she does not live as if others really exist, her own existence is circumscribed. Paradoxically, because she sees everything as self, she has no independent selfhood. It is a condition Robert Lifton describes in his book *The Broken Connection: On Death and the Continuity of Life* (1979): "The . . . absolute equation between 'my world' and 'the world' reflects a fundamental impairment in self-concept, an inability to recognize the self's boundaries, or the fact that the self *has* boundaries, in the general human dialectic of separateness and larger connection."[7] Having never experienced death or otherness, Fay is incapable of experiencing life. In a non-differentiated state, there can be no life, since the significance of life develops only with awareness of the contrasting reality of death. Thus, in a psychologically real sense, it is death that creates life, otherness that generates selfhood. Lifton has explained: "There is a clear sense of the relationship between awareness of death and a delineated self. The second is impossible without the first. Even prior to the disturbing syllogism, 'If death exists, then I will die,' is an earlier one: 'Since "I" was born and will die, "I" must exist.'"[8]

Fay's isolation from life and death is reflected in her hatred of the clock on the McKelva mantel. "It's the first thing I'm going to get rid of," she declares (p. 100). (Judge McKelva's total concentration on passing time as he lies dying is only slightly more deadly than Fay's denial of its existence.) Ignoring the reality of time, she has no time—for death or for life. The clichés that cram her mind offer further evidence of Fay's lifeless psyche. "Nature's the great healer," she opines (p. 10); "Thank you for nothing!" she screams at Dr. Courtland (p. 43). At her husband's funeral, she performs the appropriate "scene" for bereaved widows, taught by her mother (p. 111). Like the Dalzell family in the hospital, whom Fay joins in "vying and trouble-swapping" (p. 38), and like most of her own family, Fay, as Laurel comes to realize, belongs to "the great interrelated family of those who never know the meaning of what has happened to them" (p. 84). Clearly, her not knowing is tied to her incapacity for individual, authentic feeling. She is, Laurel finally recognizes, a woman "whose own life had not taught her how to feel" (p. 173).

One exception to this characterization among the Chisoms is Fay's Grandpa, who comes to Judge McKelva's funeral bearing a box of pecans—and a sack of shells because "I didn't like to leave 'em in that nice warm seat for the next passenger" (p. 77). Such a simple acknowledgement of other is re-enforced when, standing by the open casket, Mrs. Chisom, Fay's mother, asks Grandpa: "Out of curiosity, who does he remind you of?" After reflecting, the old man answers: "Nobody." As he had said to his great-grandson Wendell, "It's Mr. McKelva. I reckon he stood whatever it was long enough" (p. 77). While it is natural for all of us to experience the death of another as a rehearsal for our own dying, Grandpa Chisom will not play Mrs. Chisom's game of seeing the dead man merely as some reflection of his own family. Grandpa Chisom recognizes Judge McKelva's death as

Judge McKelva's. Young Wendell shows potential for a similar sensibility when he asks repeatedly: "Who you think it is, Grandpa?", "But who do you call the man, Dad?" (pp. 77, 81). Wendell, Laurel senses, is "young, undriven, unfalsifying, unvindictive. So Fay might have appeared, just at the beginning, to her aging father, with his slipping eyesight" (p. 76).

Welty's awareness of life's doubleness extends even to Fay, whom she treats with compassion as well as derision. Fay strikes us as being less sensitive than an animal, but like an animal she feels no guilt. At times, however, her instinctual responses seem more effective than Laurel's reasoning. For example, while Laurel tries to figure out what her hospitalized father wants, Fay places a cigarette between his lips, saying, "*There's* something" (p. 29). And when she sees Fay asleep, even Laurel, who is usually so ready to judge and so sure of the rectitude of her judgment, muses: "Is there any sleeping person you can be entirely sure you have not misjudged?" (p. 60).

Initially, Laurel sees Fay as her opponent and as her mother's rival. Because she sees her too as responsible for her father's death (in effect, Claudius to her Hamlet), Laurel is driven by a need to make Fay face that responsibility. However, as she runs from the chimney swift into her parents' bedroom, Laurel begins to understand the wrongheadedness of the simplistic vision that has made Fay practically non-existent:

> Fay had never dreamed that in that shattering moment in the hospital she had not been just as she always saw herself—in the right. Justified. Fay had only been making a little scene—that was all.
> . . . . Death in its reality passed her right over. Fay didn't know what she was doing . . . and she never will know, Laurel thought, unless I tell her. (p. 131)

Laurel is only half right here: Fay did not know what she was doing. To know requires a felt union with the object of knowledge, and Fay's world is all subject. However, for this very reason there is no hope that Laurel's telling Fay of her responsibility will make any difference. Only after Laurel has been to the dark little room and emerges will she be able to evaluate Fay fully. Then she recognizes the truth:

> . . . Fay was without any powers of passion or imagination in herself and had no way to see it or reach it in the other person. Other people, inside their lives, might as well be invisible to her. To find them, she

could only strike out those little fists at random, or spit
from her little mouth. She could no more fight a feeling
person than she could love him.

"I believe you underestimate everybody on earth,"
Laurel said. (p. 178)

Laurel finally comes to realize that she is most endangered not by what Fay might do, but by the possibility that she might become like Fay. This recognition of the basic non-dualistic principle—that we are very like our own worst enemy—is for Laurel the beginning of wisdom.[9] Detecting "Fay-ness" in herself, she can develop her un-Faylike qualities. That Fay is a kind of shadow-self for Laurel is underscored by the fact that she is close to Laurel's age and that she too is without husband or child, and, in her own way, without mother and father as well. Miss Tennyson points out that Grandpa Chisom kissed Laurel goodbye because he "thought you must be Fay" (p. 101).

Laurel arrives at her heart of darkness (where "she saw the horror"—the possibility of her transformation into a Fay: "Have I come to be as lost a soul as the soul Fay exposed to Father, and to me?" [p. 131])—immediately before she backs out of the large bedroom into the room where she had slept as a baby. Here she recognizes that the scene she had just been imagining—telling her dead mother about Fay's abuse of the Judge—"was a more devastating one than all Fay had acted out in the hospital" (p. 132). Later, she comes to see herself "pursuing her own way through the house as single-mindedly as Fay had pursued hers through the ceremony [on] the day of the funeral" (p. 177), like Fay ignoring life's complex polarity. Acting from such a simplified perspective would be "more devastating" to Laurel's selfhood than anything Fay could have done to her.

However, the truth is that since her mother's and husband's deaths, Laurel has been trying to simplify reality—including her evaluation of people and relationships—in much the same way as Fay, underestimating everyone in her own way. Laurel reacts with outrage when she hears the Judge's mourning friends eulogize him as hero, humorist, and saint. Of course, in their apotheosis his friends are reducing Judge McKelva's humanity, but Laurel is too in refusing to accommodate the idea that her father was a more complex person than she had ever acknowledged. That Laurel's impulse toward reductionism is death-directed is symbolized by its similarity to Fay's preferring the Judge neatly laid out in his coffin (she thinks he looks better this way [p. 84]) to the living Judge with all the complications of bandaged eyes and sandbags around his head. Death *is* simpler than life. And to simplify life is to deal in death.

Laurel mirrors Fay, too, in the shallowness of her emotional responses. Even at the beginning of the novel, when, alternating periods with the hospitalized Judge, Laurel and Fay sleep divided only by the thinnest of partitions, Laurel's own protective self-containment is revealed in her not wanting to see Fay as a living other, any more than Fay had wanted to know Laurel: " . . . Laurel shrank from contact; she shrank from that thin board and from the vague apprehension that some night she might hear Fay cry or laugh like a stranger at something she herself would rather not know" (p. 18).

That her father's death is the catalyst for Laurel's movement into life, away from this self-containment, is one of the most obvious embodiments in Welty's fiction of her vision of the dynamic relationship between the unified poles of reality. To emphasize the continuity of her father's movement toward death with Laurel's re-entrance into life, Welty describes Laurel's discovery of life's non-dualistic reality in imagery that parallels descriptions of significant events at the end of Judge McKelva's life. Both, for example, must learn to see backwards as well as forwards. The first symptom of the Judge's eye problem was his seeing the glittering tin bird-frighteners his first wife, Becky, had tied on the fig tree in the back yard, even though he was standing on the front porch and looking down the street: " . . . I was forced into the conclusion I'd started seeing behind me" (p. 5).

Here is a recurring vision in Welty's world: what is past is potentially always with you and before you as well. The Judge voices Welty's philosophy of the eternal presense of the past when he tells Dr. Courtland: "Never think you've seen the last of anything." He says this with a "laugh that was like [a] snarl" —an appropriate way to express an insight that combines negation and affirmation. His trip back to the past calls up its dark side—in this case, the reality of death, Becky's and (by extension into the future, since he is suffering from some of the same symptoms as Becky) his own. After the Judge makes his snarling declaration, Dr. Courtland puts the glasses back on his patient's nose, a symbolic salute to the vision he had just expressed (pp. 10-11). In developing her capacity for seeing behind her, Laurel's special challenge will be to look back at her mother's life and death, and at the life and death of her husband.[10] Confronting the darkness of this backwards glance, she will also find joy in the discovery that, to the extent that the past is accessible to memory, death is not absolute.

　　Laurel's experience also parallels her father's in that she comes to enlightenment in a small, dark room. The novel begins with Judge McKelva's walking into the windowless room where his eyes will be examined after Dr. Courtland turns out the light. His hospital room is, like the room Laurel enters, dark, a room "like a nowhere"—and, hence, like everywhere:

> Even what could be seen from the high window might have been the rooftops of any city, colorless and tarpatched, with here and there small mirrors of rainwater. At first, [Laurel] did not realize she could see the bridge—it stood out there dull in the distance, its function hardly evident, as if it were only another building. The river was not visible. She lowered the blind against the wide white sky that reflected it. (p. 14)

Laurel has difficulty seeing bridges; she is resisting the perspective that could show her the river reflected in the sky and the sky mirrored in the rooftop puddles (images doubly merging earth and heaven, the symbolic *loci* of life and death), early clues to life's unity of apparent contraries. But further evidence of this truth is all around her.

　　In fact, the darkened hospital room may be the central image of the convergence of apparent opposites. Here also life and death come together: the nurse who watches over the dying man sits knitting endless pairs of baby bootees. Furthermore, as we've seen in previous works by Welty, the attainment of vision is associated with the absence of physical illumination. Dr. Courtland holds out the hope that the darkness of the hospital room will contribute to new light for the Judge—"a little vision he didn't think was coming to him" (p. 13).

　　Whether Judge McKelva gets his vision or not we do not know. The mystery of the movement from life to death on the part of the dying person is one that even Welty is loath to penetrate. If death does have two faces (as everything else seems to have in Welty's universe), Judge McKelva shows us the visage we usually think of: death as emptiness, separation, loss— Sartrean nothingness. His way of dying strikes the reader just as it does Laurel—as heartbreaking, in the Judge's withdrawal from the external world, in the divestiture of all his senses, in the cessation of his curiosity, emotions, and desires.

The simplification that he apparently opts for at the end of his life seems, at least as far as the living can detect, but an extension of what he had attempted in his marriage to Fay. That too had been a paring down of emotions, a retreat from the complex entanglements of love and bitterness, mutual help and (during Becky's last illness) mutual destruction characterizing his first marriage.[11] His labelling himself an optimist, trying to see only the bright side even in the face of his first wife's agonizing death, evading the reality of her desperation—this had been even earlier evidence of his desire to simplify (and to falsify) life. (Laurel truly is the optimist's daughter in her previous attempts at creating a similarly simplified existence, one which effectually cuts her off from life's fullness.[12]) As his death nears, Judge McKelva's isolation from life is so pronounced that Laurel ends up sitting beside him reading, not to the patient, but—in utter helplessness—to herself. The Judge spends his last weeks looking inward, in tune, it seems to Laurel, only with the passing of time, absorbed in what appears to be a perfectly unitary reality. Indeed, his self-involvement is like death, just as Fay's is (although hers is more horrifying, since she continues among the living).

However, the Judge resists our judging him as merely like Fay, because something about his final days hints of another union of contraries. While, relative to Laurel and her world of the living, he seems "dead" (that is, cut off from them in his singularity), to the extent that he is breaking the barriers of simplistic self-involvement in another direction, he is becoming alive relative to that world. And the Judge is apparently shattering barriers, going back in memory, perhaps forward into death—but in directions that we cannot follow. We do know, however, that after his operation, Judge McKelva calls Laurel by her childhood nickname and speaks of Becky as if she were alive, responding to his own vision of the coexistence of the past and the present. Just before his operation, Laurel had thought that her father "seemed for the first time . . . a man admitting to a little uncertainty in his bearings" (p. 12). Perhaps what she sensed was the Judge's first perception of non-dual reality. Beyond this is silence.

What we do know is that in *her* small room Laurel does have a vision. This is the other face of death, its creative side. And once she has had this vision, she emerges from the darkened room into the curtainless house at the end of the book. Ironically, the house is curtainless because the bird of death has passed by: the chimney swift in flying about has dirtied the curtains, causing the housekeeper to remove them for washing. Here is the perfect emblem of death bringing light.

Indeed, the bird is itself a vivid image of death's polarity. In folklore, as in Southern superstitions, the Death Demon or the messenger of Death frequently appears in the form of a bird: Odin's ravens, the Valkyries, and the Sirens. Since birds, as Edgar Herzog points out, "in themselves belong to the heavenly, spiritual, 'light' side of things," to combine them with characteristics of the chthonic makes them in some ways even more terrifying. Welty expressed her personal sense of this horror in an interview with Martha van Noppen, in which she discussed the bird in the house in *The Optimist's Daughter*. "It is terrifying," she told van Noppen, "to think of anything with wings that can't get out—the caging of anything, a spirit."[13] However, the association of birds and death has its reassuring as well as its chilling aspect. Herzog explains:

> The bird-form shrouds the Death-Demon in the mystery of distance, and yet lifts a corner of the shroud, since through it man experiences the fact that annihilation is not merely destruction but also transformation—and this is why the birds of death have hidden knowledge like the ravens of Odin and the Sirens who sing of the wisdom of Hades.
> . . . .
> Thus these images show a deep and hidden knowledge of the polarity of death and life—of the fact that death is not only darkness, decline and ending but also light, ascent, fulfillment and blessing of life.
> There are traces of the awareness of this polarity from the earliest times—in the classical figures of the Sirens, in the original connection between Aphrodite and Persephone and in the dark myths of Hel or Freya receiving dead heroes as lovers. Again and again the polarity seems to be on the point of being made clear in the mythological images of death, but in the end it would seem to be one of those secrets of which man can only become aware for brief moments—and that when he does the revelation is so deeply disturbing that it cannot be grasped and permanently held.[14]

In *The Optimist's Daughter* we see the association of birds with life as well as death when, as the mourners leave the Judge's gravesite, "the birds settled again. Down on the ground, they were starlings, all on the waddle, pushing with yellow bills of spring" (p. 93).

Another image of the convergence of life and death appears on the night of the Judge's death in the sounds of the frogs chirping from the site of the excavation next door. As the decayed building is being torn down, life renews itself from the ruins. We also detect similar universal implications in Judge McKelva's declaration about the discovery of oil on his flooded land: "*See there?* . . . . There was never anything wrong with keeping up a little optimism over the Flood" (p. 121). That might be the moral, too, of the Biblical Flood which, in addition to death and destruction, brought hope and new beginnings.

Laurel's movement from the darkened room into the metaphorical light is foreshadowed early in the novel when Mr. Dalzell, Judge McKelva's roommate, keeps knocking the blinds (the pun is significant) from the windows that Laurel is trying to keep covered to protect her father's eyes. It is probably also symbolically significant that back in Chicago Laurel had been designing a curtain for a repertory theatre—a curtain that is meant to be lifted or to be parted. Right now she resists the lifted curtain.

Mr. Dalzell is himself blind and very confused about literal reality (he thinks the Judge is his long lost son Archie), but he is endowed with insight into a larger reality (his words have an oracular resonance, even if it is a decidedly countrified version). The first evening Mr. Dalzell pulls down the lowered blind, letting in a flood of light, he declares: "I had to pull the vine down to get the possum" (p. 21). On the night the Judge dies, the blinds are down again: " . . . inside the room's darkness a watery constellation hung, throbbing and near. [Laurel] was looking straight out at the whole Mississippi River Bridge in lights" (p. 33). The dull view she had scarcely recognized the first day—with the bridge, the emblem of connection, at the center—is now illuminated; once again celestial and earthly unite in imagery; inside and outside exist together; death is accompanied by light.

A third view of the river will sharpen Laurel's "vision." While she is in the bedroom of her infancy, she dreams of and then, waking, remembers, yet another bridge she had actually seen on the trip she and Phil made from Chicago when they came to Mount Salus for their wedding—she a native of Mississippi, he of Ohio. It is the passage Welty cites in *One Writer's Beginnings* as containing "the only kind of symbol that for me as a writer has any weight, testifying to the pattern, one of the chief patterns, of human experience"[15]:

> When they were climbing the long approach to a
> bridge after leaving Cairo, rising slowly higher until
> they rode above the tops of bare trees, she looked down
> and saw the pale light widening and the river bottoms
> opening out, and then the water appearing, reflecting
> the low, early sun. There were two rivers. Here was
> where they came together. This was the confluence of
> the waters, the Ohio and the Mississippi.
>
> They were looking down from a great elevation and
> all they saw was at the point of coming together, the
> bare trees marching in from the horizon, the rivers
> moving into one, and as he touched her arm she looked
> up with him and saw the long, ragged, pencil-faint line
> of birds within the crystal of the zenith, flying in a V
> of their own, following the same course down. All they
> could see was sky, water, birds, light, and confluence. It
> was the whole morning world.
>
> And they themselves were a part of the confluence.
> (pp. 159-60)

Memory of this journey across the bridge carries Laurel
from her past into her future. But Laurel achieves this vision of
confluence—of life's ultimately unifying polarity—only after a
long trip by memory into her past. In order to re-emerge from
the dark center of her life, from the emotional paralysis that has
seized her, from the horror of the awareness that she could become like Fay, Laurel has had to re-experience also her mother's
life and death. Here, too, she discovers the truth of convergence.

The sickness that ended in Becky's death had begun, as did
the Judge's final illness, with troubled vision. Becky too had
tried to simplify life, but whereas the Judge attempted to see it all
optimistically, she had distorted reality by viewing it too darkly.
The conflict deep within her spoke, however, of the complexity
of her passions, a complexity where opposites coexist without
cancelling each other. As Becky had neared death, she had realized that even with his love her husband could not save her and
that he would not acknowledge the hopelessness of her situation. Turning on him, she had whispered, "'Why did I marry a
coward?'—then had taken his hand to help him bear it" (p. 148).
Here was the simultaneous existence of that most difficult to accept of all polarities: love and hate, or, as Welty describes it,
"love's deep anger" (p. 148). This is an example of the human
relationship symbolized in the pigeons that had so repulsed Laurel as a child: " . . . sticking their beaks down each other's throats,
gagging each other, eating out of each other's craws, swallow-

ing down all over again what had been swallowed before . . ."
(p. 140).[16]

The Judge's response to his dying wife's anguish penetrates just as deeply to the center where opposites mingle:
"Whatever she did that she couldn't help doing was all right. . . .
But it was *not* all right! Her trouble was that very desperation.
And no one had the power to cause that except the one she desperately loved, who refused to consider that she was desperate.
It was betrayal on betrayal" (p. 176). Laurel intuits what may be
the greatest paradox of all about her parents' relationship when
she concludes that Becky herself was responsible for her husband's marriage to Fay. Just as Heraclitus saw contraries generat-
ing each other, so Laurel realizes that Becky's intense, complex
love had caused the Judge's retreat to Fay's feeble, simplistic variety.

During her life's intersection with death, Laurel becomes
aware also of the intersection of her experiences with Becky's.
Becky, who as a teenager had taken her ailing father to Johns
Hopkins Hospital in Baltimore, had been no more able to save
him than Laurel had been to save her father. (At her death,
Becky had experienced the convergence of *her* life and her father's when she whispered as her own words, before her last operation, her father's words when he was dying.) And Laurel recalls that while she had stood by her mother's bed, washed by
guilt because of her helplessness, Becky had lain there sunk in
remorse for what she felt had been *her* desertion of her mother.
Looking at her own hands, Becky had seen the bleeding hands of
her mother. In her last words to Laurel, Becky might have been
speaking to herself: "You could have saved your mother's life.
But you stood by and wouldn't intervene. I despair for you"
(p. 151). She passes on to Laurel the guilt her mother had unwit-
tingly passed on to her, willing her pain as well as love, min-
gling psychological abuse with maternal nurturance.

There is, however, a danger in receiving a vision such as
this. If Laurel were to interpret such memories as implying that
one life is no different from another—since in so many significant ways Laurel's life repeats her mother's—Laurel would truly
become like Fay and would be not much different from the animal whose life is largely a recapitulation of its parents' lives.
(Concerning the scene Fay makes at the funeral, Miss Adele re-
marks cuttingly: "I gathered from the evidence we were given
that Fay was emulating her own mother. . . . We can't find fault
with doing that, can we, Laurel?" [p. 111] Even the blundering

jack-of-all-trades, Mr. Cheek, says Laurel sounds like Old Miss [p. 166].) Indeed, to decide to relive her mother's life is the temptation that Laurel's hometown friends offer when they trivialize her work ("Laurel has no other life" [p. 112]), and invite her to return permanently to Mount Salus, so she can replace Becky in their bridge club.

How can the living respond to death so as to affirm the continuity of life without turning their backs on the dead or on their own independent existences? To "become" her mother would not do this, for to the extent that she merely duplicates her mother's life, Laurel would thwart her own individuality and creative potential. In that choice, death (destruction of her independent selfhood) would rise out of death. To repudiate, on the other hand, all the influence that her mother had on her, to erase that connection from her consciousness as Fay tries to do with her family, would likewise allow death to produce death. In such a case, Laurel would, of course, have "her own life," but such a life, isolated outside of affective continuity, would have no human meaning. Elizabeth Kübler-Ross has said: "In order to be at peace, it is necessary to feel a sense of history—that you are both part of what has come before and part of what is yet to come."[17] Robert Lifton agrees: "Survivors' psychological needs include *both* connection and separation."[18] What Laurel must do is face death and the past it connects her with, while transcending both the past and death by returning to life and using there, in her own ways, the best of that past.

Her pattern must not be the circle—a repetition of her mother's life. (Right after the Judge's death, Fay joins the "circle" of the Dalzell family, while Laurel, isolated, walks in circles.) As we saw in *Losing Battles*, the circle protects and it can expand to include identical points in its periphery, but it is a static form. Instead, Laurel's life pattern must be the spiral. While the circle is a completed form, the spiral is always in process. It is the circle put in motion, contracting to the center in order to expand, only to contract and then expand endlessly. The center of the spiral for Laurel has been the room where she slept as a child, next to her parents' room. The spiral, which Kerenyi has seen as the "dynamic-topographical map of the underworld" and a symbol of death itself, moves in a circular pattern to the center (which is simultaneously the depths). However, according to Edgar Herzog, at the center "the movement is 'transformed' so that it returns to the periphery that it may return once more to the centre. . . . [T]his process can be applied both to the life of humanity as a whole and also to that of the individual. It might be said that symbols of this kind express 'death-and-becoming.'" Herzog explains:

> The centre of the spiral is the ultimate point of the descent into death and, at the same time, the point at which new life is born: new life begins with the reversal of the movement of the spiral and the return from the depths of death. This is exactly the same idea as that contained in the image of apple or seeds as the food linking the living with the dead, since it is only when it is destroyed in the maw of earth that the seed can "unfold" and develop its power to build new life. At the same time the spiral gives form and precision to the idea, and the movement carried by its line conveys a sense of compulsion; the movement inward to the centre and outward to the circumference expresses a sense of inescapable destiny and an unending alternation of Death and Life.[19]

Laurel's working in the garden the day after her father's funeral is part of the imagery of birth spiralling out of death.

Laurel's mother (whose bird frighteners could not scare away the bird of death) is herself the perfect image of double-handed, Janus-faced life/death. The person who gave Laurel life also gave her her most vivid experience of death. As Elaine Marks reminds us: "The death of the mother is a crucial event that determines attitudes and behavior and that brings the 'child' to an awareness of human precariousness and solitude."[20] Welty shows that the mother's death can also bring awareness of human connectedness. And Edgar Herzog has said: "When the image of the mother is struck by the dark rays emanating from the experience of death, or the image of death is touched by the glow of the maternal, then that which is nearest and that which is most alien, nourishing life and devouring death, are brought together in one image."[21] Laurel sees the maternal glow touching the darkness of death when the cold, lightless little room is flooded with warmth and firelight because of her memory of her mother. Out of her mother's and father's deaths—and her husband's—Laurel is reborn into life.

Before an upward spiral is possible, however, Laurel must spiral downward to the center, plunging to the depths of her emotions. She must truly feel her own feelings, experience her despair. As the spring of her feelings begins to flow, Laurel is ready to apply to life the lesson Phil had taught her about art, in imagery again recalling the spiral: "to work toward and into her pattern, not to sketch peripheries" (p. 161). She had responded to Phil's death by freezing the memory of their perfect life to-gether—and with it freezing in the past her capacity to feel. Like the rose bush her father trimmed at the wrong time, she also had been pruned before achieving more than her first blooming as a mature woman. What her memory of her mother and fa-ther's marriage has shown her is what she and Phil had not had: in the very perfection of their brief relationship, where there had been "not . . . a single blunder," lay its imperfection. They had missed out on the fullness of a love, like her parents', that in-cludes caring and abuse, sacrifice and demands, joy and pain. Remembering her short marriage now, Laurel recalls that Phil had taught her that love was not (as she had thought) shelter, but could instead be exposure, even exposure to the greatest of all brutalities—loss of love to death. The paragraph describing Laurel's response to these memories is filled with images of be-ginnings:

> A flood of feeling descended on Laurel. She let the papers slide from her hand and the books from her knees, and put her head down on the open lid of the desk and wept in grief for love and the dead. She lay there with all that was adamant in her yielding to this night, yielding at last. Now all she had found had found her. The deepest spring in her heart had uncovered itself, and it began to flow again. (p. 154)

She knows now that "life, any life . . . was nothing but the continuity of its love" (p. 160). When she meets Fay at the end of the novel she will learn the other part of this lesson: " . . . there is hate as well as love . . . in the coming together and con-tinuing of our lives" (p. 177). Psychic wholeness comes to Lau-rel, the critic Helen Tiegreen believes, because she acquires the capacity to feel anger and to acknowledge it without guilt, accept-ing life's mixture of good and bad, pain and joy as necessary to human movement.[22] "Continuity" itself implies motion, a movement into the future, while maintaining ties to the past. Grief frozen is a denial of life and love. Hatred denied is an equal retreat from life. When Laurel awakens after the night of her vision, "the house was bright and still like a ship that has tossed all night and come to harbor" (p. 163).

But that ship will harbor here only briefly. As an artist, Laurel's business has always been to create unity out of disso-nance. Now her life's business is to create an existence out of de-struction. Before she can turn to this challenge, however, Laurel has one more encounter with the non-living: she must deal with Fay. What this meeting with Fay confirms for Laurel is the superiority of her own response to life and to death. It is now that she comes to realize that Fay is no threat to her or to the memories of her mother or father. "The past isn't a thing to me," Fay brags (p. 179), revealing one reason for her inability to affect the living—past or present. But at the moment that Laurel tells Fay, "I know you aren't anything to the past. . . . You can't do anything to it now," Laurel is hit by the awareness that she herself can do nothing to the past now, either.

At the same instant, however, she comes to understand that while the past is impervious to Fay and to her, the memory of the past never will be impervious to the feeling and remembering (the artistic or creative) mind. Laurel decides: "The memory can be hurt, time and again—but in that may lie its final mercy. As long as it's vulnerable to the living moment, it lives for us, and while it lives, and while we are able, we can give it up its due" (p. 179). This was an insight Welty voiced in an essay published the year after *The Optimist's Daughter*, when she wrote:

> Remembering is so basic and vital a part of staying alive that it takes on the strength of an instinct of survival, and acquires the power of an art. Remembering is done through the blood, it is a bequeathment, it takes account of what happens before a man is born as if he were there taking part. It is a physical absorption through the living body, it is a spiritual heritage. It is also a life's work.[23]

Here are some of the deepest secrets in Welty's labyrinth: that knowing can reside in the blood as well as in the mind; that existence in the present and movement into the future require connection with the past; that the physical and the spiritual ultimately unite.

Laurel has burned her mother's letters; now she can give up to Fay even the breadboard her husband had made for her mother, realizing that "memory lived not in initial possession but in the freed hands, pardoned and freed, and in the heart that can empty and fill again, in the patterns restored by dreams" (p. 179). This is what Laurel has achieved: an awareness of the pulsating quality of life, emptying and refilling, transforming destruction into creativity.

Notes

1 Martha van Noppen, p. 242.

2 Jean Todd Freeman, p. 198.

3 Eudora Welty, *The Optimist's Daughter* (New York: Random House, 1972), p. 132. All subsequent references to this edition will be given in the text of this chapter.

4 Welty is exploring what Robert Lifton calls, in another connection, "the lost theme" in modern life and literature: the "psychological relation between the phenomenon of death and the flow of life" and "the place of death in the human imagination" (*The Broken Connection: On Death and the Continuity of Life* [New York: Simon and Schuster, 1979], pp. 4, 7).

5 Cf. Chester E. Eisinger's "Traditionalism and Modernism in Eudora Welty" in Prenshaw, ed., *Eudora Welty: Critical Essays*, pp. 23-24. Eisinger speaks of *The Optimist's Daughter* as "a meditation upon death" in which "Welty is concerned with the difficulties and betrayals of dying." Confronting these, Eisinger says, Laurel "earned catharsis of her emotions."

6 Edgar Herzog, *Psyche and Death*, trans. David Cox and Eugene Rolfe (New York: G. P. Putnam's Sons, 1966), p. 21.

7 Lifton, p. 47.

8 Lifton, p. 69.

9 For two different interpretations of the significance of the similarities between Laurel and Fay, see Thomas Daniel Young, "Social Forms and Social Order: Eudora Welty's *The Optimist's Daughter*," in *The Past in the Present: A Thematic Study of Modern Southern Fiction* (Baton Rouge: Louisiana State University Press, 1981), p. 114, and John Edward Hardy, "Marrying Down in Eudora Welty's Novels," pp. 114-15.

10 In her discussion of Laurel as "seer," Lucinda H. MacKethan points out that "the first personal note given in the description of Laurel herself is that 'Her dark blue eyes looked sleepless.' The closing sentence speaks of 'the last thing Laurel saw' . . ." (in "To See Things in Their Time: The Act of Focus in Eudora Welty's Fiction," *American Literature*, 50 [May 1978], 272). For an illuminating discussion of Laurel's development of that "most certain vision" transcending reason, see Robert L. Phillips, "Patterns of Vision in Welty's *The Optimist's Daughter*," *Southern Literary Journal*, 14 (Fall 1981), 10-23. See also William Jay Smith, "Precision and Reticence: Eudora Welty's Poetic Vision" in *Eudora Welty: A Form of Thanks*, pp. 78-94.

11 Albert Devlin sees Laurel as one who employs what Allen Tate termed the "dialectical mode." Because of her ironic vision, she speaks, he says, as if she were listening to two voices talking, rather than using just the one rhetorical voice of traditional Southern "conversation" (*Eudora Welty's Chronicle: A Story of Mississippi Life*, p. 200). It is possible to regard the two contrary voices of her parents as the source of the two voices that unite in her.

12 On the Judge's and Laurel's involvement in the "doubleness of experience," cf. Peggy W. Prenshaw, "Woman's World, Man's Place," p. 70. See also Randisi's discussion of "Laurel's progress toward an acceptance of ambiguity, or double-vision" and her "acceptance of imperfection" (pp. 142-50).

13 *Conversations*, p. 241.

14 Herzog, pp. 64, 83.

15 *One Writer's Beginnings*, p. 102.

[16] Michael Kreyling locates the "heart of the novel" in the contradictions of this pigeon passage. However, Kreyling identifies the conflict between Becky and the Judge as part of the battle between self and group that he sees as the theme of the novel (p. 169).

[17] Elizabeth Kübler-Ross, *Death: The Final Stage of Growth* (Englewood Cliffs, NJ: Prentice-Hall, 1975), p. 167.

[18] Lifton, p. 96.

[19] Herzog, pp. 93, 95.

[20] Elaine Marks, *Simone de Beauvoir: Encounters with Death* (New Brunswick, NJ: Rutgers University Press, 1973), p. 100.

[21] Herzog, p. 100.

[22] Tiegreen bases her analysis on a comparison of the original *New Yorker* version of *The Optimist's Daughter* and the Random House version of the novel (pp. 190-91, 204).

[23] "Some Notes on Time in Fiction," *The Eye of the Story*, p. 171; originally published in *Mississippi Quarterly*, 26 (Fall 1973), 483-92.

Afterward

A strange passage appears in Eudora Welty's essay "Writing and Analyzing a Story" (1955). Welty is arguing for the independence, in the writing, of an author's creations. They are not composed "in any typical, predictable, systematically developing, or even chronological way," she insists; "no past story bears recognizably on a new one or gives any promise of help. . . ."[1] Then comes the intriguing concession:

> Yet it may become clear to a writer in retrospect (or so it did to me, although I may have been simply tardy to see it) that his stories have repeated themselves in shadowy ways, that they have returned and may return in future, too—in variations—to certain themes. They may be following, in their own development, some pattern that's been very early laid down. Of course, such a pattern is subjective in nature; it may lie too deep to be consciously recognized until a cycle of stories and the actions of time have raised it to view.[2]

Welty's statement offers a happy example of how she makes language itself work to break dualistic boundaries. If we read the passage carefully, we notice that the time-table Welty predicts for an author's recognition of thematic confluence is an unusual one. "In retrospect," she says, a writer may discover patterns of connections not only in past writings, but in those of the future too. Taking away intervening phrases, we have this: "Yet it may become clear to a writer in retrospect . . . that his stories . . . have returned and may return in future . . . to certain themes." Of course, the explanation for the temporal oddity here may simply be that Welty nodded at the pen. But even then, it is a fascinating slip.

A time—or vantage point—has been posited from which the writer can see both backwards and forwards: it is a time that comes after both past works and future compositions, since it can look at the future retrospectively. This feat is worthy of the land through the looking-glass, where Alice hands round the cake and then slices it. Welty's juggling of time in this essay—until like three balls, past, present, and future are suspended in orbit without a first and last—is appropriate for a writer whose fiction returns continually to the theme of the union of apparent opposites, denying in work after work ultimate distinctions between past and future.

What is more, this Alice-in-Wonderland procedure seems to have been something like the pattern of Welty's recognition of the role of holism in her own work. One such moment of Janus-faced retrospection seems to have taken place very close to the beginning of her career, in her essay on Ida M'Toy. Here Welty explicitly associated creativity with non-dualistic vision. It is tempting to think that Welty was describing not just creative people or writers in general, but her own future artistic self in the midwifery and witchery, the self-contained merchant and showering comet—and above all in the victory over dualism— of the malignly tender Ida M'Toy. In a looking-glass world this would, of course, be possible: write the description of oneself and one's art and then live the life and create the work. The handful of stories published before the 1942 essay (including "Death of a Travelling Salesman" and "The Wide Net") foreshadowed this thematic focus in her works; those that came after made good the premonition. At the other end of her career, in *One Writer's Beginnings*, Welty looked for the pattern, "very early laid down," in her life and found at its center the idea of confluence.

The works focused on in this study, examined from a more ordinary chronological retrospective than Welty evoked in "Writing and Analyzing a Story," show Welty's variations on the idea of life's multiple comings together over a lifetime of artistic creation. The unity of theme in these works, linked with the variety of distinct and original expressions of that insight, is itself an astonishing statement of Eudora Welty's holistic vision.

Notes

[1] *The Eye of the Story*, pp. 107-8.
[2] *The Eye of the Story*, p. 108.

Works Cited

Allen, John. "The Three Moments." *A Still Moment: Essays on the Art of Eudora Welty*. Ed. John F. Desmond. Metuchen, NJ: The Scarecrow Press, 1978, pp. 12-34.

Arnold, Marilyn. "Eudora Welty's Parody." *Notes on Mississippi Writers*, 11 (Spring 1978), 15-22; rpt. in *Critical Essays on Eudora Welty*. Ed. W. Craig Turner and Lee Emling Harding. Boston: G. K. Hall, 1989, pp. 32-38.

Arnold, St. George Tucker. "The Raincloud and the Garden: Psychic Regression as Tragedy in Eudora Welty's 'A Curtain of Green.'" *South Atlantic Bulletin*, 44 (January 1979), 53-60.

Barfield, Owen. *Evolution of Consciousness: Studies in Polarity*. Ed. Shirley Sugerman. Middletown, CT: Wesleyan University Press, 1976.

—. *The Rediscovery of Meaning, and Other Essays*. Middletown, CT: Wesleyan University Press, 1977.

Belenky, Mary Field, et al. *Women's Ways of Knowing: The Development of Self, Voice, and Mind*. New York: Basic Books, 1986.

Berman, Morris. *The Reenchantment of the World*. Ithaca: Cornell University Press, 1981.

Bettelheim, Bruno. "Fairy Tales as Ways of Knowing." *Fairy Tales as Ways of Knowing: Essays on Märchen in Psychology, Society, and Literature*. Ed. Michael M. Metzger and Katharina Mommsen. Bern: Peter Lang, 1981.

—. *The Uses of Enchantment: The Meaning and Importance of Fairy Tales.* Harmondsworth, England: Penguin Books, 1978.

Bohm, David. *Causality and Chance in Modern Physics.* London: Routledge & Kegan Paul, 1957.

—. *Wholeness and the Implicate Order.* London: Routledge & Kegan Paul, 1980.

"Briefly Noted Fiction." *The New Yorker,* XVIII (October 24, 1942), 82.

Briggs, John P. and F. David Peat. *Looking Glass Universe: The Emerging Science of Wholeness.* New York: Simon and Schuster, 1984.

Bryant, Joseph Allen, Jr. *Eudora Welty.* Minneapolis: University of Minnesota Press, 1968.

—. "Seeing Double in *The Golden Apples.*" *Sewanee Review,* 82 (Spring 1974), 300-15.

Buber, Martin. *The Writings of Martin Buber.* Ed. Will Herberg. New York: World, 1973.

Bunting, Charles T. "'The Interior World': An Interview with Eudora Welty." *Conversations with Eudora Welty.* Ed. Peggy Whitman Prenshaw. Jackson: University Press of Mississippi, 1984, pp. 40-63.

Campbell, Joseph. *The Hero with a Thousand Faces.* Bollingen Series XVII. Princeton: Princeton University Press, 1973; 1st edition, 1949.

—. *Myths to Live By.* New York: Viking Press, 1972.

Campbell, Joseph and Bill Moyers. *The Power of Myth.* Ed. Betty Sue Flowers. New York: Doubleday, 1988.

Capra, Fritjof. *The Tao of Physics.* New York: Bantam Books, 1984.

Chodorow, Nancy. *The Reproduction of Mothering: Psycho-analysis and the Sociology of Gender.* Berkeley: University of California Press, 1978.

Cirlot, J. E. *A Dictionary of Symbols.* Trans. Jack Sage. New York: Philosophical Library, 1962.

Clemons, Walter. "Meeting Miss Welty." *The New York Times Book Review,* 12 April 1970, 2+; rpt. in *Conversations with Eudora Welty.* Ed. Peggy Whitman Prenshaw. Jackson: University Press of Mississippi, 1984, pp. 30-34.

Coleridge, Samuel Taylor. *The Friend.* Ed. B. E. Rooke. Princeton: Princeton University Press, 1969.

Cooper, J. C. *Yin and Yang: The Taoist Harmony of Opposites.* Wellingborough, Northamptonshire: The Aquarian Press, 1981.

Craige, Betty Jean. *Reconnection: Dualism to Holism in Literary Study.* Athens: University of Georgia Press, 1988.

Daly, Mary. *Gyn/Ecology: The Metaphysics of Radical Feminism.* Boston: Beacon Press, 1978.

Davenport, F. Garvin, Jr. "Renewal and Historical Consciousness in *The Wide Net.*" *Eudora Welty: Critical Essays.* Ed. Peggy Whitman Prenshaw. Jackson: University Press of Mississippi, 1979, pp. 189-200.

Davies, Paul. *God and the New Physics.* New York: Simon and Schuster, 1983.

—. *Other Worlds: Space, Superspace and the Quantum Universe.* London: Sphere Books, 1982.

Dégh, Linda. "Grimm's *Household Tales* and Its Place in the Household: The Social Relevance of a Controversial Classic." *Fairy Tales as Ways of Knowing: Essays on Märchen in Psychology, Society, and Literature.* Ed. Michael M. Metzger and Katharina Mommsen. Bern: Peter Lang, 1981.

Devlin, Albert J. *Eudora Welty's Chronicle: A Story of Mississippi Life.* Jackson: University Press of Mississippi, 1983.

—. "Meeting the World in *Delta Wedding*." *Critical Essays on Eudora Welty*. Ed. W. Craig Turner and Lee Emling Harding. Boston: G. K. Hall, 1989, pp. 90-110.

—. *Welty: A Life in Literature*. Jackson: University Press of Mississippi, 1987.

Dollarhide, Louis and Ann J. Abadie, eds. *Eudora Welty: A Form of Thanks*. Jackson: University Press of Mississippi, 1979.

Drake, Robert Y., Jr. "The Reasons of the Heart." *Georgia Review*, 11 (Winter 1957), 420-26.

Eisinger, Chester E. "Eudora Welty and the Triumph of the Imagination." *Fiction of the Forties*. Chicago: University of Chicago Press, 1963, pp. 258-83.

—. "Traditionalism and Modernism in Eudora Welty." *Eudora Welty: Critical Essays*. Ed. Peggy Whitman Prenshaw. Jackson: University Press of Mississippi, 1979, pp. 3-25.

Eliade, Mircea. *Rites and Symbols of Initiation: The Mysteries of Birth and Rebirth*. Trans. Willard Trask. New York: Harper & Row, 1958.

—. *The Two and the One*. Trans. J. M. Cohen. Chicago: University of Chicago Press, 1965.

Eliot, C. *Japanese Buddhism*. New York: Barnes and Noble, 1969.

Fitzgerald, F. Scott. *The Crack-up*. Ed. Edmund Wilson. New York: New Directions, 1945.

Freeman, Jean Todd. "An Interview with Eudora Welty." *Conversations with Eudora Welty*. Ed. Peggy Whitman Prenshaw. Jackson: University Press of Mississippi, 1984, pp. 172-99.

French, Warren. "All Things Are Double: Eudora Welty as a Civilized Writer." *Eudora Welty: Critical Essays*. Ed. Peggy Whitman Prenshaw. Jackson: University Press of Mississippi, 1979, pp. 179-88.

Garry, Ann and Marilyn Pearsall, eds., *Women, Knowledge, and Reality: Explorations in Feminist Philosophy*. Boston: Unwin Hyman, 1989.

Gilligan, Carol. *In a Different Voice: Psychological Theory and Women's Development*. Cambridge: Harvard University Press, 1982.

Glenn, Eunice. "Fantasy in the Fiction of Eudora Welty." *A Southern Vanguard*. Ed. Allen Tate. New York: Prentice-Hall, 1947, pp. 78-91.

Glennon, Lynda. "Synthesism." *Women and Dualism: A Sociology of Knowledge Analysis*. New York: Longman, 1979.

Gray, Richard. "A Dance to the Music of Order: Eudora Welty." *The Literature of Memory: Modern Writers of the American South*. Baltimore: Johns Hopkins University Press, 1977, pp. 174-85.

Gretlund, Jan Nordby. "The Terrible and Marvellous: Eudora Welty's Chekhov." *Eudora Welty: Eye of the Storyteller*. Ed. Dawn Trouard. Kent, OH: The Kent State University Press, 1989, pp. 107-18.

Griffin, Dorothy G. "The House as Container: Architecture and Myth in *Delta Wedding*." *Welty: A Life in Literature*. Ed. Albert J. Devlin. Jackson: University Press of Mississippi, 1987, pp. 96-112.

Gross, Seymour. "A Long Day's Living: The Angelic Ingenuities of *Losing Battles*." *Eudora Welty: Critical Essays*. Ed. Peggy Whitman Prenshaw. Jackson: University Press of Mississippi, 1979, pp. 325-40.

Grudin, Robert. *Mighty Opposites: Shakespeare and Renaissance Contrariety*. Berkeley: University of California Press, 1979.

Harding, Sandra and Merrill B. Hintikka. *Discovering Reality: Feminist Perspectives on Epistemology, Metaphysics, Methodology, and Philosophy of Science*. Dordrecht, Holland: D. Reidel, 1983.

Hardy, John Edward. "*Delta Wedding* as Region and Symbol." *Sewanee Review*, 60 (July-September 1952), 397-417.

—. "Marrying Down in Eudora Welty's Novels." *Eudora Welty: Critical Essays.* Ed. Peggy Whitman Prenshaw. Jackson: University Press of Mississippi, 1979, pp. 93-129.

Heilbrun, Carolyn. *Writing a Woman's Life.* New York: W. W. Norton, 1988.

Herzog, Edgar. *Psyche and Death.* Trans. David Cox and Eugene Rolfe. New York: G. P. Putnam's Sons, 1966.

Hinton, Jane L. "The Role of Family in *Delta Wedding, Losing Battles,* and *The Optimist's Daughter.*" *Eudora Welty: Critical Essays.* Ed. Peggy Whitman Prenshaw. Jackson: University Press of Mississippi, 1979, pp. 120-31.

Jackson, Katherine Gauss. "In Brief: Fiction." *Harper's Magazine,* CLXXXVI (December 1942), n.p.

Jones, Alun. "A Frail Travelling Coincidence: Three Later Stories of Eudora Welty." *Critical Essays on Eudora Welty.* Ed. W. Craig Turner and Lee Emling. Boston: G. K. Hall & Co., 1989, pp. 181-92.

Jung, Carl. *Civilization in Transition. The Collected Works of C. G. Jung.* Vol. 10. Trans. R. F. C. Hull. London: Routledge & Kegan Paul, 1964.

Jung, Carl G., ed. *Man and His Symbols.* London: Pan Books, 1978; first edition, 1964.

Kazin, Alfred. "An Enchanted World in America." *New York Herald Tribune Books* (October 25, 1949), 19.

Keller, Evelyn Fox and Christine R. Grontkowski. "The Mind's Eye." *Discovering Reality: Feminist Perspectives on Epistemology, Metaphysics, Methodology, and Philosophy of Science.* Ed. Sandra Harding and Merrill B. Hintikka. Dordrecht, Holland: D. Reidel, 1983, pp. 207-24.

Koestler, Arthur. *Janus: A Summing Up.* London: Hutchinson and Co., 1978.

Kreyling, Michael. *Eudora Welty's Achievement of Order.* Baton Rouge: Louisiana State University Press, 1980.

Kübler-Ross, Elizabeth. *Death: The Final Stage of Growth.* Englewood Cliffs, NJ: Prentice-Hall, 1975.

Kuehl, Linda. "The Art of Fiction XLVII: Eudora Welty." *Conversations with Eudora Welty.* Ed. Peggy Whitman Prenshaw. Jackson: University Press of Mississippi, 1984, pp. 74-91.

Landers, T. H. "More Trouble in Mississippi: Family vs. Anti-Family in Miss Welty's *Losing Battles.*" *Sewanee Review,* LXXIX (Autumn 1971), 626-34.

Lehmann-Haupt, Christopher. "Too Slow and Not Terrific Enough." *New York Times Book Review,* 10 April 1970, 37.

Lewis, Thomas. *The Lives of a Cell.* New York: Viking, 1974.

Lifton, Robert Jay. *The Broken Connection: On Death and the Continuity of Life.* New York: Simon and Schuster, 1979.

Lockerd, Benjamin G., Jr. *The Sacred Marriage: Psychic Integration in 'The Faerie Queen.'* Lewisburg: Bucknell University Press, 1987.

Lyons, Nona. "Two Perspectives on Self, Relationships and Morality." *Harvard Education Review,* 53, 125-45.

MacKethan, Lucinda H. "To See Things in Their Time: The Act of Focus in Eudora Welty's Fiction." *American Literature,* 50 (May 1978), 258-75; rpt. in *The Dream of Arcady.* Baton Rouge: Louisiana State University Press, 1980, pp. 181-206.

McLuhan, Marshall. *The Gutenberg Galaxy: The Making of Typographic Man.* Toronto: University of Toronto Press, 1962.

Marks, Elaine. *Simone de Beauvoir: Encounters with Death.* New Brunswick, NJ: Rutgers University Press, 1973.

Miller, Jean Baker. *Toward a New Psychology of Women.* Boston: Beacon Press, 1976.

Moore, Carol. "Aunt Studney's Sack." *The Southern Review,* 16 (Summer 1980), 591-96.

Moreland, Richard C. "Community and Vision in Eudora Welty." *The Southern Review*, 18 (Winter 1982), 84-99.

Nicolas of Cusa. *The Vision of God.* Trans. Emma Gurney Salter. New York: Frederick Ungar, 1960.

Ong, Walter. *Orality and Literacy: The Technologizing of the Word.* London: Methuen, 1982.

Pei, Lowry. "Dreaming the Other in *The Golden Apples*." *Modern Fiction Studies*, 28 (Autumn 1982), 415-33.

Phillips, Robert L. "Patterns of Vision in Welty's *The Optimist's Daughter*." *Southern Literary Journal*, 14 (Fall 1981), 10-23.

Pitavy-Souques, Danièle. "A Blazing Butterfly: The Modernity of Eudora Welty." *Welty: A Life in Literature.* Ed. Albert J. Devlin. Jackson: University Press of Mississippi, 1987, pp. 113-38.

Polanyi, Michael. *Personal Knowledge.* Chicago: University of Chicago Press, 1958.

Prenshaw, Peggy Whitman, ed. *Conversations with Eudora Welty.* Jackson: University Press of Mississippi, 1984.

—. *Eudora Welty: Critical Essays.* Jackson: University Press of Mississippi, 1979.

—. "Woman's World, Man's Place: The Fiction of Eudora Welty." *Eudora Welty: A Form of Thanks.* Ed. Louis Dollarhide and Ann J. Abadie. Jackson: University Press of Mississippi, 1979, pp. 46-77.

Price, Reynolds. "The Onlooker, Smiling: An Early Reading of *The Optimist's Daughter*." *Shenandoah*, 20 (Spring 1969), 58-73.

Pugh, Elaine Upton. "The Duality of Morgana: The Making of Virgie's Vision, the Vision of *The Golden Apples*." *Modern Fiction Studies*, 28 (Autumn 1982), 435-51.

Rabkin, Norman. *Shakespeare and the Common Understanding.* New York: Free Press, 1967.

Randisi, Jennifer Lynn. *A Tissue of Lies: Eudora Welty and the Southern Romance.* Lanham, MD: University Press of America, 1982.

Reuther, Rosemary Radford. *New Woman, New Earth: Sexist Ideologies and Human Liberation.* New York: The Seabury Press, 1975.

Reynolds, Larry J. "Enlightening Darkness: Theme and Structure in Eudora Welty's *Losing Battles.*" *Journal of Narrative Technique,* 8 (Spring 1978), 133-40.

Roszak, Betty and Theodore Roszak, eds. *Masculine/Feminine.* New York: Harper and Row, 1969.

Rothenberg, Albert. "Einstein's Creative Thinking and the General Theory of Relativity: A Documented Report." *American Journal of Psychiatry,* 136 (January 1979), 38-43.

—. *The Emerging Goddess: The Creative Process in Art, Science and Other Fields.* Chicago: University of Chicago Press, 1979.

—. "Janusian Thinking and Creativity." *The Psychoanalytic Study of Society.* Ed. W. Muensterberger, et al. New Haven: Yale University Press, 1976.

Rothman, Nathan. "The Lost Realm." *The Saturday Review of Literature,* XXV (November 14, 1942), 16.

Sather, Margarette. "Man in the Universe: The Cosmic View of Eudora Welty." Unpublished doctoral dissertation. University of Louisville, 1976.

Skaggs, Merrill Maquire. "Morgana's Apples and Pears." *Eudora Welty: Critical Essays.* Ed. Peggy Whitman Prenshaw. Jackson: University Press of Mississippi, 1979, pp. 220-41.

Sleuthaug, Gordon E. "Initiation in Eudora Welty's *The Robber Bridegroom.*" *Southern Humanities Review,* 7 (Winter 1973), 77-87.

Smith, William Jay. "Precision and Reticence: Eudora Welty's Poetic Vision." *Eudora Welty: A Form of Thanks.* Ed.

Louis Dollarhide and Ann J. Abadie. Jackson: University Press of Mississippi, 1979, pp. 78-94.

Snead, James A. *Figures of Division: William Faulkner's Major Novels.* New York: Routledge, Chapman & Hall, 1987.

Stevens, Anthony. *Archetype: A Natural History of the Self.* London: Routledge & Kegan Paul, 1982.

Stroup, Sheila. "'We're All Part of It Together': Eudora Welty's Hopeful Vision in *Losing Battles.*" *Southern Literary Journal,*15 (Spring 1983), 42-58.

Tiegreen, Helen Hurt. "Mothers, Daughters, and One Writer's Revisions." *Welty: A Life in Literature.* Ed. Albert J. Devlin. Jackson: University Press of Mississippi, 1987, pp. 188-211.

Trilling, Diana. "Fiction in Review." *The Nation,* CLXII (May 11, 1946), 578.

Trilling, Lionel. "American Fairy Tale." *The Nation,* CLV (December 19, 1942), 686-87.

Trouard, Dawn, ed. *Eudora Welty: Eye of the Storyteller.* Kent, OH: The Kent State University Press, 1989.

Turner, W. Craig and Lee Emling Harding, eds. *Critical Essays on Eudora Welty.* Boston: G. K. Hall, 1989.

van Noppen, Martha. "A Conversation with Eudora Welty." *Conversations with Eudora Welty.* Ed. Peggy Whitman Prenshaw. Jackson: University Press of Mississippi, 1984, pp. 236-51.

Vande Kieft, Ruth M. *Eudora Welty.* New York: Twayne, 1962; revised, 1987.

—. "Further Reflections on Meaning in Eudora Welty's Fiction." *Critical Essays on Eudora Welty.* Ed. W. Craig Turner and Lee Emling Harding. Boston: G. K. Hall & Co., 1989, pp. 296-309.

—. "The Vision of Eudora Welty." *Mississippi Quarterly,* 26 (Fall 1973), 517-42.

Warren, Robert Penn. "Love and Separateness in Miss Welty."
    Kenyon Review, 6 (Spring 1944), 246-59.

—. "Out of the Strong." *Shenandoah*, 20 (Spring 1969), 38-39.

Watkins, Floyd C. "Eudora Welty's Natchez Trace in the New
    World." *The Southern Review*, 22 (October 1986), 709-10.

Watts, Alan. *The Two Hands of God: The Myths of Polarity.*
    New York: Collier Books, 1963.

Weiner, Rachel. "Eudora Welty's *The Ponder Heart*: The Judg-
    ment of Art." *Southern Studies*, 19 (Fall 1980), 261-73.

Welty, Eudora. *The Collected Stories of Eudora Welty.* New
    York: Harcourt, Brace and World, 1980.

—. *Delta Wedding.* New York: Harcourt, Brace & World,
    1946.

—. *The Eye of the Story: Selected Essays and Reviews.* New
    York: Random House, 1978.

—. *The Golden Apples.* New York: Harcourt, Brace, 1949.

—. "How I Write." *Virginia Quarterly Review*, 31 (1955), 240-
    51.

—. "Looking Back at the First Story." *Georgia Review*, 33
    (Winter 1979), 751-55.

—. *Losing Battles.* New York: Random House, 1970.

—. *One Time, One Place: Mississippi in the Depression, A
    Snapshot Album.* New York: Random House, 1971.

— *One Writer's Beginnings.* Cambridge, MA: Harvard Uni-
    versity Press, 1984.

—. *The Optimist's Daughter.* New York: Random House,
    1972.

—. *The Ponder Heart.* New York: Harcourt, Brace, 1954.

—. *The Robber Bridegroom.* Garden City, NY: Doubleday,
    Doran, 1942.

—. "Some Notes on Time in Fiction." *Mississippi Quarterly*, 26 (Fall 1973), 483-92.

Westling, Louise. *Eudora Welty*. Totowa, NJ: Barnes and Noble Books, 1989.

—. *Sacred Groves and Ravaged Gardens*. Athens: The University of Georgia Press, 1985.

Wilber, Ken. *The Spectrum of Consciousness*. Wheaton, IL: The Theosophical Publishing House, 1977.

Young, Thomas Daniel. "Social Forms and Social Order: Eudora Welty's *The Optimist's Daughter*." *The Past in the Present: A Thematic Study of Modern Southern Fiction*. Baton Rouge: Louisiana State University Press, 1981, pp. 87-115.

Zukav, Gary. *The Dancing Wu Li Masters: An Overview of the New Physics*. New York: William Morrow, 1979.

Index